THE AMERICAN CATHOLIC
PEACE MOVEMENT
1928-1972

This is a volume in the
Arno Press collection

THE AMERICAN CATHOLIC TRADITION

Advisory Editor
Jay P. Dolan

Editorial Board
Paul Messbarger
Michael Novak

See last pages of this volume
for a complete list of titles.

THE AMERICAN CATHOLIC PEACE MOVEMENT 1928-1972

Patricia F. McNeal

ARNO PRESS
A New York Times Company
New York ● 1978

First publication 1978 by Arno Press Inc.

Copyright © 1974 by Patricia F. McNeal

THE AMERICAN CATHOLIC TRADITION
ISBN for complete set: 0-405-10810-9
See last pages of this volume for titles.

Manufactured in the United States of America

Library of Congress Cataloging in Publication Data

McNeal, Patricia F.
    The American Catholic peace movement, 1928-1972.

    (The American Catholic tradition)
    Originally presented as the author's thesis, Temple
University, 1974.
    Bibliography: p.
    1. Peace—Societies, etc.—History—20th century.
2. Catholic Church and world politics—History—20th
century. I. Title. II. Series.
JX1952.M184 1978   261.8'73'06273   77-11297
ISBN 0-405-10840-0

TEMPLE UNIVERSITY

THE AMERICAN CATHOLIC PEACE MOVEMENT 1928 - 1972

A DISSERTATION

SUBMITTED TO THE FACULTY OF THE HISTORY DEPARTMENT

IN CANDIDACY FOR THE DEGREE OF

DOCTOR OF PHILOSOPHY

BY

PATRICIA F. MCNEAL

PHILADELPHIA, PENNSYLVANIA

MAY, 1974

TABLE OF CONTENTS

INTRODUCTION

This dissertation developed from a study that was first undertaken in the fall of 1969 when Dr. Allen F. Davis, in a research seminar on peace, invited me to venture into contemporary history and write a historical biography of Reverend Daniel Berrigan, S.J., who was then on trial for the destruction of draft files in Catonsville, Maryland. The trial greatly interested me and I previously had heard Dan Berrigan speak and had read a few of his books.

Agreeing to the project, I traveled to Baltimore for an eyewitness account of the events of the trial and to arrange interviews with Daniel Berrigan, his friends and supporters, and even his opponents. The attempt to interview him proved to be a considerable task, since he was arrested and placed in jail two hours before my arrival in Baltimore.

That night there was a rally at St. Ignatius Hall in Baltimore in support of the Catonsville Nine. One of the speakers was Dorothy Day. When she arose to speak, a young student next to me turned to his friend and asked who the old lady was. The friend replied, "I don't know, but she sure means a hell-of-a-lot to all the Catholics here." After Miss Day's speech, I rushed up to her to conduct my first interview and asked her about the relationship of Daniel Berrigan

1

to the Catholic Worker. Her reply was sharp. "Dan isn't a
Catholic Worker, he came to us and stole our young men away
into the peace movement." I was shocked and confused, for
most Catholics know that Dorothy Day is the "Mother" of all
American Catholics who are involved in social concerns. I
continued my interviews, travels, correspondence, and reading.

The process had awakened my own desire for peace and
had convinced me of the necessity to actively try to stop
the war in Vietnam. It also had enabled me to meet and
become friends with a network of people who were known in the
American press as the Catholic Left. Fringe benefits of the
process were a raid on my home by the F.B.I. for supposedly
harboring The East Coast Conspiracy to Save Lives, and a sub-
poena to appear in Harrisburg to testify before a grand jury
concerning the destruction of draft files on the East Coast,
the planned kidnapping of Henry Kissinger and the blowing-up
of heating tunnels in Washington, D.C. The end products of
the process were this dissertation and a Ph.D.

Catholics have not played a leading role in the American peace movement. A nucleus of Catholics, however, did
rise to a prominent position in peace activity in the 1960's.
Their prominence resided in the fact that the Catholic Church
in the United States prior to 1960 was predominantly a highly
conservative and patriotic body whose hierarchy exhorted its
members to obey the nation's lawfully constituted government
in matters of war and peace.[1] The Catholic Church, as Dorothy
Dohen has pointed out, "has long been under the onus to prove

its congruence with American life. Religion has been used
to sanction the nationalistic goals, to support them."[2]
With the exception of Lutherans, Catholics were the most militaristic religious group in the United States prior to World
War II.[3] In light of these facts, I have attempted to focus
my study on the history of the Catholic peace movement in
America. In other words, to locate and trace the antecedents
that account for the emergence, on an unprecedented scale, of
Catholic peace activists during the 1960's.

When a Catholic looks to the Church for guidance on
the issues of war and peace, he finds only general principles
that can be applied in various ways. The reason for the
absence of any direct answer is that in its formal creed or
doctrine, the Catholic Church has no proscription against
participation in war. At best the concern of the popes for
peace can be qualified as "pastoral": they do not speak to
the fundamental issue of the rightness or wrongness of war.
Rather, what a Catholic discovers are centuries-old justifi-
cations for three ethical positions: pacifism, just war, and
the crusade. Pacifism was the dominant position maintained
by Christians down to the fourth century. With the conversion
of Constantine and the union of church and state, the pacifist
position lost its popularity and the just war became the normative position. The Catholic architects of this theory in the
fourth century were St. Ambrose and St. Augustine. During
the Middle Ages the code of the just war was violated in practice and the Church sought new ways to bring peace and unity

to Christendom. Out of this dilemma emerged the crusade, a
holy war waged in the name of God for the cause of peace.
Its aim was to achieve peace at home by directing bellicosity
to a foreign land.[4] The crusade failed to restore peace and
unity and it was eventually discontinued as a peace-making
policy. With the emergence of the nation-state in the late
Middle Ages, St. Thomas Aquinas attempted to resolve the issue
of war and peace. The failure of the crusades and the failure
of pacifism to relate to secular events led St. Thomas to
refine the just war doctrine with such precision that his
formulation has remained the normative position of the Church.
By the twentieth century it formed the basis for the peace
appeals of the Popes, from Benedict XV to Pius XII.[5]

The first Catholic peace organization in American
history based its concern on the normative just war position.
In 1928, Reverend John A. Ryan founded the organization and
called it the Catholic Association for International Peace,
(CAIP). It grew in size to 500 members prior to World War II.
When the United States entered World War II in 1941, the organization sanctioned the actions of the government and declared
that the nation was engaged in a just war. After the war, the
CAIP declined in significance as a peace group.

The first Catholic group in America to challenge the
just war theory was the Catholic Worker founded in 1933.
Dorothy Day, its co-founder, adamantly proclaimed that the
Catholic Worker Movement was pacifist and maintained this posi-
tion during World War II and all subsequent wars involving the
United States.

One perspective of this dissertation will be a general study of the growth of Catholic interest and action in peace. This will be seen primarily by examining the formation, purpose, and limitations of the CAIP and the Catholic Worker. Emphasis will be placed on concrete actions performed in response to American governmental action and Catholic hierarchical action or inaction.

The study will also focus on other Catholic peace organizations, all of which were offsprings of the Catholic Worker Movement. PAX was the first such organization and it was formed in 1936. Its aim was to form a "mighty league of CO's [conscientious objectors]." In 1940 PAX was reorganized and given a new name, the Association of Catholic Conscientious Objectors, (ACCO). After World War II, the ACCO ceased to function, believing that the Catholic Worker could adequately carry on its work and message. Another separate peace group was not formed until 1962 when PAX was re-activated.

In 1964, a Catholic peace group, the Catholic Peace Fellowship, (CPF), for the first time in American history was formed not solely under Catholic auspices, but also with the support of the Fellowship of Reconciliation, (FOR), the oldest non-denominational pacifist peace group in America. Daniel Berrigan and his brother Philip were mainly responsible for its formation. With the draft board action in Catonsville, Maryland in 1968, these two brothers became the leading peace figures in the Catholic Left. From 1928 to 1969 Catholics had moved from a marginal status in the American peace movement

to a position of central importance. The history of this
change forms the framework for this study.

The second perspective of this dissertation will be a
study of four Catholic peacemakers: Dorothy Day, Thomas
Merton, and Daniel and Philip Berrigan. A close look at
Dorothy Day explains why pacifism was first adopted by the
Catholic Worker as an alternative to war. Although the
Catholic Worker did face strong opposition in its pacifist
stance, it did provide the only viable peace witness in
American Catholicism even during a time of war until the
1960's.

I have chosen to study Thomas Merton because of his
theological writings on peace. An analysis of his thought
provides a clear understanding of the relationship of Catholic
theology to the American Catholic peace movement. It was not
what Merton did, but what he wrote that was significant. More
than anyone else, he was able to account for the demise of the
ethics of the just war and pacifism and he also pointed toward
non-violent resistance as the way to develop a new theology
of peace.

The study ends with the Berrigan brothers who rose to
prominence in the 1960's. As public figures, they stood in
the vanguard of the entire American peace movement. They also
had become the architects of a new political and theological
movement labelled the Catholic Left. Their thought and action
tested the strengths and limits of non-violent resistance as
a viable alternative to war. Studies of these self-conscious
peacemakers provide insights not only into their personal

motivation but into the changes in thought and action of American Catholics concerned about peace.

The limitations of this study are evident. It deals with a small nucleus of Catholics. Books, periodicals, correspondence, and specific actions of these Catholics do not necessarily reflect the opinion of the entire Catholic community. Nor is their influence on the political and social behavior of Catholics at large subject to precise measure. Despite these limitations, one can still derive a comprehensive view of what Catholics have done for peace in America.

One cannot complete a study of this type without expressing the sincerest gratitude to the many people who make it possible. In the first place I wish to thank all people who make the Catholic Left happen in the 1960's. I am especially indebted to Philip Berrigan for his friendship and his labors for peace. Most especially I want to thank Professor Allen F. Davis of Temple University who directed my work and who with his buoyant optimism continually stimulated me "to seek the new" in American history. I am also indebted to Dr. Herbert Bass of Temple University whose thoroughness as a scholar and perceptive grasp of political history taught me to appreciate the significance of the power of the state in history.

There were other people who also assisted me in completing this study. James Forest of the Catholic Peace Fellowship shared his memories, library and correspondence with me. James Douglas gave me his private collection of statements

and correspondence while at the Second Vatican Council. Carol
and Jerome Berrigan were most gracious in their concern and
hospitality and allowed me access to their basement archives
on Daniel and Philip. Gordon C. Zahn, professor of sociology
at the University of Massachusetts and David O'Brien, professor of American history at Holy Cross College, both aided
portions of this study with a critical reading and valuable
insights. I also wish to thank my husband, Jay P. Dolan who
as an historian provided much criticism and constantly prod-
ded me toward completion of this work. And finally to the
archivists at Marquette University, the University of Notre
Dame, the Catholic University of America, and the Peace
Collection at Swarthmore College, I am also very grateful.

REFERENCES

[1]John Tracy Ellis, "American Catholics and Peace: A Historical Sketch," (Washington, D.C., 1970), 25, reprint from James S. Rausch (ed.), The Family of Nations (Huntington, 1970).

[2]Dorothy Dohen, Nationalism and American Catholicism (New York, 1967), p. 127.

[3]D. D. Droba, "Churches and War Attitudes," Sociology and Social Research, XXIV (July, 1932), p. 552.

[4]Roland H. Bainton, Christian Attitudes Toward War and Peace (New York, 1960), p. 112.

[5]Harry C. Koenig (ed.), Principles for Peace, (Washington, D.C), pp. IX-X.

CHAPTER I

ORIGINS OF THE CATHOLIC PEACE MOVEMENT

On April 5, 1917, the day before Congress declared
war, James Cardinal Gibbons stated in the name of the Catholic
hierarchy:

> In the present emergency it behooves every
> American citizen to do his duty and uphold
> the hands of the President . . . in the solemn
> obligations that confront us. The primary
> duty of a citizen is loyalty to country. This
> loyalty is exhibited by an absolute and unre-
> served obedience to his country.[1]

As the leading official spokesman for the American Catholic
Church, Gibbons reaffirmed its loyalty to the nation on the
eve of the First World War. During the war, 814,768 Catholics
demonstrated their patriotism by serving in the Armed Forces
and more than 16,000 of them gave their lives for their
country.[2] This "tradition of patriotism in wartime," wrote
one historian, "has been a hallmark of the American Catholic
community."[3] As members of an immigrant Church, Catholics in
the United States have continually sought to dispel the label
of foreigners put on them by American nativists,[4] and their
enthusiastic support of the nation's wars "has remained one
of the most frequently used, if not logical, retorts to answer any aspersions on Catholic loyalty to American principles."[5]

The principal Catholic effort during World War I was
the formation of the National Catholic War Council. Founded
in August, 1917, it functioned throughout the war "as a highly
effective medium in almost every phase of Catholic participation in the war effort, from providing material assistance to
chaplains serving with the troops to acting as an official
agency designated by President Wilson to promote the war-loan
drives."[6] The success of the war council as a national coordinating agency for the Church persuaded its supporters,
principally, Bishop Peter J. Muldoon of the Diocese of Rock-
ford, Illinois, to continue its operation after the war. The
name was changed to the National Catholic Welfare Council
(NCWC) and despite initial opposition from some members of the
hierarchy, the NCWC eventually emerged as the main organizational agency of the Church.

The NCWC originally had five departments: education,
lay activities, press, missions and social. But the one
department "that has probably impinged more than any other
on the national consciousness is the Social Action Department."[7]
Catholics had been concerned with social issues for many
decades and in the late nineteenth and early twentieth centuries this traditional concern was transformed to face the
new problems raised by an emerging industrial nation. One of
the leading figures in this emerging social Catholicism was
John A. Ryan, a priest professor at Catholic University.

Ryan first received public attention in 1906 when he
published A Living Wage, Its Ethical and Economic Aspects, a

work defending the right to a just living wage. Thereafter
he gradually emerged as the principal architect of Catholic
social concern. When the hierarchy established the Social
Action Department in 1920, they chose John A. Ryan as its
director. Under his leadership the department helped to
make American Catholics aware of social and economic questions.

Ryan wrote the Bishop's Program of Social Reconstruction in 1919, a very progressive document for its time. Its
publication "constituted a distinct advance on earlier American Catholic social thought."[8] Its main focus was the reconstruction of American society through the principles of
justice and charity. In spite of avid criticism from some
segments of the Catholic community who labelled the 1919
statement as "partisan, pro-labor union, or socialistic propaganda,"[9] it pointed the direction toward which many Catholics
were moving in the years after World War I. One visible
omission in this quest for social reform was the international
issues of war and peace.

As was evidenced in World War I, Catholics were eager
to prove their loyalty to the United States but in seeking
social reform they never challenged the place of the nation
in the international community. The mentality of an immigrant
community, eager to prove its loyalty to the adopted homeland,
did not allow Catholic reformers to challenge the country's
basic social system. They wanted reform, but only within
the boundaries of the accepted American tradition. They
looked to the government for help, not to criticize it. Thus,

it was inevitable that one of the last issues Catholic reformers would confront was the responsibility of the United
States in war and for peace.

"One hundred percent Americanism" is not the whole
story. The failure of the Catholic social movement to consider the issues of war and peace requires an additional
explanation: the uncritical acceptance of the just war
tradition on the part of American Catholics. The architects
of the just war theory were St. Ambrose and St. Augustine
who wrote in the fourth century. Later in the Middle Ages,
St. Thomas Aquinas refined the doctrine with such great
precision that his formulation has remained the traditional
interpretation of the just war theory. The moral criteria
set forth by Aquinas consisted of four points: 1) a sovereign
authority must declare war; 2) the cause must be just; 3)
there must be a right intention and 4) the good sought should
outweigh the evil rendered.[10] In this theory the presumption
of justice is granted to the state. All responsibility for
war is placed on the state. The state, thereby, becomes the
decision maker for all individual consciences, and where the
individual disagrees with the decision of the state, the
burden of proof rests with him. American Catholics' acceptance of the just war theory reinforced the 100 percent
Americanism and made legitimate the Catholic acceptance of
the state in the issues of war and peace.

Although the majority of Catholics did not question the
attitude of their government on the issues of war and peace,

some individuals after World War I began to recognize the
need for the church in America to address the international
issues of war and peace. It was the League of Nations debate
that prompted these Catholics to attempt to move the Church
in this direction. Individuals identified with the Social
Action Department of the NCWC initiated the move. Their aim
was not to criticize the actions of the United States government, but rather to encourage the government to move toward
establishing world peace. Though the men in the Social
Action Department were primarily concerned with social
reform at home, they attempted for the first time to link
their quest for social justice to the broader international
issues of war and peace. The Catholic tradition, after all,
had always stressed the inseparable link between justice and
peace.

Pope Benedict XV initiated Catholic involvement in the
League of Nations debate with his encyclical "To the Leaders
of the Belligerent Peoples" (1917). He advocated the League
and offered his moral support and presence in such an under-
taking.[11] Three years later the American Catholic hierarchy
reinforced the opinion of Benedict XV and called for an association of nations to restore peace to the world.[12] Nevertheless, the majority of American Catholics supported the
popular movement towards isolationism and rejected any idea
of collective security. Efforts to reform the world had been
disillusioning and now Americans generally hoped to pursue
peace and prosperity by having the nation mind its own
business.

Popular and often bitter opposition met the efforts
of Catholic spokesmen for the League. Charles Fenwick, a
Bryn Mawr professor and a nationally known Catholic, spoke
out in favor of the League before Catholic audiences in the
East and Midwest. Reinforcing his talks with quotations
from Augustine, Thomas Aquinas and the popes, he found that

> not only were Irish Catholics upset because of
> the failure of President Wilson to do anything
> about the independence of Ireland, but that German
> Catholics felt that Germany was being choked to
> death by the loss of needed territory like the
> busy Rhine, the iron and coal of the Saar and
> Alsace-Lorraine, the valuable mines of Silesia
> and reparations that would last until 1987.
> Italian Catholics were incensed at the loss of
> Fiume.

Fenwick also reluctantly admitted "I never won a single
debate, or converted a single audience."[13] Similar experiences were related by Francis McMahon, a professor at the
University of Notre Dame, who was met when he talked on
behalf of the League with the charge that it "was invented
by Wilson and taken to Geneva, the ancient city of Calvin,
to make it anti-Rome." Others told him that "its instigators
were the international Masons." Another charge against the
League was "its failure to include the Vatican in its organization," McMahon reported.[14]

Father John A. Ryan was a foremost Catholic advocate
of the League. Ryan had given one of the first talks in
support of the League at a meeting of the Knights of Columbus
in Louisville in December, 1918, five months before the
covenant of the League was written into the Treaty of Versailles.

In May, 1919, he stated that the League was "the only means
in sight (to save the people of Europe from experiences
perhaps worse than those of war)."[15]

    In 1922 Ryan travelled to Europe and while visiting
England he met a British peace advocate, Father Joseph
Keating, S.J., from whom he learned about England's Catholic
Council for International Peace. After returning to the
United States, Ryan discussed with some of his friends the
idea of founding a similar Catholic peace organization in
the United States. He got support from Carlton J. H. Hayes
of Columbia, Sidney L. Gulick of the Federal Council of
Churches for Prevention of War, who all urged him to organize a peace movement among Catholics.[16] At this time, Ryan
was on the board of the NCPW. The diversity of positions
later evidenced by these individuals concerning collective
security and pacifism reveal how loosely related peace
societies were in the twenties and how undefined was Ryan's
position on peace. Not until the thirties did the peace
societies align in two blocs. One side would be led by
Clark Eichelberger and the League of Nations Association,
financed by the Carnegie Endowment for International Peace;
at that time it increasingly supported collective security
even at the risk of American involvement. The other side
consisted of a coalition of pacifist leaders in the Fellowship of Reconciliation, the Women's International League,
the American Friends Service Committee and the National
Council for Prevention of War. The latter agitated for

strict neutrality with nondiscriminatory embargoes against all belligerents in order to keep America out of war.[17] In the thirties Ryan himself resigned from the NCPW because it was too pacifist. He would lead the Catholics into the camp of collective security.

In 1922 Ryan was not interested in organizing Catholics into a peace movement. His first goal was the issue of social action. Yet, Ryan did agree with the judgment of Bishop Peter J. Muldoon, episcopal chairman of the Social Action Department, that "the department was not doing enough to educate Catholics on world affairs. It concentrated on domestic social justice alone."[18] Another priest, Father Joseph Burke, C.S.P., finally pushed Ryan in the direction of organizing a peace movement among Catholics. He suggested that Ryan and his assistant, Father R. McGowan, "get leading Catholics together at the 28th Annual Eucharistic Congress to be held in Chicago in 1925,"[19] and together they could begin to discuss the issue of international peace.

The proposed meeting took place in the morning and afternoon following the close of the Congress with fifty Catholic leaders assembling in the Law School of Loyola University. The assembled group did not draw up any specific plans for the future, but they expressed a desire to meet again to discuss the issue of peace. An organizing committee headed by Colonel P. H. Callahan of Louisville, Kentucky, was established. The next conference took place in Cleveland on October 6, 1926. A committee system was

adopted to study, report upon and help promote Catholic
understanding and action on problems of world peace. An
organizational meeting was then scheduled for April, 1927,
at the Catholic University of America in Washington, D.C.[20]
This meeting finally realized the goal of a Catholic peace
organization; it adopted a constitution and elected officers
and chose a name for the society, the Catholic Association
for International Peace (CAIP). Its motto was that of Pope
Pius XI's reign, "The Peace of Christ in the Kingdom of
Christ." It was the first Catholic peace organization in
American history.

The Association did not look for mass support, but
planned

> to seek to educate Catholics and non-Catholics
> on the Catholic point of view on international
> affairs, as drawn from what the Holy Fathers,
> the Bishops of the United States, and Catholic
> scholars had said on the principles of attain-
> ing world peace through justice and charity. [21]

Studies were to be made by experts, reports published on the
principles of peace and their application to current issues.
In addition, the Association would promote annual conferences,
lectures and study circles to present Catholic opinion upon
subjects relating to international morality. The CAIP was
allotted office space in the NCWC headquarters in Washington
as an independent branch of the Social Action Department and
was given the use of NCWC facilities, including the news
service.

In attempting to analyze the ideology, structure and tactics of the CAIP, it is impossible to separate the Association from the Social Action Department of the NCWC because of the central roles of Ryan and McGowan in both organizations. During this period, Ryan's reputation as "American Catholicism's foremost social reformer,"[22] enabled him to link American Catholics and liberal, progressive groups. Father McGowan, however, assumed primary responsibility for the CAIP's organization and vision.[23] Both men believed that "highly trained laymen and laywomen would join priests in furnishing the material for the program of education for and the actual recreation of the social order. Catholics should remake social institutions by gaining positions of power in business organizations and civil life."[24] Thus, the structure of the CAIP was elitist from the beginning though it intended to reach the general population of the laity. People invited to participate in the formation of the CAIP and later to serve on its committees were leaders from church, business and university life.

Bishop Thomas J. Shahan, rector of the Catholic University of America, was elected honorary president. The first secretary was Francis Riggs who served but a short time before he left to become chief of police in Puerto Rico. Other prominent people in the early activities of the CAIP were Professors Parker T. Moon and Carlton J. H. Hayes of Columbia; the Reverend John La Farge, S.J., editor of America; the Reverend Francis Haas of Grand Rapids, later bishop of

that diocese; Miss Marie Carroll, librarian of the World
Peace Foundation; Sister Vincent Ferrer, O.P., of Rosary
College; Archbishop Robert E. Lucey of San Antonio, then a
priest of the Archdiocese of Los Angeles; and George Shuster,
editor of Commonweal and later president of Hunter College.[25]
These prominent and influential people belonged to an institutional world of decision-making which spoke in political
terms of compromise and mediation, later they would advocate collective security.[26]

The key organizational component of the CAIP was the
committee. Men and women of intellect and influence were
appointed to these committees formed to present "a united
front against isolationist mentality."[27] Among committee
statements, for example, presented at a general organization
meeting, was a report on International Ethics formulated by
the Ethics Committee chaired by Ryan. This report, in rejecting the pacifist position, stated that "righteousness would
surely not be protected if wicked men were permitted to have
a monopoly on physical coercion." It was the consensus of
the committee that the just war tradition of St. Thomas
Aquinas provided the theological position on issues of war
and peace for the CAIP. Besides the Ethics Committee, the
five other committees originally established were Pan-American
Relations, the United States and Europe, the United States
and Asia, and Education and Dependencies of the United States.
Later other committees were added.[28] Through the 1930's
committee reports warned against fascism, nazism, communism,
nationalism and anti-Semitism.

These committees expressed the internationalist viewpoint of the CAIP. It opposed interwar isolationism and sought to awaken in Catholics a sense of collective responsibility as well as support for a world organization. In emphasizing the international order the Association developed a concept of internationalism that was based on the desire for cooperation among individual nations through a world organization. This view depended on a concert of power in the political realm. The degree of collective cooperation among nations would determine the type of security that could be devised to prevent war. The CAIP, therefore, supported America's entrance into the League of Nations and the World Court.

As early as 1930, the Ethics Committee issued a pamphlet on The Causes of War. It argued that the primary cause of illegal warfare was the action of unmoral states. An unmoral state was defined as one dominated by excessive nationalism and aggressive materialism. In the CAIP the major critic of excessive nationalism was Carlton J. H. Hayes whose pamphlet Patriotism, Nationalism and the Brotherhood of Man stated that Catholics were all too quick to subordinate their loyalty to Catholic principles to those of nationalism, chauvinism and antiforeignism. Hayes, one of the most prominent scholars of the 1930's and one of the most influential members of the CAIP, went on to argue that there was no basic difference between the selfishness of America's political and economic policy and that of other nations. He did point out, however, that fascism and nazism were the twentieth century's most extreme forms of virulent nationalism. He also stressed that such political philosophies were unacceptable to the Catholic Church since they exalted the state as the supreme and exclusive object of man's loyalty.

The Association also attacked aggressive materialism. In the economic reports of the committees, aggressive materialism was cited as a major source of discord and distrust among nations. In 1938 the Association issued a report, World Trade Patterns, in which it demonstrated that the economic life of the world in the 1930's was moving, not toward a just distribution of the goods of nature, but toward divisive ideological political blocs of economic control. This was true of all forms of government, democratic, fascist or communist. The most blatant example, according to the report, was Germany's domination of Eastern Europe. Like other conservative peace groups the CAIP in 1937 urged that a World Economic Conference be held to remedy the economic ills that seriously contributed to Europe's major troubles. The proposed guiding principle for the conference was the "reaffirmation of the moral unity of mankind and that an injustice done to one nation is an injustice done to all."[29]

Prominent in the CAIP's international position is the legitimacy of a just war. In 1932 Father Cyprian Emmanuel, chairman of the Ethics Committee, wrote a pamphlet, The Ethics of War, presenting the conditions of a just war for

the moral nations of the twentieth century. The criteria
for such a justifiable war included the four traditional
conditions of the just war theory.[30] Because it adopted
the just war theory, the CAIP was able to endorse the
Stimson doctrine and the Geneva Disarmament Conference. It
also supported the denunciation of nazism, the revision of
neutrality legislation and ultimately the acceptance of World
War II as a just war.

The person most responsible for coordinating this work
was Elizabeth Sweeney, secretary of the Association. Miss
Sweeney had previously been a secretary in the Social Action
Department of the NCWC. Extremely competent as a secretary,
she was an active member of many Catholic organizations. This
experience as well as her knowledge of Washington, D.C.,
equipped her well to coordinate the work of the CAIP. One of
her principal accomplishments was directing publication of
twenty-eight pamphlets between 1928 and 1938. The funds
needed to publish these pamphlets were donated by institutions
that held membership in the CAIP such as Mount St. Joseph's
College, Rosary College and Rosemont College.[31]

The CAIP also received contributions from organizations who sympathized with the Association's principles and
work such as the National Catholic Welfare Conference (NCWC),
National Council of Catholic Men (NCCM), National Council of
Catholic Women (NCCW), National Federation of Catholic College
Students (NFCCS) and Newman Club Federations. The tactic of
infiltrating to Catholic colleges and "official" Catholic

organizations also prevailed in the CAIP's attempts to
disseminate the reports of committee work.

Its first effort in disseminating peace education
material consisted of distributing pamphlets to already
existing discussion groups. In this way they hoped to
have these discussion groups focus on the issue of international peace and ultimately to become members of the CAIP.
Elizabeth Sweeney applied these tactics when she addressed
the annual convention of the NCCW in 1933. The executive
secretary of the organization had invited Miss Sweeney to
deliver an address on international peace. After the address,
the NCCW adopted the topic of international peace as the discussion theme for the year. CAIP pamphlets were then used
as source material for the NCCW discussion groups which met
in dioceses throughout the United States.[32]

The CAIP also worked with existing nondenominational
organizations in order to recruit new members. In Los
Angeles Father Lucey, a young parish priest, established an
active branch of the CAIP out of the existing League of
Nations Association. After Father Lucey left the diocese
in 1932, Mary Workman, an active member in the parish,
attempted to coordinate activities, but without strong
clerical leadership, the group became increasingly less
active.[33]

On the college level, the CAIP devoted most of its
energies to Catholic institutions. As early as December 7,
1928, Elizabeth Sweeney proposed to facilitate the distribution of CAIP material to peace study groups in Catholic

colleges. Two years later the executive committee suggested
that all Catholic colleges should encourage student participation in peace programs on Armistice Day. The first program
was organized at the College of Notre Dame of Maryland by the
CAIP; it was led by Dr. Elizabeth Morrissey, a member of
the CAIP on the college faculty.[34] In the early thirties
more than 150 Catholic colleges adopted Peace Week Programs.
There were attempts to initiate CAIP chapters on every campus,
but there was also an alternative policy of affiliating
existing clubs with the CAIP. Often the Student Mission
Crusade, the Catholic Action Movement or the International
Relations Club affiliated with the CAIP.[35] Affiliate members
were then organized into geographic units known as Student
Peace Federations. In 1936 the Association sponsored two
Student Peace Federation Conferences modeled on the CAIP's
annual conference.[36] The Middle Atlantic colleges met at St.
Elizabeth College in New Jersey and the Middle Western col-
leges met at Rosary College in River Forest, Illinois.

During the 1930's the CAIP faced the question of
whether or not the Reserved Officers Training Corps (ROTC)
programs which began to emerge on Catholic campuses were
compatible with the CAIP. In 1931 only three Catholic
universities had an ROTC program: Boston College, Fordham
University, and Georgetown University. All three colleges
offered it as an elective and the total number of students
involved was 1,169.[37] However, by 1937 many more Catholic
universities had adopted the program. Reverend E. V. Stanford, O.S.A., President of Villanova University, writing

to the CAIP reflected the Association's position. "[I see]
no conflict between an ROTC Unit in a college and an active
interest in CAIP . . . I see no reason why military men
could not hold membership in a conservative peace association like the CAIP."[38] The CAIP saw no basic conflict with
the ROTC mainly because of its just war presupposition and
its commitment to collective security.

The CAIP also tried to bring the message of peace to
the secondary and elementary levels of education.[39] That
such a need existed was obvious from the results of a study
made by Monsignor Maurice Sheehy on "National Attitudes in
Children." published by the CAIP. The study surveyed elementary and high school students in large metropolitan
centers of thirty states and Puerto Rico and was among the
first to reveal the consciousness of racial or national differences among children and youth.[40] These findings were
supplemented two years later by a pamphlet, Peace Education
in the Curriculum of the Schools written by Monsignor J. M.
Wolfe of Dubuque, Iowa, chairman of the Peace Education
Committee. Wolfe hoped that the new curriculum would present
a broad, comprehensive program for cultivating "peace minded-
ness" among young people.

The CAIP also attempted to gain support for its principles in Congress. Since this was the main arena of action
for Catholics in the Social Action Department, the CAIP
attempted the Department's tactics. In 1930 the Association
wrote a letter to the editor of the Congressional Digest

concerning the omission of the role of Catholic theologians, Vitoria and Suarez, in a _Digest_ article on freedom of the seas.[41] The CAIP regretted such overlooking of the Catholic peace tradition. The CAIP also attempted to influence national legislation on war and peace issues. In 1933 when Congress voted on the Arms Embargo bill, ten Catholic Democrats and all seven Catholic Republicans voted against the bill. Members of the Association were distraught because five of these legislators were on the sponsoring committee of the annual conference of the CAIP which had just met and endorsed the Arms Embargo bill.[42] Such voting on certain legislative issues reflected the lack of accord of some CAIP members with statements endorsed by the committee system.

Differences between the CAIP and Catholic legislators continued through the 1930's and reflected the situation among the members of Congress. Yet, after 1935 the Roosevelt administration was able to gain support for its move from neutrality legislation to collective security. As this support increased, the CAIP, with its internationalist ideology, endorsed the policies of the president in spite of the administration's continuing differences with some members of Congress.

The main reasons for the Association's support of the Roosevelt administration's opposition to mandatory neutrality legislation were the presuppositions of the CAIP which committed the organization to collective security and the just war ethic. This is most clearly seen in the CAIP's role

concerning neutrality legislation. The CAIP grew increasingly critical of the pacifist position and sought to replace
the pacifists' quest for strict neutrality with legislation
favoring collective security.

As early as 1937 the CAIP demonstrated its opposition
to the Neutrality Act by contending that the act made no
distinction between the aggressor nation and its victim.[43]
In 1938 it reiterated its position by objecting to the
"narrow conception of national interest upon which [the]
Neutrality Act was based -- [an] attitude of washing our
hands of responsibility in present crime -- [and it was]
concerned primarily not with the prevention of war but with
[the] avoidance of its consequences."[44] This paved the way
for the CAIP to embrace wholeheartedly Roosevelt's move away
from neutrality toward collective security.

The only stumbling block for the CAIP in this process
was the Spanish Civil War and the ensuing debate between 1937
and 1939 over the Embargo Act. During this time President
Roosevelt did not advocate a change in the Neutrality Act of
1937 and a lifting of the Embargo Act. Yet, in his "Quaran-
tine Speech" at Chicago on October 5, 1937 he discarded the
doctrine of neutrality for the United States and espoused
the idea of collective security -- the cardinal principle
of internationalism. Despite his espousal of collective
security he never lifted the Embargo. The administration's
ambiguity was also reflected in the CAIP. It seemed logical
by 1937 that the CAIP was ready to reject strict neutrality.

But, the American bishops and the "official" Church statements from the NCWC came out in support of Franco in Spain
and were against the repeal of the Embargo which would favor
the Loyalists. Because of the CAIP's close relationship
with the NCWC, it chose to remain silent rather than confront the position of the "official" Church. The Association would not disobey the "official" Church in order to
support collective security by advocating a lifting of the
Embargo. With Franco's victory in Spain in 1939, such a
conflict of loyalties would never again confront the CAIP.
The "official" Church opposed nazism. This Catholic position cleared the way for the CAIP to speak out against
strict neutrality when it touched on the German situation.

The shift of the CAIP from support of neutrality
legislation to endorsing collective security reflected the
transformation taking place among other non-pacifist peace
groups such as the Carnegie Endowment for International
Peace, the Church Peace Union, the World Alliance for International Friendship through the Churches and the League of
Nations Association. All these organizations rallied around
the concept of collective security and formed the Non-
Partisan Committee for Peace Through the Revision of the
Neutrality Law. Through this organization and others, the
non-pacifist peace groups prepared the nation for war by
emphasizing collective security rather than a position of
neutrality. As a spokesman for the Non-Partisan Committee
for Peace Through the Revision of the Neutrality Law in late

1939, John A. Ryan expressed the consensus of the group
when he stated in a radio broadcast that all Americans were
"morally obliged to do all they reasonably can to defeat
Hitler and Hitlerism."[45] When the United States declared
its formal participation in World War II, the CAIP unhesi-
tatingly continued the Catholic tradition of patriotism in
wartime.

Though the CAIP urged its members to work within the
framework of all existing organizations devoted to the cause
of peace in the world, it did little more than send pamphlet
material upon request or provide a speaker for a peace rally.
Some individual members did serve on national committees of
various peace organizations. The CAIP worked most closely
with the Carnegie Endowment for International Peace and the
Church Peace Union.[46] In May, 1936, Monsignor Ryan served
as the CAIP representative on the National Peace Conference,
a committee set up in Washington, D.C., to keep various
organizations informed regarding the legislative situation
in Congress.[47] Prior to this, Ryan had resigned from the
National Council for the Prevention of War because it was too
pacifist in orientation.[48]

This basic attitude toward non-Catholic staunchly
pacifist peace organizations was also reflected in an inter-
office communication from Elizabeth Sweeney to Mr. Caravati:

> National Council for Prevention of War -- Mr. Frederick
> Libby:
> They have done a great deal in dissemination of
> usable material on international questions which

is obviously lacking in any ethical or
spiritual significance. I would be for
cooperating with them in matters such as
questionnaires, etc., but would not recom-
mend the general use of literature in the
schools when the CAIP publications are
available.[49]

The CAIP's relations with peace organizations outside
the United States reflected its domestic tactics. Wanting
to establish contact with Europe, Elizabeth Sweeney, as early
as June, 1929, wrote on behalf of the CAIP to Father Franziskus
Stratmann, O.P., head of the German Catholic Union for Peace,
who in turn urged the need to prepare the way for an International Peace Conference. Father Stratmann held that no
modern war could be a just war and also urged that war service and military service be declared an absolute contradiction of the teachings of Christ and of the Catholic Church.[50]
From this position he urged Miss Sweeney to contact Joseph
Clayton in England who had written on peace for the English
Dominican periodical, Blackfriars, the Polish Jesuit, Graf
Rostoworowski, Professor Ude of Graz University, Professor
Keller of Freiburg University and the War Resisters' Inter-
national. The CAIP, however, gave little cooperation because
those Catholics were staunch pacifists. It did publish a
pamphlet, though, called Catholic Peace Organizations in
Europe. It also worked with the Carnegie Endowment for
International Peace in publishing for American readers a
500-page work on internationalism and Catholicism. The work,
The Catholic Tradition of the Law of Nations, was written by

John Eppstein under the auspices of the Catholic Council
for International Relations of Great Britain.

Prior to World War II, the CAIP never claimed a membership of more than 500,[51] but because of the prestige of
its members, the ideals of the Association reached a wide
audience. The CAIP's identification with the NCWC opened
the doors to all other recognized Catholic organizations.
Most of the work was coordinated by Elizabeth Sweeney whose
influence cannot be overestimated. She strove to help the
CAIP achieve its purpose "to further accord, with the teachings of the Church, the 'Peace of Christ in the Kingdom of
Christ' through the preparation and dissemination of studies
applying Christian teaching to international life."[52]

The CAIP's focus on peace education accorded well
with the Catholic liberal social philosophy of Ryan and
McGowan: "prevent social problems through legislation or,
when you can't prevent them, ease them by the intelligent
application of Christian organized social work."[53] Thus,
Father McGowan's desire to avoid "the danger of seeking a
central panacea"[54] for peace prevailed in the committee
system's development of a general body of Catholic thought
on international peace. The Association's best work was
done in presenting the just war tradition within Catholicism
and in attempting to combat isolationism. The CAIP by adopting the structure of the NCWC "was to eschew anything like
direct action . . . and to pursue rather a 'campaign of peace
education.'"[55]

Though the CAIP was an autonomous organization, its
relationship with the NCWC only compounded its problems.
The CAIP like the NCWC favored the organizational approach
of issuing statements from the top of the Catholic hierarchical structure rather than working directly with Catholics
on a grass roots level. Neither the CAIP nor the NCWC could
in any way control the jurisdiction of the local bishop in
the hierarchical Church structure nor could either claim to
be "official" in the strict sense of the term. Thus, other
movements seeking to further the mission of peace in the
Church could achieve equal status within a diocese if their
leaders managed to secure episcopal approval. Catholics
might significantly diverge from the CAIP's "official" plans
and maintain an "unofficial" movement as a source of continuing personal initiative. The identification of the CAIP
with the NCWC profited the Association little. George
Shuster, a member of the Association, wrote that "the CAIP
was at its best when the NCWC kept its hands off."[56]

The CAIP claimed to be the "official" peace organization seeking to present a never actualized unified program
of peace within the Catholic Church. Nevertheless, by the
1930's other movements, representing alternative perspectives
on war and peace issues, began to emerge. As was true in the
case of the CAIP, these movements traced their roots back to
the social question, the principal concern of Catholics
between the two great wars. The crash of 1929 and the ensuing
depression focused the concern of Americans on social issues

and more than one citizen had devised a plan for rebuilding
the nation. Among those who gained unusual national prominence was Father Charles E. Coughlin, a pastor in Royal Oak,
Michigan.[57] Equipped with his own program of social reconstruction, Coughlin, unlike Ryan, soon challenged the New
Deal policies of Franklin D. Roosevelt. Like Ryan, however,
Coughlin's concern for social justice eventually led him
into the international arena of war and peace.

Coughlin was an ardent nationalist and believed that
the United States was synonymous with Christendom; anything
that sapped the strength of this "Christian Commonwealth"
had to be eradicated. Believing as firmly as he did in this
unique version of the American dream, Coughlin regarded what
he thought to be the two principal evils of the depression,
capitalism and communism, as forces to be eliminated from
American society.

By 1938 his belief in the threat of "International
Jewry" reinforced his views of capitalism and communism and
what at one time was a domestic threat now emerged as an
international conspiracy. In his opinion, Jewry advanced
the evils of capitalism and communism and all three forces
threatened the "Christian Commonwealth" both from within
and without. An equally passionate isolationism reinforced
Coughlin's view of America's place in the world community
and until the advent of World War II Coughlin was a principal
figure in the debate on war and peace.

The one constant in Coughlin's strategy was his own personality which he conveyed over the radio. This factor alone accounts for the demagogic quality of his following. Members of his movement were his radio listeners, the majority of whom lived in Eastern and Midwestern cities. The radio provided the vehicle through which Coughlin, a powerful orator, rose to national prominence. In his addresses, this "shepherd of discontent" was able to put into words the fears and frustrations of his listeners.

Surfacing during the depression as a social reformer, Coughlin eventually emerged for some Catholics as a spokesman against World War II. Anything that diverted the energies of the nation away from its reconstruction was to be opposed, and World War II did just that. Coughlin's main concern was not peace but war as a threat to the Christian nation, America. His opposition to the war became a moral crusade.

One might legitimately ask why Coughlin is being mentioned in a study of the Catholic peace movement. The reason is that Coughlin opposed the participation of the United States in World War II. Yet, at no time did he identify himself with any of the existing peace groups, though at times he found himself standing with them on a particular issue. In order to understand the complexity and diversity of Catholic opposition to World War II, Coughlin must be viewed in a historical perspective with Catholic peace groups. His isolationism which led him to adopt the position of strict neutrality during the 1930's presents a total picture of Catholic responses. This picture reveals an identical pattern of the conflicts among advocates of collective security, pacifists and isolationists found in the broader context of American responses to neutrality legislation.

Most significantly, Coughlin's stance against America's entry into World War II represented a new departure in American Catholicism. In challenging America's participation in World War II, Coughlin represents a significant break with the Catholic patriotic tradition. Coughlin's motives were not rooted in a concern for peace. Rather, he challenged the role of the state in this particular war because American participation would support the wrong side -- a side that was dominated by British capitalists and Russian communists. This side was inconsistent with Coughlin's view of America as the new Christendom. Thus, despite his extreme nationalism, Coughlin was able to challenge the role of the United States government in World War II. Some of his followers even became conscientious objectors during the war.

The third group of Catholics who addressed themselves to the issues of war and peace was centered in the Catholic Worker Movement. Founded in 1933 in New York City, the Catholic Worker was unique in the history of American Catholicism. Unlike the Coughlin crusade or the CAIP, the Catholic Worker was fundamentally a movement of Catholic lay people. Moreover, the Catholic Worker, as it moved into the arena of war and peace, was to adopt a position of pacifism and thus become the first Catholic group in the United States to follow this ideal. Like Coughlin and the social actionists of the CAIP, however, the Catholic Worker first emerged as a group of Catholics who were concerned about the social reconstruction of America.

The cofounders of the Catholic Worker Movement were Peter Maurin and Dorothy Day. Maurin was a French itinerant peasant who had abandoned the Christian Brothers in France to join the Sillon movement. Disillusioned with the Sillon movement and seeking to escape the draft in France, he emigrated to Canada. These experiences had helped to form Maurin's philosophy of Christian personalism. He believed that at the core of Christianity was personal responsibility which the chaotic conditions of modern society destroyed. Maurin believed that man could affirm his personal responsibility by integrating the spiritual and material aspects of life by actively participating in the political, economic and social concerns of the world. If each individual Christian pursued this course, a restoration of unity in the Christian world would result.[58] Peter Maurin, wanting to share his vision with everyone, became a peripatetic teacher. Eventually he made his way to the United States.

Dorothy Day was by occupation a journalist. In her early days, after dropping out of college for financial reasons, she was involved with radical movements such as the Industrial Workers of the World and the communists; she also became a feminist.[59] At the time she first met Peter

Maurin, she was a recent convert to Catholicism and was on
assignment for America and Commonweal in Washington, D.C.
She was also in the midst of writing a novel which George
Shuster, the editor of Commonweal, claimed was excellent.[60]
Peter Maurin stopped by the office of George Shuster one
day to share his ideas. Upon hearing Maurin, Shuster
encouraged him to meet Dorothy Day. As soon as Dorothy heard
Maurin speak, she quit her job as a journalist and stopped
writing her novel. Her sole desire was to join Maurin in
building the Catholic Worker Movement. As Dorothy Day
herself was to say many times of Peter Maurin, "He was my
master and I was his disciple."[61] Dorothy managed to find
concrete ways of embodying Maurin's ideas. First, she
began a penny a copy newspaper, The Catholic Worker. She
also opened a House of Hospitality on Mott Street in New
York City. "Round-table discussions" where workers and
intellectuals could meet were held at the House. Later,
she began a farm commune in Easton, Pennsylvania.

The Catholic Worker Movement was not an organization
but rather a gathering of diverse people. Those who joined
the movement were cosmopolitan scholars and reformers who,
unlike members of the CAIP, identified themselves with the
disinherited.[62] They embraced a life-style of voluntary
poverty and focusing their attention on economic and social
changes that were consistent with the goals of nomic and
social changes that were consistent with the goals of
Christian personalism. These people did not wait for

clerical leadership. Nevertheless, the Catholic Worker was recognized by the Church hierarchy and the Archdiocese of New York requested its members to accept a chaplain. The founders did so, but the chaplain stayed very much in the background. Dorothy Day, then as always, followed the directives of her Church superiors. The Catholic Worker Movement, however, was never dependent upon the Church or any other institution for financial support. Voluntary contributions provided what monetary assistance was necessary to continue.

Because of the depression, Catholic Workers focused all their energies on ways to relieve human suffering and to remedy the injustices of American society. They based their program of social reconstruction on Christian personalism and upon the Holy Father's injunction to "go to the workingman, especially to the poorest of them." Catholic Workers favored a new economic system to replace what they viewed as a decadent capitalism. Though steeped in the thought of American and European social and liturgical thinkers, they centered the core of their beliefs on the Gospel.[63] The way to show their love for God was by love of their fellows through embodying the Sermon on the Mount. Thus, in their call for a new social order based on the program outlined by the popes in Rerum Novarum and Quadragesimo Anno, members favored direct action aimed at countering the evils of industrial society and demanded an unbloddy revolution. An explicit concern for peace was

not apparent in the early days of the Catholic Worker.[64]
But, as Dorothy Day was to say before the outbreak of World
War II:

> For eight years we have been opposing the use
> of force -- in the labor movement, in the class
> struggle, as well as in the struggles between
> countries. . . . By working for a better social
> order in our own country, by working for the
> 'tranquility in order' which is the definition
> of peace, we are working for peace.[65]

The Catholic Worker saw the incidents of aggression
during the 1930's and the world's response to them as the
play of power politics. In its view the League of Nations
and the concept of collective security to prevent war seemed
to fail each successive test. Thus, the Movement developed
and acted upon an evangelical pacifist rationale.

The Catholic Worker's pacifist position became explicit at the time of the Spanish Civil War. The Catholic
establishment was decidedly pro-Franco but the Catholic Worker
did not support his cause. Its newspaper condemned every
aspect of Franco's revolt in an attempt to show why it could
not follow the position of the Catholic establishment. In
doing this The Catholic Worker stated that it was adopting
a position of strict neutrality since it would support
neither Franco nor his opposition. Yet by remaining neutral,
it was already in opposition to the mainstream of Catholics
in the United States. The Catholic Worker took a pacifist
stance since it believed there was too much right and too
mich wrong on both sides during the war. The paper printed

the message of love and Christian pacifism: "Love your
enemies; do good to them that hate you, and pray for them
that persecute and calumniate you."[66] This position remained
constant and in 1939 <u>The Catholic Worker</u> opposed the lifting
of the Arms Embargo and declared that the United States
"should not export arms to any country in peace or at war.[67]

Strict neutrality became for the Workers the only
viable way to prevent America's entrance into World War II.
It was this stance that most clearly revealed the ideological
differences between the Catholic Worker and the CAIP. After
1939 the CAIP supported the policy of collective security
pursued by the Roosevelt administration. Ironically, the
Catholic Worker found itself aligned with Coughlin in advocating strict neutrality. Catholic Workers, however, were
internationalists and the Coughlinites were isolationists.
It is also true that these differences and similarities which
emerged among Catholics over the issue of neutrality legislation were identical to those found among all pacifist
groups, all advocates of collective security and all isolationists in America during the 1930's. Once America
entered the war, the pacifist rationale of the Catholic
Worker logically required its members to reject participation
in the war as a means of resolving the conflict. This was
also true of all pacifist peace groups.

Because of the Catholic Worker founders' commitment
to Christian personalism which required them to assume
personal responsibility for God's law of service to man, it
was natural for them to move to the Christian tradition of

pacifism with its emphasis on obedience to the spirit and word of the New Testament. In evangelical pacifism the fusion of vigorous social action with an absolute rejection of violence based on loving service and the solidarity of human brotherhood was complete.

Articles published in The Catholic Worker revealed the movement's concern for peace during the 1930's.[68] By 1935 the distribution of the movement's newspaper had increased from 2,500 copies to 110,000 copies and it was also appearing in England and Australia.[69] The paper consistently opposed efforts to involve the United States in war. It provided clear statements of its peace position, interspersed with articles on the popes' messages on peace, on the morality of war and on conscription. It denounced Roosevelt's foreign policy and opposed preparedness measures. It urged Catholic Workers not to manufacture munitions and later also not to purchase defense bonds. Individual Catholic Workers also joined demonstrations and boycotts, appeared before Congressional hearings and attempted to organize Catholic pacifists in resistance to conscription.

The Catholic Worker itself did not cooperate directly with other groups during the 1930's.[70] The articles in The Catholic Worker provided what little cooperation there was. In December, 1934, The Catholic Worker ran an ad for its readers to join the CAIP and to purchase its pamphlets. The newspaper also utilized the NCWC news service on items relating to peace. As late as 1939 in its October editorial, the newspaper asked:

> How many Catholics know that in Washington we
> have a Catholic Association for International
> Peace . . . an association which is headed by
> Most Reverend Edwin V. O'Hara, Bishop of Kansas
> City? Among the vice presidents there are many
> friends of The Catholic Worker. . . . It is
> absolutely necessary that our groups and cells
> and as many of our readers as possible should
> write and obtain literature that is available
> and form study groups to prepare themselves
> for the work of peace.

Individual Catholic Workers did their most effective work in organizing study clubs for resistance to conscription.[71]

The Catholic Worker's pages also praised the work of Women's International League for Peace and Freedom (WILPF)[72] and the work of the National Council for the Prevention of War,[73] both of which were as pacifist as the Catholic Worker. The paper often used resource material from the Council on the escalation of war. Monsignor Paul Hanley Furfey, a sociology professor at the Catholic University of America and an active member of the Catholic Worker Movement, was also a member of this board, but he remained after Monsignor Ryan resigned.

The Catholic Worker was allied with Commonweal in its neutral position on the Spanish Civil War. In fact, there was only one diocesan Catholic paper, The Echo, in Buffalo, New York, which not only was neutral during the Spanish Civil War, but like The Catholic Worker also professed pacifism. The Catholic Worker's only criticism of the secular press on the peace issue was a call for a boycott of Hearst papers because they were "imperialist warriors."[74] The paper

also reflected its contact with international newspapers
when it reported that students in Rome had protested the
stand of The Catholic Worker on the Ethiopian situation and
had defended Mussolini's occupation with quotes from the
sixteenth-century Catholic just war theorist, Vitoria.[75]

The Catholic Worker also touched on issues crucial to
peace in its attempt to offset the influences of anti-
Semitism and anticommunism among American Catholics. Peter
Maurin argued in his newspaper articles that "America is big
enough to find a refuge for persecuted Jews."[76] Dorothy Day
stated that The Catholic Worker "defended Jews during times
of stress."[77] And in 1939 it reported Archbishop Stritch
of Chicago as decrying "the slanders and untruths being
printed about the Jews" and Archbishop Stritch's condemnation of the anti-Semitism of Father Coughlin and the
Christian Front.[78]

The Catholic Worker's founders deplored red-baiting
as much as anti-Semitism, especially among Catholics. Dorothy
was convinced by her early association with communists "that
often the Communist more truly loves his brother, the poor
and oppressed, than many so-called Christians."[79] In July,
1937, The Catholic Worker replied to Father Coughlin's charge
that its members were communists. Dorothy contended that
The Catholic Worker was not communistic and affirmed that
the only true "international" was the Catholic Church.[80]
Both the anti-Semitism and the anticommunism of Coughlin
and the Christian Front were condemned in The Catholic Worker's
pages.

The founders were also aware of the great fear on
the part of Catholics of communism and saw it often as the
real motive behind Catholic statements on war and peace
issues. In October, 1936, The Catholic Worker agreed to
cooperate with John Noll, Bishop of Fort Wayne, in his anti-
communist drive, but explained its participation by stating
that "it joined mainly because it believed that man was not
subject to the state but to Christ and that this message
should be delivered to the leaders of all nations not just
the communist leaders." The pages of The Catholic Worker were
just as firm in their opposition to peace groups controlled
by communists such as the American League Against War and
Fascism.[81] The Catholic Worker's opposition rested on the
grounds that these groups still advocated class war and
warned their readers against them. People interested in
joining these groups were advised to contact The Catholic
Worker for more information. They also urged Catholics to
start their own peace groups so that communists would not
be the only ones claiming to work for peace.

The pages of The Catholic Worker in 1936 pleaded with
bankers not to lend money to nations at war.[82] It opposed
the cash-and-carry clause of the Neutrality Act of 1937
because it "only served to line up Fascist against Democratic
powers."[83] It also admitted, with the defeat of the Ludlow
Resolution in the House by only twenty-one votes, that there
was no way left for the American people to prevent a presidential declaration of war. "War is coming" for the United

States declared <u>The Catholic Worker</u>.[84] In 1939, it again
held to its position of strict neutrality and opposed the
lifting of the Embargo Act and the proposed neutrality with
its cash-and-carry provision. <u>The Catholic Worker</u>'s position was clear and consistent and like other pacifist peace
groups in America supported the Keep America Out of War
campaign after 1939 and increasingly turned to the needs of
its own constituents, particularly to the needs of Catholic
conscientious objectors to war. Pearl Harbor was anticlimac-
tic for Catholic Workers. President Roosevelt had already
won approval to extend American military and economic goods
to the Allies, had accepted an anti-German naval commitment
in the Atlantic and had removed most of the fetters from
neutrality legislation.[85] Unable to alter national legislation and defeated in their demands for strict neutrality,
<u>The Catholic Worker</u> remained faithful to its pacifism and
refused to participate in war when it was finally declared.

The Catholic Worker Movement like the CAIP and Coughlin
was led into the arena of war and peace through its concern
for social justice. By moving to the left on the political
spectrum in America, the Catholic Worker stepped out of the
whole intellectual and social ethos of Americanism. Strengthened by deep religious faith, the Catholic Worker Movement
gradually worked out its stance of evangelical pacifism. Any
degree of intellectual sophistication concerning this position
would not be reached until after World War II. The significance of the Catholic Worker for American Catholic history in

the 1930's is that it provided a pacifist alternative to
war. The basis of this ideal was rooted in the church and
could stand up against the pressures of the state. Yet,
the Movement was not expecially effective. Although
evangelical pacifism seemed irrelevant to events both within
the United States and in the international scene, the
Catholic Worker was not shaken by ineffectiveness and continues to flourish to this day.

The internationalism of the CAIP, on the other hand,
left the Association with no alternative to war once it was
declared by the government of the United States. Ryan and
his associates wished to achieve world peace through social
justice. They believed that social reform at home was an
important means of achieving world peace, and the greatest
strength of their approach to international problems was
their economic interpretation and their clear recognition
of the necessity of worldwide planning and control. In the
absence of a strong international organization and with no
ethic but the just war theory which placed all responsibility
for war and peace on the state, the CAIP ended up with the
nation as its criterion. For all the Association's opposition to extreme nationalism and to the Coughlin hysteria,
the CAIP accepted the decisions of its nation for international
ends. In face of Hitlerism its way to peace was through war.

Despite Coughlin's moral crusade against political
evils, especially the evil of World War II, he was unable
to stop the United States from entering World War II. At

best Coughlin's hatreds and isolationism provided the
rationale for his opposition and nonparticipation in the
war effort. The irony of this stance is that Coughlin was
mainly condemned for his extreme nationalism, yet, at the time
of World War II, he stood in opposition to his nation.

The structure and tactics of all three Catholic groups
managed to influence and attract as members portions of the
American Catholic public. The CAIP, the "official" Catholic
peace organization, attracted middle- and upper-class
Catholics and once war was declared reflected the majority
opinion, not only of Catholics, but of all Americans. Coughlin's demagogic approach appealed to the lower class and the
more disaffected members of society in his offer to provide
more justice and to raise their standard of living by rooting
out evil. The Catholic Worker attracted those Catholics seeking an intensified life-style of commitment to the Gospel
message of "love of neighbor." In all three groups it was
only the Catholic Worker which offered a life-style and a
supportive community that enabled its members to provide a
Christian witness to peace, an alternative to the American
way of life.

Neither Coughlin nor the Catholic Worker were able to
influence national legislation to the extent of maintaining
strict neutrality, even though minor victories were achieved,
such as the 1939 delay of the lifting of the Arms Embargo
during the Spanish Civil War. The defeat of strict neutrality
and the United States entrance into World War II cancelled

out the minor victories. Coughlinites and the Catholic
Worker, together with all isolationist and pacifist groups
during the 1930's, could not determine national legislation
and despite their protestations America went to war.

The CAIP's move to collective security in national
legislation placed them in the victorious camp of the Roosevelt
administration and ultimately in the midst of World War II.
The belief that Hitler had to be stopped, even by war, was a
greater cause than the maintenance of peace. In this case,
the CAIP was no different than the other peace groups which
advocated collective security.

The diversity in American Catholicism's quest for
peace represented by these three groups contradicts the
generally accepted view of a united Catholic front on the
issues of war and peace. It was not primarily any ethical
position that caused this diversity among Catholics. It was
rather the three positions of pacifism, internationalism and
isolationism supported with a Catholic ethical rationale,
that provided the basis for ideological diversity. These
three positions marked not only the diversity among Catholics
but among all Americans during the 1930's. The difference
between Catholics and other Americans was that Catholics
re-inforced these positions with a Catholic theological
rationale.

Until the 1930's the just war theory had been the
normative ethical position in American Catholicism. With
the appearance of the Catholic Worker Movement this theory

50

was seriously challenged by the centuries-old tradition of
pacifism. After the war, the ethical stance of pacifism
has become more widespread among Catholics and as a result
the just war theory is considerably less acceptable.[86] The
demagogic rhetoric of the crusader, Charles Coughlin, has
disappeared and one reason for its demise is the emphasis
on hatreds and negativism rather than on positive ethical
values. Though the CAIP continued to publish pamphlets and
issue statements on war and peace, it had little impact on
the Catholic peace movement after the opening of World War
II.

The group that would provide the American Catholic
peace witness during World War II and for the next forty
years in American history would be the Catholic Worker. In
order to understand the place of pacifism within the Catholic
Worker Movement it is necessary to know more fully the
thought and action of Dorothy Day. Through the Worker, she
offered a new direction in the American Catholic peace movement and launched what she described as a "permanent revolution" im American Catholicism.[87]

REFERENCES

[1] Ellis, "American Catholics and Peace . . . ," p. 25.

[2] *Light and Truth* (Chicago, June, 1925), p. 27.

[3] Henry J. Browne, "Catholicism in the United States," in Smith and Jamison, *The Shaping of American Religion* (New Jersey, 1961), p. 77.

[4] John Higham, *Strangers in the Land: Pattern of American Nativism, 1860-1925* (New York, 1966), p. 218.

[5] Browne, "Catholicism in the United States," p. 77.

[6] John Tracy Ellis, *American Catholicism* (Chicago, 1969), p. 141.

[7] Ibid., p. 144.

[8] David J. O'Brien, *American Catholicism and Social Reform: The New Deal Years* (New York, 1968), p. 42.

[9] Ibid., p. 43.

[10] John K. Ryan, *Modern War and Basic Ethics* (Milwaukee, 1943), pp. 41-52.

[11] Koenig, *Principles . . .* , pp. ix-x.

[12] Pastoral Letter of U.S. Bishops 1920 (dated 1919) cited in "Notes on CAIP" by Raymond McGowan, August 4, 1958, to be found in the Archives at Marquette University (AMU), CAIP Collection.

[13] Harry W. Flannery, "CAIP Fights for International Peace," *U.S. Catholic* (September, 1963), 25. The correspondence received by Flannery while researching the CAIP is located in the CAIP Collection at AMU.

[14] Ibid., 25 and 26.

[15]Idem. See also John A. Ryan's autobiography, Social Doctrine in Action (New York, 1941), pp. 140, 141, 145.

[16]Francis Broderick, Right Reverend New Dealer, John A. Ryan (New York, 1963), p. 136.

[17]Charles Chatfield, For Peace and Justice: Pacifism in America, 1914-1941 (Tennessee, 1971), p. 101.

[18]AMU, CAIP Collection, "Notes on CAIP" by Raymond McGowan, August 4, 1958.

[19]Idem.

[20]Idem.

[21]AMU, CAIP Collection, "CAIP Constitution," Section 2.

[22]O'Brien, American Catholicism and Social Reform . . . , p. 121.

[23]AMU, CAIP Collection, Letter dated March 1, 1963, Mrs. R. M. Patterson to Harry W. Flannery.

[24]Dennis Robb, "Specialized Catholic Action in the United States, 1936-1949: Ideology, Leadership, and Organization" (Ph.D. Dissertation, University of Minnesota, 1972), p. 32.

[25]Flannery, "CAIP Fights . . . ," p. 27.

[26]This point about type of membership is similar to the thesis of Sondra R. Herman, Eleven Against War: Studies in American International Thought, 1898-1921 (California, 1969), p. ix.

[27]Flannery, "CAIP Fights . . . ," p. 27; Broderick, Right Reverend New Dealer. . . , pp. 137-38 contends that Ryan drew substantially from the book of Franziskus Stratmann, O.P., The Church and War. It should be noted, however, that Stratmann believed no modern war could be just.

[28]The CAIP committees expanded from its original seven to committees on Ethics, History, Inter-American Relations, World Order, Juridical Institutions, Economic Life, Social Welfare, Agriculture, Asia, Africa, Dependent Areas, Education, Religion and Culture, Adult Education and School and College Education cited in Norman Krause Herzfeld, "Working for Peace," The Voice of St. Jude (December, 1954), n.p.

[29]AMU, CAIP Collection, "Summary of CAIP Committee Work," Section 1, 6.

[30]AMU, CAIP Collection, "A History of the Catholic Association for International Peace 1927-1953," by Clarence L. Hohl, Jr., Ph.D., 22; see John A. Ryan's International Ethics, fourth edition.

[31]AMU, CAIP Collection, "Correspondence," Letters to Miss Elizabeth Sweeney.

[32]AMU, CAIP Collection, "Correspondence," Letters during 1930's, Anna Dill Gamble to Elizabeth Sweeney.

[33]AMU, CAIP Collection, "Correspondence," Letters during 1930's, Mary Workman to Elizabeth Sweeney.

[34]AMU, CAIP Collection, "Minutes of the Executive Committee," December 27, 1928, and April 22, 1930.

[35]AMU, CAIP Collection, "Correspondence," Letter dated April 5, 1935, Sister Rose de Lima to Miss Elizabeth Sweeney.

[36]AMU, CAIP Collection, "Correspondence," Letters dated May 9, 1935, and October 28, 1936, Sister Rose de Lima to Miss Elizabeth Sweeney. Also a typed page announcing the two meetings on November 20.

[37]Congressional Record, 71st Congress, 3rd Sess., 1931, LXXIV, 2263-67.

[38]AMU, CAIP Collection, "Correspondence," Letter dated February 1, 1937, Rev. E. V. Stanford to Miss Elizabeth Sweeney.

[39]AMU, CAIP Collection, "Correspondence," Letter dated April 5, 1934, Monsignor J. M. Wolfe to Committee Members.

[40]Herzfeld, "Working for Peace," n.p.

[41]AMU, CAIP Collection, "Correspondence," Letter dated February 3, 1930, Elizabeth Sweeney to Librarian of Navy Department; Broderick, Right Reverend New Dealer . . . , p. 138, points out that from the inception of the CAIP, Ryan wanted the CAIP to function as an American Catholic pressure group for international peace, working alongside Protestant and secular groups and lobbying before congressional committees.

^{42}AMU, CAIP Collection, "Correspondence," Letter
dated April 19, 1933, Patrick J. Ward to Miss Elizabeth
Sweeney; Ryan, Social Doctrine in Action, pp. 214-15, contends that he had been a member of the National Council for
the Prevention of War "when the Council took a strong stand
against President Roosevelt's recommendation to Congress in
1939, to lift the embargo on the sale of arms in favor of
Great Britain and France, I am certain I should have then
withdrawn."

^{43}AMU, CAIP Collection, "Summary of CAIP Committee
Work 1927 to 1952," 7.

^{44}Idem.

^{45}New York Times, October 16, 1939, cited in Charles
J. Tull, Father Coughlin and the New Deal (Syracuse, 1965),
p. 217.

^{46}AMU, CAIP Collection, "Correspondence." This is
revealed in the letter of Miss Elizabeth Sweeney. It is
never explicitly stated. Broderick, Right Reverend New
Dealer. . . , p. 137, points out that "Groups with strong
Protestant backing, like the National Study Conference on
the Church and World Peace, wanted to draw the NCWC in, but
Bishop Muldoon warned Ryan to avoid the type of official
cooperation with Protestant organizations that might draw a
rebuke from Rome and would certainly outrage the more conservative American bishops. The hierarchy even steered clear
of the National Council for the Prevention of War, a group
less intimately associated with Protestant churches as such.
Ryan himself moved cautiously, for a tinge of pacifism sur-
rounded the peace movement generally; he was always wary of
extremist views because he was willing to support war measures
under some circumstances."

^{47}AMU, CAIP Collection, "Correspondence," Letter dated
November 17, 1936, Walter Van Kirk to Miss Elizabeth Sweeney.

^{48}Ryan, Social Doctrine in Action , p. 214.

^{49}AMU, CAIP Collection, "Correspondence," Letter dated
May 17, 1934, Miss Elizabeth Sweeney to Mr. Caravati.

^{50}AMU, CAIP Collection, "Correspondence," Letter dated
June 26, 1929, Franziskus Stratmann, O.P., to Miss Elizabeth
Sweeney.

[51]AMU, CAIP Collection, Hohl, "A History of the Association . . . ," p. 55.

[52]AMU, CAIP Collection, "CAIP Constitution."

[53]Letter dated February 29, 1972, Paul H. Furfey to
author.

[54]AMU, CAIP Collection, "Notes on CAIP" by Raymond
McGowan, August 4, 1958.

[55]AMU, CAIP Collection, "Correspondence," Letter
dated February 18, 1963, Rev. Charles C. Miltner, C.S.C.,
to Harry W. Flannery.

[56]AMU, CAIP Collection, "Correspondence," Letter
dated February 2, 1963, George Shuster to Harry W. Flannery.

[57]In this article I have presented a general interpre-
tation of Coughlin's relationship to the Catholic peace
movement. To achieve this interpretation I have consulted
a number of studies on Coughlin. See O'Brien, American
Catholicism and Social Reform . . . ; Tull, Father Coughlin . . .
David H. Bennett, Demagogues of the Depression: American Radi-
cals and the Union Party, 1932-36 (New Jersey, 1969); Aaron
Abell, American Catholicism and Social Action (1960, rpt. Notre
Dame, Ind., 1963); Craig A. Newton, "Father Coughlin and His
National Union for Social Justice," Southwestern Social Science
Quarterly, XLI (December, 1960), 341-49 and James P. Shenton,
"The Coughlin Movement and the New Deal," Political Science
Quarterly, LXXIII (September, 1958), 353-73. I have also
consulted twenty pamphlets written by Coughlin and his news-
paper, Social Justice, 1937-1942. Pamphlets and newspaper
are located in the Archives at the University of Notre Dame.

[58]The Catholic Worker, September, 1933, and April,
1935, cited in O'Brien, American Catholicism and Social
Reform . . . , p. 195.

[59]Dorothy Day's books are mainly autobiographical:
From Union Square to Rome (Maryland, 1939), Houses of
Hospitality (New York, 1939), The Long Loneliness (New York,
1952) and Loaves and Fishes (New York, 1963). There is no
autobiography of Peter Maurin. There is one biography,
however, Arthur Sheehan, Peter Maurin: Gay Believer: The
Biography of an Unusual and Saintly Man (New York, 1959).

[60]Presentation by Rev. James T. Burtchaell of Laetare Medal to Dorothy Day at University of Notre Dame's Commencement, May, 1972.

[61]Day, The Long Loneliness, p. 166.

[62]Herman, Eleven Against War . . . , p. ix.

[63]The major influences were Benedictine Virgil Michel, Monsignor Paul Hanley Furfey, Tolstoy, Berdyaev and Emmanuel Mounier and many other personalist thinkers.

[64]It is important to note that there is nothing in the closed Catholic Worker Collection at AMU which deals directly with peace. Both Dorothy Day and her chosen biographer, William Miller, so report.

[65]The Catholic Worker, June, 1940, and October, 1939.

[66]A complete study of American Catholics' reaction to the Spanish Civil War is found in the works of J. David Valaik: "American Catholic Dissenters and the Spanish Civil War," The Catholic Historical Review, LIII (January, 1968), 537-546 and "Catholics, Neutrality, and the Spanish Embargo, 1937-1939," Journal of American History, LIV (June, 1967), 73-85.

[67]The Catholic Worker, October, 1938.

[68]Letter dated February 29, 1972, Paul Hanley Furfey to author.

[69]The Catholic Worker, May, 1935.

[70]Interview with Dorothy Day, June 24, 1971: Dorothy stated that there was never any significant cooperation with other peace groups until the 1950's.

[71]See author's article, "Catholic Conscientious Objectors During World War II," soon to appear in The Catholic Historical Review.

[72]The Catholic Worker, April, 1934.

[73]Ibid., January, 1936, and March, 1937.

[74]Ibid., July-August, 1935.

[75]Ibid., May, 1936.

[76]Ibid., December, 1935.

[77]Ibid., July-August, 1939.

[78]Idem.

[79]Ibid., December, 1934, also cited in O'Brien, American Catholicism and Social Reform . . . , p. 202.

[80]Ibid., May, 1934.

[81]Ibid., July-August, 1935; July, 1936; May, 1937; January, 1938.

[82]Ibid., May, 1936.

[83]Ibid., January, 1938.

[84]Idem.

[85]Chatfield, For Peace and Justice . . . , p. 325.

[86]"War," The Catholic Encyclopedia, XV (New York, 1913), gives Charles Mackey's definition of the just war criteria and presents it as normative. "War," The New Catholic Encyclopedia, XIV (New York, 1967), quotes Paul Ramsey: "It has been observed that according to recent papal teaching (Pius XII and John XXIII) there is no longer any just war theory, because these popes have withdrawn the right of war in the situations to which these tests or conditions had reference, i.e., offensive war. This means that contemporary moral teaching represents both a continuation and a radical adjustment of traditional teaching on just warfare."

[87]"Dorothy Day Describes the Launching of The Catholic Worker and the Movement Behind It, May, 1933," cited in John Tracy Ellis, (ed.), Documents of American Catholic History, II (Chicago, 1967), p. 629.

CHAPTER II

DOROTHY DAY AND PACIFISM

Pacifist groups alone were able to remain steadfast
in their peace position once the United States government
officially declared its involvement in World War II. The
only Catholic group to espouse pacifism during this period
of American history was the Catholic Worker. Though not a
peace group it represented the only Catholics who as a group
opposed World War II. It becomes evident that in order to
understand the role of the Catholic Worker in the American
Catholic peace movement, special emphasis must be placed on
the thinking and action of Dorothy Day, the co-founder of
the Catholic Worker Movement. There are two reasons for
this: first, she has been the foremost exemplar of the
Worker ideal and second, it is Dorothy Day who introduced
the spirit of pacifism to the Catholic Worker Movement. Miss
Day has directed the movement's constant opposition to war
from the time of the Spanish Civil War through the Second
World War, the Korean War to the War in Vietnam.

It was a long journey for Dorothy Day to reach her dual
position of Catholic and pacifist. Ironically, the journey
would not even be begun until she had firmly formed herself
as a radical. It would not be until Miss Day had explored

58

every radical position and participated in a variety of
radical causes that she would begin her long and lonely
journey as a radical who was also Catholic and pacifist.

Dorothy Day was born in Brooklyn Heights on November
8, 1897, the daughter of John I. Day, a sportswriter. Essentially a conservative, Mr. Day contrived to combine respect-
ability with journalism, as have his three sons. There were
also two daughters, one of whom early settled down to married
life in Rye, New York and the other, Dorothy, who in the eyes
of her father, was a black sheep from the start. The Days
were Scotch-Irish Calvinists who belonged to the Presbyterian
Church. Dorothy Day found the family pattern unsatisfying.
"There was never any kissing in our family, and never a close
embrace," she wrote years later. There was only a firm and
austere kiss from my mother every night. . . . We were like
most Anglo-Saxons."[1]

Unable to embrace her parents, Miss Day embraced the
poor and the oppressed. As a young girl in Chicago, where
her father was a sports editor of Inter Ocean, she began
reading radical literature. Kropotkin especially influenced
her and alerted her to the plight of the poor. At fifteen
she believed she had discovered a direction to her life that
would bring her happiness. It was empathy with the poor and
oppressed more than political considerations that formed the
basis of Dorothy's radicalism.

Dorothy Day was sixteen years old when World War I
began, and she was unaffected by it. Her main concern at the

time was going away to school. In 1914 she entered the
University of Illinois at Urbana on a scholarship which
she supplemented by caring for children and doing house
work. She remained in college only two years. Formal academic disciplines did not capture her interest. She missed
classes, disdained the customary patterns of college social
mixing, and with singular determination went forward to
grapple with the universe. She read everything by Dostoevsky,
who impressed her profoundly, and the stories of Gorky and
Tolstoy. She became preoccupied with poverty, misery and
the class war, and eventually joined the campus Socialist
club. "I was in love with the masses," she wrote. Dorothy
made one close friend during her college days, a classmate
and fellow rebel, the wealthy and brilliant Rayna Simon.[2]
Rayna used to laugh at Dorothy's absorption in Socialism,
but ten years later Rayna gave her life to the cause.

Leaving college in 1916 because of academic dissatisfaction and financial need, Dorothy Day moved with her family
to New York, where her father had taken a job on the Telegraph.
Soon after they arrived she went to work as a reporter and
columnist on the Socialist Call. Her father's disapproval
led her to rent a room on Cherry Street, in the slums of the
lower East Side, and never again did she live with her family.

On her own at nineteen, Miss Day spent the next ten
years in the tumult of Greenwich Village life. The job on the
Call was followed by one with the Anti-Conscription League;
the United States was at war with Germany by then, and she

was assigned the task of pasting "peace" stickers on the venerable façade of the Union League Club. Presently she joined the Industrial Workers of the World, because she shared its anarchistic verve and distrust of Marx. In the summer of 1917 she became Floyd Dell's assistant on the Masses. Her job ended that fall when the radical magazine was suppressed. During this same year she joined sixty other women who picketed the White House to protest against the treatment of some suffragettes sho had been imprisoned in Washington after staging a demonstration. Miss Day and others were arrested and when they refused bail were sentenced to thirty days in the Occoquain prison. Confinement, a physical struggle with a guard, and the hunger strike to which the suffragists had committed themselves brought her close to despair. On the fourth day an attendant brought her a Bible, and she read it. The psalms comforted her, yet she decided that the comfort received from religion was a sign of weakness.[3] After her confinement she returned to New York City and her next job was on the Liberator, the successor to the Masses. She liked it well enough but found it more fun to be with the group at the Provincetown Playhouse where Eugene O'Neill and other of her friends had plays in rehearsal.

In 1918 Miss Day took a job as a probationary nurse at King's County Hospital. The reason for the job was given in a note to a friend at the time, "I hate being Utopian and trying to escape from reality. Now that we are in the thick

62

of war and there is so much to be done, I might as well try
to do it instead of sitting around playing at writing."[4]
When the war ended she returned to her village haunts. It
was also during this time that she became engaged to Mike
Gold, a dedicated Communist and writer. The marriage never
took place because Dorothy could not accept his hard-line
Marxist interpretation of history.

In the early twenties, Miss Day spent her time between
New York and Chicago, working as a reporter, a proofreader,
a librarian, and even as a clerk at Montgomery Ward's. In
1923 A. & C. Boni published her first novel. It was about
Village life and was not very successful. But the publisher
had titled it The Eleventh Virgin and sold it to Hollywood
on the strength of the name. When the movie people got it,
they had it rewritten to include sex beyond the title. Miss
Day, however, did get $2,500 out of it, which she used to
buy a cottage on the shore of Raritan Bay, at Huguenot, Staten
Island.[5]

Several months after moving into her cottage, she began
to live with Forster Battingham, a young biology instructor.
He had been in the service during World War I and had been
taken ill with influenza in 1918 and spent practically the
duration of his military service in the hospital. He was an
anarchist; yet, he was not a part of the literary or radical
groups with whom Dorothy Day had been associated. His sister,
Lily, however, had married Kenneth Burke, the philosopher and

literary critic, and it was Dorothy's friendship with Lily
that brought the two together.[5] Their first meeting had been
at Malcolm Cowley's Village apartment. Cowley had just
recently married Peggy Baird, Dorothy's friend who had gone
with her to the suffragette demonstration in Washington, D.C.
Dorothy Day, however, never pretended to dwell in the inner
circle of the intellectual and literary set that lived in
Paris and the Village in the twenties. Though she enjoyed
their company, she had a basic aversion to intellectual and
abstract discussion. She preferred simple and direct human
contact in live flesh and blood situations, especially among
the poor and the oppressed.[6] She viewed herself as a writer,
however, and within a year after her marriage, her second
novel, What Price Love? was bought by the Bell Syndicate
for newspaper serialization.

On March 3, 1927 she gave birth to her daughter Tamar.
She was happy though Forster was not. He wondered what point
there was to bringing another person into a world of hope-
lessness and injustice. In her autobiography, Dorothy tells
how the birth of her child compelled her to become a Catholic.

> Forster had made the physical world come alive
> for me and had awakened in my heart a flood of
> gratitude. The final object of this love and
> gratitude was God. No human creature could
> receive or contain so vast a flood of love and
> joy as I felt after the birth of my child. With
> this came the need to worship and adore. I had
> heard many say they wanted to worship God in
> their own way and did not need a Church in which
> to praise Him. . . . But my very experience as
> a radical, my whole make-up, led me to want to

associate myself with others, with the masses,
in praising and adoring God. Without even
looking into the claims of the Catholic
Church, I was willint to admit that for me
she was the one true Church.[7]

This choice on Dorothy Day's part meant that she
would have to leave her mate, who was deeply irreligious
and found all that he needed in nature and felt no need to
justify the natural world in terms of religion. Her choice
of Catholicism also meant parting with her life-long radical
friends. In some aspects, Miss Day's choice is not entirely
incomprehensible. She ultimately seemed to be searching for
something that her past experiences had not satisfied. She
had never been attracted to the intellectual life, she had
found the class-conflict interpretation of Marx inadequate
to explain the plight of the masses, and one-issue causes
such as women's rights did not long hold her attention.
Journalism and writing were still her profession, but she
didn't view herself as really successful in these areas.
Her conversion signified a belief in a deeper reality. This
belief was so strong that she was willing to leave all.

First she had her child Tamar baptized. Then on
December 28, 1927, Dorothy Day was baptized a Catholic in
the Church of Our Lady, Holy Christians in Totenville, Staten
Island. The action was almost wholly mechanical. There was
no consolation. It had been done and that was that. From
the first she knew that what she sought in the Church was an
involvement with man that went beyond anything she had

experienced during her association with her radical friends. Looking at the Catholic Church in America she found little or no vision beyond the traditional boundaries of the local parish. The kind of involvement she sought would not be available for the next five years of her life. It would have to wait until she met Peter Maurin.[8]

During the five year interval, Miss Day explored her faith, raised her daughter, wrote, at times did manual labor jobs, and traveled. Her writing at first took her to Hollywood where she received a contract to write dialogues for pictures. She found it depressing and when her three month contract was up she was dismissed. She bought a ticket for herself and Tamar to Mexico City. There she wrote graphically about the life of the poor among whom she lived. She returned to New York and in 1931 went to visit her mother in Florida and for the first time saw the life of the Southern Blacks. Back in New York she was off again on a writing assignment for *America* and *Commonweal* to cover the Washington hunger march. Though she had lost touch with most of her radical friends, Mike Gold still dropped by to see her. It was Mike's brother, George Granich, who was working with the Communist-dominated unemployment councils who encouraged her to go to Washington, D.C. Witnessing the hunger marches and the total absence of the Church's presence on behalf of the poor, she knew that somewhere the faith that she had embraced had been turned aside from its true historic mission. She became determined to discover how the mission of the Church could

become vital. "And when I returned to New York," she wrote,
"I found Peter Maurin -- Peter, the French peasant, whose
spirit and ideas will dominate. . . .the rest of my life."[9]

It is doubtful that anything as significant as the
Catholic Worker Movement would have enveloped the energies
of Dorothy Day if she had not met Peter Maurin. For five
years Miss Day had been a Catholic and as always a radical.
But how she would blend the two aspects into a life's work
was still unclear. She needed a vision, an intellectual
rationale, and a program. Peter Maurin had all of this in
what he termed "Utopian Christian Communism." Miss Day was
able to bring to it journalistic experience that would
enable his message to reach other people. She had a practical approach and a talent for leadership that would find
ways to give reality to the vision. As much as Miss Day
needed Peter Maurin, so too did he need her or else he would
have remained an ineffectual eccentric. Thus, these two
people co-founded the Catholic Worker Movement in America.[10]

In order to understand the way in which Miss Day introduced the spirit of pacifism and non-violence into the
movement, it is first necessary to understand how Maurin's
vision presented a synthesis of Catholicism and radicalism.
The issue of pacifism was never explicitly discussed in the
initial formation of the Catholic Worker Movement.

By the time Dorothy had met Maurin, he had acquired an
extraordinary knowledge of political theory, Church history,
economics, and law, both canon and secular. From this

knowledge, he had developed an ideology that he expressed orally and in writing. He developed a form of writing which he termed the "Easy Essay." Its purpose was to simplify abstract ideas and communicate them in an almost child-like manner. Maurin's message, whether oral or written, was essentially that of Catholic radicalism. This primarily meant that the Worker ideal was total -- it subsumed all. Thus, it was antithetical to liberalism which of its very nature flows in and out of the currents of time and contains the acceptable humanism of progress. It was also unlike liberalism because the Worker ideal did not accept the national state as the primary source of community which holds together the change and flow of the phenomenal world. Technology, the means of assuring progress in the world was also rejected in the radical vision. In place of the liberal myths of nation state, technology and progress, Maurin posited the Christian myths of the Garden of Eden, the Fall, the light of the Beatitudes, the darkness of oblivion, sacred community, and sinful alienation. Thus, the radical ideal of the Catholic Worker was rooted not in the material world but in the realm of the spiritual. The goals of the Catholic Worker would be achieved at the end of time -- with the second coming of Christ. Thus, the vision was eschatological and therefore, beyond history. It demanded that history submit to it and not the reverse.[11]

With the presentation of Maurin's vision to Dorothy Day, she for the first time found a radicalism which she believed to be sufficient for the crises at hand.

Besides radicalism the other distinctive feature of the Worker ideal which Maurin presented to Dorothy Day was personalism. "The personalist idea holds that the primacy of Christian love should be brought from its position of limbo where human affairs are concerned and infused into the process of history. The central fact of existence should not be process, with men holding on in whatever spot he found most tolerable, love should redeem process itself. Workers faith in love is the ultimate reality."[12] This concept of personalism coupled with a view of freedom that meant the capacity of an individual to turn from the tyranny of sense toward the spirit involved suffering and even tragedy. It basically meant that each individual would re-enact in his own life the mystery of the crucifixion of Christ.

Personalism rather than political analysis appealed greatly to Dorothy Day. She had been attracted to radical groups mainly because of the plight of the masses. She turned toward political groups such as Socialists and the Industrial Workers of the World in her youth in hopes of finding solutions to the plight of the poor. In them she never found an adequate answer. In Christian personalism, however, the solution resided with the individual and was not dependent on material circumstances. Victory also was assured though it was not confined to human history but to a power beyond history -- Christ.

Maurin was also careful to point out in the presentation of his vision what he believed to be the greatest enemies to attaining the Worker ideal in contemporary America. The enemies were nationalism and capitalism. Maurin spent a great deal of time protesting these dehumanizing aspects of American life. According to him, the nation had become the symbol of community and had put too much of its use to the ends of competitive power. Capitalism like nationalism was opposed because of its glorification of struggle. Capital always in pursuit of its own aggrandizement had used the nation for its own imperialist ends. Maurin did not believe that there was anything new in his analysis of the twin-enemies, nationalism and capitalism, but he did believe that his solution was new. The Worker ideal presented a viable alternative to the American way of life. He had no blue-print for the decentralization and simplification of American society -- it was all very vague. At best, all he could offer were a few general principles.[13]

Yet, these general principles were all that Dorothy Day needed to begin her work. She believed that the Worker ideal was a positive Christian alternative and that it should be made available to every individual who desired to embrace it. For this to occur, it was first of all necessary to present the ideal to others. Dorothy Day's first effort was to do what she knew how to do best -- start a newspaper. She entitled it, The Catholic Worker, to announce a Catholic presence and concern for the poor and oppressed which had mainly been the concern of Communists and other radicals. The publication of the first issue caused Maurin to disappear

for a few months. He had wanted the paper to devote itself
solely to the printing of his "Easy Essays." Dorothy held
firm and Peter finally returned.[14]

Miss Day also managed to find ways of carrying out
other aspects of Peter's vision. She managed to open a House
of Hospitality on Mott Street in New York City which would be
the beginning of a voluntary community. Round-table discussions between workers and intellectuals were also held there.
She managed to raise enough money to buy land to start a
farming commune in hopes of achieving a simplified way of
life in contrast to the dehumanizing aspects of the capitalistic economy. These three endeavors provided visibility,
place, and work for individuals who also desired to embrace
the Worker ideal. The main work of Catholic Workers was
administering food, clothing, and shelter to the poor. As
they performed these Corporal Works of Mercy, they also spent
much time protesting the dehumanizing aspects of nationalism
and capitalism through their newspaper, by participation in
strikes, and by demonstrations against social injustice. All
of these services were in great demand during the depression.

Within a few years of the founding of the Catholic
Worker Movement, it became evident that it was not the depression, but war that was the major crisis confronting Americans.
The Catholic Worker mentioned that during a time of war the
nation state was invested with all the marks of power in the
form of military might. At a time of war, the cohesive power
of the state reached its zenith.[15] For Dorothy Day, war

meant a colossally organized extreme opposition to active
love. It was clear to her that the Gospel message was peace
and it was during such a time of conflict that the Catholic
Worker suffered the most. The only alternative to state
violence was non-violence. Sarcastically, she began to refer
to the government of the United States as "Holy Mother, the
State."

The nation state's decision to declare war was thus
the ultimate question to be faced by the individual. Maurin
who was completely a man of peace never reached the point of
making his pacifism a pronouncement. Perhaps to have gone
this far would have offended his personalist sense; yet, to
be consistent with the vision he presented, man seemed to
have no alternative if true to that spirit of peace.[16] John
C. Cort, a young Catholic Worker of the thirties writes that
"Dorothy says that Peter was a pacifist, but I don't recall
seeing anything he ever wrote or hearing anything he ever
said that supports that. The subject didn't seem to interest
him, or else he didn't feel confident enough to challenge the
traditional Catholic view that there are just wars and there
are unjust wars."[17]

Maurin's reluctance, however, did not prevent Miss Day
as editor of The Catholic Worker from announcing through its
pages that pacifism was its position. It is important to
emphasize that Dorothy Day viewed pacifism as a part of the
total vision that was presented to her by Peter Maurin. The
Catholic Worker was a total way of life and to be consistent

with the Worker ideal during a time of war, the response of
pacifism and non-violence flowed naturally and perhaps super-
naturally from the totality. The Catholic Worker was never
concerned only with peace; its concern was a whole way of
life. As early as October, 1933, the newspaper states that
its "delegates" would "be among those present at the United
States Congress Against War" and they would be representing
"Catholic Pacifism." Since this was the first such collective statement in American history of a group of Catholics,
they well knew that they scarcely represented more than
themselves. As to what was meant by "Catholic pacifism" in
terms of an intellectual rationale, that was still undefined.

The intellectual rationale of pacifism that was operative during the 1930's was that of the just war theory.
Because of the dominance of the just war theory in the Catholic
tradition, it was logical for Catholics to attempt to apply
it to pacifism. Thus, pacifism at this time was based on the
fact that the war in question was not just. The main theoreti-
cian, at least for all practical purposes, of the just war
rationale for Catholic Worker pacifism was the young Bill
Callahan. He was the managing editor of the paper during
much of the decade. His persistent talk of pacifism greatly
influenced Miss Day. In December, 1935, he gave a talk to
the Catholic Social Club of Brooklyn, entitled "Catholics
Should be Conscientious Objectors in Time of War."[18] Then
in October, 1936, he announced through The Catholic Worker
"the formation of a Catholic organization of conscientious

objectors." Four months later the group was named PAX and
Bill Callahan headed the organization. Again, the logic of
the group was based on the presupposition that the war in
question was not just.

These news items went virtually unnoticed. Catholic
pacifism would not become an issue of concern until the
Spanish Civil War. When the war erupted in July, 1936,
Dorothy Day proclaimed pacifism and neutrality in the pages
of The Catholic Worker. Ironically, the issue of pacifism
was overshadowed by anti-Communism. American Catholics had
found a rallying point for their anti-Communism in the war.
Thus, it was not The Catholic Worker's voicing of Dorothy
Day's position of pacifism and refusal to take sides in the
war that raised the ire of American Catholics, but that the
Catholic Worker was not defending the Spanish Fascists who
were fighting for the Church against Communist persecution.
In the Catholic Worker's attempt to offer a reflective
Catholic counter-opinion to the "propaganda in favor of
Franco and Rebel Spain" it provoked the strongest reaction
to The Catholic Worker since its inception. A clearer
emphasis on Catholic pacifism would not emerge until the outbreak of World War II, but even then the issue of Catholic
pacifism would be blurred by historical interpretations of
the causes of the war and conscientious objection.[19]

The Catholic Worker's preoccupation with the twin
enemies of nationalism and capitalism affected their interpretation of the cause of World War II. The Worker contended
that wars were the work of the big capitalists. In its

interpretation that World War II resulted from a conspiracy
of high finance, the Worker was joined by the Coughlinites
and by a notable member of the American hierarchy, Archbishop John T. McNicholas of Cincinnati. The latter two,
however, added the proposition that it was also of Communist
inspiration. When the war did break out, the Worker continued to insist that it was a repetition of 1914. It gave
its position in a front page statement: "We Are to Blame
for New War in Europe." Whatever the fault of Dorothy Day
in this matter, it was not a fault of the spirit but of a bad
reading of history.[20]

This interpretation of World War II did, however, have
an effect on her pacifist rationale. Through 1939 Dorothy Day
and The Catholic Worker had used history-based arguments to
justify Worker pacifism. This was understandable because of
the just war tradition in Catholicism. This tradition had
taught Catholics to distinguish between a just war and an
unjust war in history. Once that decision was reached, then
the individual could or could not participate in the war.
Catholic Workers had tried to adapt the just war criteria to
their pacifist position in hopes of developing a theological
rationale for their pacifism. By 1940, however it became evident that World War II was not a repetition of World War I and
that Catholic pacifism could not be based solely on the just war
tradition whose criteria was based on the actions of a nation in
the objective material world. Dorothy Day recognized the dilemma

of the just war tradition. In World War II, the application of the just war criteria for the individual as well as for the nation state during a time of war had no end for either in its actions but violence.

By 1940, Dorothy Day believed that the Worker's pacifist position had to be put to the test of close theological analysis. She also knew that she was not equipped to provide such reasons herself. She was dependent on others to provide the rationale. She increasingly relied for spiritual direction on Father John Hugo, a Pittsburgh cleric and young theologian. Father John Hugo, sent her a note: "No doubt [pacifism] is all clear to you; but then you have not tried to work it out doctrinally. If you knew no theology, it would probably be simpler to make a solution. Yet the decision must be based on doctrine. Pacifism must proceed from truth, or it cannot exist at all. And of course this attack on conscription is the most extreme form of pacifism."[21] The lack of development in the rationale, however, did not prevent her from continuing to proclaim Catholic pacifism. Peace was the Gospel message and it was the truth of the spirit that should shape history. It was to this point that she moved as the root of certainty for her pacifist convictions.

Her view of nationalism and capitalism had as twin enemies led her to an incorrect interpretation of the cause of World War II, but the Gospel message and Christian personalism would not let her err in the realm of the spirit in

her proclamation of pacifism -- of that she was convinced.
Thus, by 1940 there was no developed rationale for Catholic
pacifism. There were only the actions of individuals some
of whom like Dorothy Day were Catholic Workers who witnessed
to pacifism. Dorothy Day as an individual and as a leader
of a group of Catholics provided this type of Catholic witness
for the first time in American History.

The cost of such witness to Dorothy Day and the Catholic Worker Movement was great. Her pronouncement of pacifism
caused dissension among members of the Movement across the
country. The Chicago house of hospitality in particular was
not pacifist. The house with John Cogley as editor had been
publishing its own newspaper, The Chicago Catholic Worker and
it did not reflect the pacifist position of the New York paper.
At the St. Francis House of Hospitality in Seattle, the
Workers stopped distributing The Catholic Worker because it
was filled almost entirely with pacifism and instead distributed The Chicago Catholic Worker. In June, 1940, Dorothy
Day sent a letter to all Workers concerning the issue of
pacifism.

> We know that there are those who are members
> of 'Catholic Worker' groups throughout the
> country who do not stand with us in this issue.
> We have not been able to change their views
> through what we have written in the paper, or
> by letters, or by personal conversation. They
> wish still to be associated with us, to perform
> the corporal works of mercy.

"And that, she said, was all right. But there had been other
cases when some associated with the Movement had taken it on

themselves to suppress the paper. In such instances she
felt it would be necessary for those persons to disassociate
themselves from the movement."[22]

Despite all of the debate and mounting tensions over
the war, the Catholic Worker Movement went on and Dorothy Day
would not relinquish the pacifist position. The issue of
pacifism may have closed some of the houses but other closed
because of the shortage of manpower. Julian Pleasants in
South Bend wrote to Dorothy Day explaining that "no people
were coming to the house and he thought he would soon be
drafted away."[23] By the end of 1942 sixteen of the houses
or one half of them had been closed.[24] In the May, 1942
issue of The Catholic Worker, Dorothy Day noted that she
had been accused of splitting the Movement from top to bottom
by her pacifism.

As the war progressed the issue that was to involve
Catholic Worker's more than anything else was the draft.
Dorothy's pacifism made her an advocate of total resistance
to the draft; her respect for the individual, the heart of
Christian personalism, enabled her to reach out and assist
all men, regardless of their degree of resistance who became
conscientious objectors in World War II.[25] Thus, it was the
Catholic Worker Movement alone, among all American Catholic
groups, who offered assistance to individuals who conscientiously objected to World War II.

Ironically, it would not be any specifically Catholic
peace group, but the Catholic Worker Movement that would

provide the backbone of the Catholic peace movement for the next forty years in American history. The reason is Dorothy Day who as co-founder of the Catholic Worker Movement would proclaim during her entire life the message of pacifism.

REFERENCES

[1] Dwight MacDonald, "The Foolish Things of the World - II," The New Yorker, XXVII (October 11, 1952), 38. This was the second of two articles appearing in the Profiles section of the magazine. It was the first biography of Miss Day published and remains to date the best available biographical source. The author is greatly indebted to MacDonald for the first eight pages of this chapter.

[2] William D. Miller, A Harsh and Dreadful Love: Dorothy Day and the Catholic Worker Movement, (New York, 1973), pp. 40-43. Miller gives a detailed account of the friendship between Dorothy Day and Rayna Simon and also of Rayna Simon's death. Miller is the only scholar to whom Miss Day has granted access to the closed Catholic Worker papers located in the archives at Marquette University. This book is the best history of the Movement to date.

[3] Ibid., pp. 49-50.

[4] MacDonald, "The Foolish Things . . . ,"39.

[5] Ibid., 40.

[6] Miller, Harsh and Dreadful . . . , p. 56.

[7] As quoted in MacDonald, "The Foolish Things . . . ," 40-41.

[8] Miller, Harsh and Dreadful . . . , pp. 59-60.

[9] Ibid., 62.

[10] Dwight MacDonald, "The Foolish Things of the World - I," The New Yorker, XXVII (October 4, 1952), 46.

[11] This is basically a synthesis of Miller's thesis of the philosophy of the Catholic Worker Movement presented in his "Introduction," Harsh and Dreadful . . . , pp. 3-16.

[12] Ibid., pp. 5-6.

[13]Ibid., p. 14.

[14]Ibid., p. 65.

[15]Ibid., p. 3.

[16]Ibid., pp. 158-59.

[17]John C. Cort, "Dorothy Day at 75," Commonweal, XCVII (February 23, 1973), 476.

[18]Miller, Harsh and Dreadful . . . , p. 159.

[19]Ibid., pp. 138-39.

[20]Ibid., pp. 160-62.

[21]As quoted in Miller, Harsh and Dreadful . . . , p. 166.

[22]Ibid., p. 168.

[23]Ibid., p. 174.

[24]Idem.

[25]Gordon Zahn, "Leaven of Love and Justice," America, CXXVII (November 11, 1972), 383.

CHAPTER III

CATHOLIC DISSENT DURING WORLD WAR II

The attack on Pearl Harbor, December 7, 1941 left no doubt in the minds of most Americans that the United States was now the victim of an aggressor nation and the duty to defend and preserve American interests was paramount. Francis J. Spellman, Archbishop of New York, reflected this same belief on the part of American Catholics when he said,

> With fire and brimstone came December 7, America's throat was clutched, her back was stabbed, her brain was stunned; but her great heart still throbbed. America clenched the palms of those hands oft-stretched in mercy to the peoples of the nations that struck her. America's brain began to clear. America began the fight to save her life.[1]

Despite this seeming unity occasioned by the declaration of World War II, some Americans raised their voices in dissent.

The Catholic Worker Movement was the focal point of Catholic opposition. When war was first declared in Europe, opposition focused on the issue of conscription; as the war progressed opposition centered on obliteration bombing and the dropping of the atomic bomb on Hiroshima and Nagasaki. Of these three issues, however, the principal concern during

the war and the one that most directly challenged the pacifist ideals of the Catholic Worker was conscription.

The roots for the opposition on the part of the Catholic
Worker Movement can be traced to its pacifism. There is no
doubt that because of Dorothy Day, the Movement and especially its newspaper were pacifist. The problem with its
pacifism, however, was that it lacked clarity in its theological rationale. The prevalence of the just war theory in
Catholicism had also predominated the thinking of Catholic
Workers. Initially, they attempted to adapt the just war
rationale to their pacifism. Dorothy Day, not being able
to provide the theological rationale herself was influenced
by these attempts, though she adamantly proclaimed that
pacifism was an integral part of the whole Catholic Worker
ideal.

Paul Hanley Furfey, a pacifist priest educator from
the Catholic University of America and a friend of the Movement, foreshadowed the theological rationale that was eventually to emerge for Catholic Worker pacifism in an article he
wrote for its newspaper in 1935. The article centered on an
imaginary debate between Christ and a patriot. Furfey based
the theological principle for pacifism in the debate, not on
the just war theory, but on the Christian's calling to a
kingdom of love and peace which takes precedence over his
calling to obedience to the state. This was the first statement of the evangelical pacifism that would eventually
characterize the Catholic Worker Movement. A young Worker

of the sixties wrote in retrospect that "with that single article the American Catholic peace movement was born."[2]

Despite Furfey's article which reflected the evangelical spirit of the Worker ideal, the just war theory dominated Catholic Worker pacifism during the thirties. The first program the Catholic Worker developed for conscientious objectors was PAX. Modelled on the PAX organization in England, it got its start in 1935 at a meeting organized by a young Worker, Bill Callahan. The purpose of the American PAX group was to organize Catholic pacifists into a "mighty league of CO's." In 1936 a three-page mimeographed statement of the group's position was distributed which was entitled the "PAX Manifesto of Principles, Aims, and Methods."[3] Its central principle was that a just war was impossible in the present age. Its aims were the formation of a permanent group that would offer assistance to Catholic CO's and promote Catholic teaching on peace. The primary methods of achieving these goals were: the refusal to bear arms in any war, cooperation with existing peace groups to spread Christ's teaching, and the triumph of love.

During this same period Archbishop John T. McNicholas of the diocese of Cincinnati called forth men to become conscientious objectors. In March, 1938 Archbishop McNicholas issued a pastoral letter urging the formation of "A Mighty League of CO's." The Catholic Worker published the full text of the letter.

"The duty of prayer for Catholics," McNicholas said, "is so urgent and binding because they must consider the justice and injustice of war." He went on to say that "Governments that have no fixed standards of morality, and consequently no moral sense, can scarcely settle the question of war on moral grounds for Christians who see and know the injustice of practically all wars in our modern pagan world." McNicholas also denounced the "war makers" who were advancing the present capitalistic system and who "did not deserve the name of patriots."[4]

This statement coming from a member of the Catholic hierarchy, encouraged the members of PAX to redouble their efforts in forming the "mighty league of CO's." McNicholas' pastoral, however, was the only American episcopal statement on which PAX could base its support for CO's.

Through a regular monthly column in The Catholic Worker, PAX attempted to secure signatures to support a Catholic's right to conscientious objection. Moreover, they dared to print a box in The Catholic Worker urging men not to register for the draft. The government chose to ignore this legal offense; the Catholic ecclesiastical authorities did not. They thought Dorothy Day and The Catholic Worker "had gone too far" in this instance and Dorothy was called to the New York Chancery and told, "Dorothy you must stand corrected." She remarked that

> I was not quite sure what that meant, but I
> did assent, because I realized that one should
> not tell another what to do in such circumstances.

> We had to follow our own consciences, which
> later took us to jail; but our work in get-
> ting out the paper was an attempt to arouse
> the consciences of others, not to advise
> action for which they were not prepared.[5]

The PAX group was more or less active until 1940 when
military conscription became imminent. By that time Bill
Callahan had left the Catholic Worker and Arthur Sheehan, a
Catholic Worker in New York, was given the job of directing
and reorganizing the group. The name was changed to the
Association of Catholic Conscientious Objectors (ACCO) in
order to be self-explanatory. By not forbidding the name,
the Church tacitly recognized the association and with it
the right of practicing Catholics to be conscientious objectors.[6] The group received many requests for information
about conscientious objection and attempted to keep informed
of Catholics who were CO's and those who had gone to jail for
non-cooperation with the draft.

By 1940 the issue of military conscription also made
apparent to Catholic Workers that there were at least two
types of Catholic pacifism: just war pacifism and evangelical
pacifism. In both cases the end result was the same. More
importantly, both emphasized the right of the individual conscience to refuse participation in war. This right had long
been part of Catholic teaching and modern popes and traditional defenders of the just war theory professed to uphold
individual conscience when the issue of conscription and war
were matters of public concern. This right of individual

conscience would provide the basis of unanimity among
Catholics concerning conscription before a formal declaration of war by the United States.

It was the proposed Burke-Wadsworth Bill in 1940 that
confronted the American public in a new way concerning the
issue of conscription. Conscription had been operative in
the Civil War and again in World War I. The Burke-Wadsworth
Bill, however, favored the use of conscription in a time of
peace and to many Americans this was a complete break with
their democratic tradition and an indication of the government's desire to enter the European conflict. At this point
in history, too, it must be remembered that as a bill it did
not have the obligatory force of law; nor was the country
officially at war. Considering these circumstances, Catholic
response to the proposal was that of almost unanimous opposition. The hierarchy, the intellectuals, and Catholic Workers
stood together on the issue.

Their argument against peace-time conscription was
basically the same. The Church always maintained both the
right of man to choose his vocation and the duty of every man
to serve his country. It taught further that when the conscience of a citizen prevented him serving in a military
vocation, the man's conscience should be respected. Another
principle invoked against conscription was that a defensive
war required no draft. Peace-time conscription would indicate that the United States was moving toward a war of aggression. A final objection was that war did not assure peace.

For these reasons, the great body of the Catholic hierarchy put themselves on record as opposed to the Burke-Wadsworth Bill. On July 30, 1940, Monsignor Michael J. Ready, their official spokesman, testified before the House of Representatives Committee on Military Affairs.

Though Ready raised the major objections of Catholic opposition to peace-time conscription, his main concern was the consciences of a limited group of Catholics. He stated before the committee that "the bishops are opposed to provisions in this bill which include for compulsory military service students for the priesthood and those under vows to serve the works of religion."[7] Since the Burke-Wadsworth Bill would cause serious damage to the religious, educational, and charitable institutions of the Church, the hierarchy opposed it. Others who testified either before the House or Senate Committees on Military Affairs were Monsignor G. Barry O'Toole of the Catholic University of America, Dorothy Day and Joseph Zarrella, both of the Catholic Worker. Monsignor O'Toole[8] asked for five minutes before both the House and Senate committees to put before them the moral issue that compulsion is not a way of freedom. Day and Zarrella[9] spoke before the House committee in behalf of the unemployed as those would be the most affected by the passage of the bill. All four Catholics maintained the right of freedom of conscience in their testimonies.

On September 16, 1940, after eighty-six days of emotional congressional debate, the Burke-Wadsworth Bill was

passed by a narrow margin. Although this new law was to be
valid for only one year, it officially established the Selective Service System. The act limited the number of men who
could be in training at one time to 900,000, restricted their
period of service to one year or less, and prohibited their
being posted outside the Western Hemisphere, except in American
territories and possessions.[10] When it expired, the House of
Representatives passed the Selective Service Extension Act on
August 18, 1941, by a single vote, 293 to 292.[11]

After the attack on Pearl Harbor, December 7, 1941,
attitudes changed dramatically. Congress quickly responded
to the attack by passing within six days an amendment to the
Selective Service Act which removed the restriction that
limited the service of draftees to the Western Hemisphere and
stipulated that their period of military service would continue from the time of induction until six months after the
end of the war.[12]

American Catholics responded to Pearl Harbor in a
similar fashion. Prior to the attack the hierarchy, intellectuals, and Catholic Workers were united in their opposition
to peace-time conscription. But after the day of infamy,
there was little doubt as to how most Catholics as well as
most Americans would react. In times of war Catholics had
continually proven to be the nation's most loyal supporters.
In December, 1941, the fires of patriotism once again swept
across the landscape and enveloped Catholics in the nation's
new crusade. Concern for the rights of individual conscience,

evident in 1940 receded into the background and the obligation of the individual to obey the state and support its just cause now became apparent.

Neither the Catholic hierarchy nor Catholic intellectuals denied the right of an individual to be a conscientious objector after World War II was declared; they also did nothing to support these individuals. In face of the evil of Hitler and the Japanese attack on Pearl Harbor, these historical events left little doubt in the minds of most Catholics, as in the minds of most Americans, that World War II was a necessary and just war. Thus, the centuries old just war tradition that had been used to provide the theological rationale for those who claimed a just war was being waged was applied once again to World War II. The just war provision for the right of individual conscience was all but forgotten by most. The obligation to obey lawful authority and defend one's country seemed sufficient reason for most Catholic consciences to participate in and to support World War II.

These events also revealed the weakness of the Catholic emphasis on the right of individual conscience in hypothetical situations. America, the Jesuit weekly, in November, 1939, published the results of a survey of 54,000 Catholic students of both sexes in 141 Catholic colleges and universities. They were asked to respond to a statement of Francis J. Beckman, Archbishop of Dubuque, who declared, "Catholics should give serious thought to the question of whether or not they should be conscientious objectors if this country should enter the war."[13] The results of the survey showed that twenty per cent of young Catholics would volunteer in military service, forty-four per cent would accept conscription, while thirty-six per cent would conscientiously object.[14] Such statistics illustrated the emphasis in Catholic education on the right of individual conscience. But once World War II was officially declared, the hypothetical one-third of Catholic conscientious objectors quickly evaporated.

To Catholic Workers, especially Dorothy Day, it became evident that individual conscience when linked with the just war tradition would not result in pacifist conclusions for most Catholics. Within the Catholic Worker Movement itself, the effects of World War II viewed as a just war had their effects. Dorothy Day acknowledged this, and confessed that "It is a matter of grief to me that most of those who are Catholic Workers are not pacifists, but I can see too how good it is that we always have this attitude represented among us. We are not living in an ivory tower."[15] Most Catholic Workers entered military service. John Cogley, one of this group, later remarked about the war years, "most of us still feel that the war on Nazism was a morally justified enterprise -- it was better to have fought that evil, even at the price of a slaughter, than to have acquiesced in it."[16] Tom Sullivan, an editor of The Catholic Worker, went to war and served in the Pacific. He did not call himself a pacifist and said nothing about means and ends; he left that to the

theologians. Jack English was a gunner on a bomber and was
shot down and spent a year in a Rumanian prison camp. He
was rescued by the Russians only to go through the blitz in
London. Dorothy Day's comment on Jack was, he "has theologian
friends whose opinions keep him away from the extreme pacifist position."[17] Other young men helped at the Catholic
Worker as long as the draft board permitted and, Dorothy Day
said, "talked the issue over constantly." She maintained
that their discussions raised the following questions:

> Can there be a just war? Can the conditions
> laid down by St. Thomas ever be fulfilled?
> What does God want me to do? And what am I
> capable of doing? Can I stand out against
> state and Church? Is it pride, presumption,
> to think I have the spiritual capacity to use
> spiritual weapons in the face of the most
> gigantic tyranny the world has ever seen?
> Am I capable of enduring suffering, facing
> martyrdom? And alone? Again the long
> loneliness to be faced.[18]

Neither Dorothy Day nor The Catholic Worker were able
to supply adequate arguments in response to the evils of
Hitler and Japanese agression, in fact, the pages of the newspaper reflect a conspicuous absence of attempting to deal
with these historical realities. Instead what is found in
its pages is undaunted pacifism and advocacy of conscientious
objection. "We are still pacifists," the editorial read,
"and our manifesto is the Sermon on the Mount, which means
that we will try to be peacemakers."[19] Thus, this small
nucleus of Catholics, divided within itself, stood alone in
the Church in opposition to war and in support of Catholic

conscientious objectors throughout World War II. Because of
its pacifist position The Catholic Worker decreased in circulation from 130,000 copies a month in 1939 to 50,500 copies
a month in November, 1944. This low ebb in circulation was
not revealed by The Catholic Worker until April, 1948, when
73,000 copies of the issue were again printed. Even as late
as 1971 it would not exceed a circulation of 88,000 copies.

Though the Catholic Worker would not shift from its
position of pacifism once the United States officially
declared war, it did shift in its theological rationale for
pacifism. The just war theory declined in significance and
the Catholic Worker now placed greater emphasis on the
evangelical counsels, the core of the Worker ideal, as the
reason for its pacifism. Even during World War II, it was
unable to develop a sophisticated theological argument for
its evangelical style of pacifism which had been foreshadowed
by Furfey. At best, it offered to readers of its paper a
wide variety of arguments for conscientious objection. The
paper was filled with the writings of American and European
Catholic intellectuals[20] who based their positions for conscientious objection either on the just war theory, the
evangelical counsels, or on a straight moralist approach of
God's command, "Thou Shalt Not Kill."

In practice, the Catholic Worker followed the same
pattern by supporting all types of conscientious objectors.
Initially the Catholic Worker opposed participation in a
program for conscientious objectors (CO's) who registered

Their dissent within the law. Dorothy Day considered such programs a form of cooperation with the war and conscription; she advocated refusal to register. Committed though she was to the most extreme form of conscientious objection, non-cooperation with the law, she was ready to respect and support those who were not ready to go that far and wanted to register their dissent within the law.[21] The evangelical counsels were sufficient reason to move the group into developing specific programs of support.

It was not only to Catholic Workers who were con-scientious objectors that support was given, but to every Catholic conscientious objector throughout America who desired its assistance. Many Catholic individuals who had never heard of the Catholic Worker emerged as conscientious objec-tors during World War II. For those Catholics who had chosen this route, the journey began with direct confronta-tion of the United States government and the Selective Service Act, originally the Burke-Wadsworth Bill of 1940. Everyone eligible for military service in World War II was required to fill out a selective service questionnaire. The religious objector, whether Catholic or not, was recognized by the Selective Service Law since the government exempted from combatant service those who, "because of religious training and belief" were opposed to all war in "any form."[22] In completing the questionnaire the individual was allowed to request a special form for conscientious objector if he so

desired, and this form (DDS-Form 47)[23] became the basis for
Selective Service classification.

Under the operation of the over-all conscription program,
there were three distinct types of conscientious objection.
First, there were the men who, on the basis of religious
opposition to war, refused all combatant military service or
training, but were willing to perform non-combatant military
service under military direction within the armed forces.
They were classified as I-A-O objectors by the Selective
Service. Secondly, there were also men whose opposition to
World War II involved the actual violation of the Selective
Training and Service Act by either refusing to register or
failing to report for induction or assuming some other posture
of non-cooperation; they were thereby imprisoned and considered draft "delinquents." The third group was opposed to war
and to all military service, combatant or non-combatant.
They were inducted into the Civilian Public Service camps
which were under civilian direction and classified IV-E.

It is important to note here that this complex means
of classification applied to but a small percentage of the
United States population. The highest estimate of the total
number of CO's during World War II was 2.4 per cent of the
population. The highest estimate of the number of Catholic
CO's was 223 out of a Church whose membership then numbered
19,914,937 or .0001 of that membership. This was a tremendous
increase over World War I where, at most, four known Catholics
had been CO's,[24] all of whom were sentenced to twenty-five

years imprisonment. In World War I, 345 different churches
were listed by CO's as the source of their religious grounds
for objection. Despite this increase Catholics who were CO's
were such a minority of Catholics that they could easily be
ignored by Church authorities.

Although the Selective Service System did not keep
accurate or complete records on CO's during World War II, it
estimated that during the six and a half year life of the
Selective Training and Service Act of 1940, it ordered the
induction of 25,000 men classified 1-A-O, 11,887 classified
IV-E, and imprisoned 6,086 CO's. Thus 42,973 of the 10,022,
367 males ordered to report for induction into the armed
forces were CO's. During World War I, 3,989 out of a total
of 2,810,296 men inducted were CO's or .0014 which was only
one-third of the World War II record of .0042. Even more
striking was the increase in the number of imprisoned CO's
which jumped from 450 in World War I to 6,068 in World War
II, an increase of 1200 per cent. Every sixth man in the
federal prisons during World War II was a CO.[25]

Because of this lack of accurate records, there is
also no way to determine the number of Catholics who were
classified 1-A-O. Statistics are available on the number of
Catholics imprisoned and the number of Catholics in the
Civilian Public Service camps. The National Service Board
for Religious Objectors (NSBRO) compiled a list of sixty-one
Catholics imprisoned in sixteen of the twenty-eight federal
prisons. The Danbury Federal Prison had the largest number

of Catholic CO's -- eighteen men. These sixty-one men were
sentenced anywhere from eighteen months to five years; the
largest number, thirty, were sentenced to three years imprisonment. Furthermore, on the entire list only one man was
cited as being released from a five-year prison sentence to
serve in the army.[26] At various times, Arthur Sheehan and
other members of the Association for Catholic Conscientious
Objectors, which had its headquarters at the Catholic Worker
on Mott Street in New York, arranged to have parole talks for
Catholic CO's in the prisons. Success was apparent at Danbury
where all but two of the seventeen men at the meeting called
by Warden Alexander had one-third of their sentences commuted
and were assigned to hospitals in New Haven, Boston, and
Baltimore.[27] When paroled, a CO was assigned to a hospital
and required only to appear for work each day. Thus, these
men fared better than the CO's in the Civilian Public Service
(CPS) camps.[28]

The idea for founding the CPS camps originated on
January 10, 1940, when peace groups concerned about the pro-
tection of the rights of CO's supported the leaders of the
Quakers, Mennonites and Church of the Brethren, who met with
President Roosevelt to propose a program for CO's. These
denominations, known as the Historical Peace Churches, suggested the establishment of an alternative service program
under their direction in which CO's could perform work of a
humanitarian nature.[29]

The actual establishment of the alternative service
system, however, forced the pacifist leaders to compromise
in a number of ways. First of all, American law would recognize conscientious objection solely on religious grounds.
Secondly, no exemption would be granted to men who in good
conscience could not accept compulsory government service
even if it were in the form of labor in the CPS camps. While
final plans were being made for the establishment of the CPS
camps, certain unwanted conditions were imposed on the
Historical Peace Churches concerning the administration of
the camps. President Roosevelt suddenly expressed opposition
to the proposed system of camp autonomy and "advocated putting
all the men to work under army direction."[30] The leaders of
the Historical Peace Churches became fearful and agreed to
assume all costs of the alternative service program in order
to eliminate military control. This meant that CO's in the
CPS camps would work without pay. In the end the government
granted that old Civilian Conservation Corps (CCC) camps
would be converted into CPS camps with the operational expenses
still borne by the Historical Peace Churches. The government,
nevertheless, maintained final supervision over the camps.
When Brigadier General Lewis B. Hershey was asked to explain
in 1941 the way funds were provided for the CPS camps, he
stated before the Congressional Subcommittee on Conscientious
Objection, "You see, we have three major historical creeds.
They underwrite those costs. If the boy has $35.00 a month,
he pays it; and if he has not, his church pays it; if neither
has it, the three religious groups pay it."[31] In total the

administration cost to the Historical Peace Churches for
the CPS camps amounted to $7,000,000. There were 12,000
pacifists in 151 CPS camps from 1940 to 1946 with a sum of
8,000,000 man-days of free work for the United States.[32]

The leaders of the Historical Peace Churches formed
the National Service Board for Religious Objectors to
administer the CPS camps. Arthur Sheehan, head of the ACCO,
which now had 800 members, felt a responsibility toward
these Catholics and, therefore, became the self-appointed
Catholic representative on the NSBRO, and consequently he
approached the Selective Service for permission to operate
a camp in the interest of Catholic CO's. The government
granted a forestry camp at Stoddard, New Hampshire, that
would accommodate fifty men, the Catholic Worker, through
small donations, attempted to meet the yearly expenditure
estimated to be $12,000. The camp was opened on August 15,
1941, with sixteen men. Dwight Larrowe was camp director
and Joseph Zarella assisted him.

There were many hardships to be faced by the men at
Stoddard. The daily schedule was as follows: 5:45 rise,
6:05 breakfast, 6:35 make bed, 6:50 meditation, 7:15 work
project, 12:00 lunch, 4:30 free time, 5:30 dinner, 6:00 free
time, 7:00 rosary, 7:30 recreation and classes, 10:00 lights
out.[33] Saturdays and Sundays were free. There also was the
problem of the camp's location -- a virtual Siberia. It was
sixteen miles from the nearest small town, so that acquiring
supplies and attending Mass was difficult. Government trucks

were available for work, but the Selective Service refused
to permit the trucks to be used for relifious purposes, even
that of traveling to Mass on Sundays. The lack of finances
for the camp caused additional problems.[34] Even adequate
food, especially meat, was not provided for the men. Dorothy
Day told the following story of the camps in Loaves and
Fishes: "At first the boys themselves did the cooking. Then
began the era of apple dumplings, apple strudel, apple frit-
ters, apple sauce, apple pie. The camps were in the middle
of an apple orchard and nothing went to waste. The fellows
even sat around at night and sliced apples for drying so
that they could be assured of their diet of apple pies for
the duration."[35]

There were also the psychological and emotional strains
on the men of doing work for which they were not trained pro-
fessionally, which they did not believe to be of "national
importance," and for which they were not paid. Internecine
conflicts arose within the group, evident in the antagonism
caused by the Christian Front group (anti-Semites who were
supporters of Father Charles E. Coughlin), and by the chapel
group (deeply religious men who believed the others were not
"Catholic" enough and whose sole aim was to erect a chapel
at the camp).[36] Because of the hardships and the injustice
of the alternative service system, a few men believed that
they could no longer cooperate in any way with military conscription; this led them to leave the camps and assume the
extreme position of non-cooperation with the selective service
system.[37]

The Catholic Church, unlike the Historic Peace Churches, did not support the CPS.[38] This absence of moral and financial assistance inflicted grave hardships on the CO's. Since the ACCO was a creation of the Catholic Worker Movement and financially dependent on it for support, the ACCO's source of revenue became as precarious as the Catholic Worker's which depended on the personal contributions of its readers and people familiar with its houses of hospitality. The CPS was never far removed from absolute poverty at Stoddard or in the other Catholic camp at Warner.

By October of 1942 Stoddard was large enough, (forty-seven men) to permit its closing and the opening of a new camp at Warner, New Hampshire, the latter camp remaining in existence until it was permanently closed on March 17, 1943. The highest population in the Warner camp ever achieved was 63 in December, 1942. At the time of the closing 62 CO's were transferred. On March 5, 1942, twelve men from the Catholic CPS camp went to the Alexian Brother's Hospital in Chicago. This was the first instance in which CO's were able to leave the camps and work elsewhere as a form of alternative service; the practice became more frequent after 1942. A unique aspect of this program was that living expenses for the CO's was not paid by the Historical Peace Churches but by the agency where the men worked.[39]

Many reasons explain the closing of the camp at Warner and the cessation of the ACCO to attempt to maintain a separate Catholic CPS camp. One reason for the general dissatisfaction

of the men with the CPS camps as a form of complicity with
the Selective Service System. A second factor was the demean-
ing work at the camps and the new opportunities opening up
for CO's in the hospitals. Finally residents of New Hampshire wanted the camp removed. Dorothy Day remarked about
the camps, "There were two camps in New Hampshire, and Bishop
Peterson was very friendly and gave us help every now and
then. But the Army did not think so highly of the camp. It
was the food that seemed to bother them, not having meat.
The camps were closed down and the boys went to other camps
around the country."[40] Finally, there was the fact that the
ACCO was not financially capable of operating the camp.[41]

After the camp closed, over 100 of the Catholic CO's
went to Swallow Falls near Oakland, Maryland, CPS #89. In
June, 1944, Rosewood Training School in Maryland opened and
took many Catholic CO's. At Rosewood the men spent twelve
hours a day caring for the mental patients, and received a
salary of $15.00 a month. Other Catholic CO's went to
Cheltenham, Maryland, and worked in a training school for
Negro boys. Still another group, known as the "Chapel" group,
went to a CPS camp designated to work on a soil reclamation
project. It was sponsored by the American Friends Service
Committee for Indians in North Dakota. During their stay in
North Dakota some Catholic CO's finally realized their dream
of building a chapel; Bolton Morris, a member of the "chapel"
group and in later years a well-known Philadelphia architect,
designed the building. When the Catholic CO's moved from

Warner, the NSBRO willingly accepted the financing of the men.
In the NSBRO records, the expense absorbed for Catholic CO's
by the Mennonites was $5,975.34 and by the Quakers, $32,
707.31.[42]

Besides working in the camps, over 500 CO's served as
"guinea pigs" for medical research for which several Catholic
CO's volunteered. Also over 2,000 CO's served in forty-one
mental hospitals and seventeen schools for the mentally
deficient.[43] Over 100 Catholic CO's served in the hospitals
after 1943. The peace churches had originally been training
some CO's in the camps for overseas work, but wartime hatred
of CO's induced Congress to attach a rider to an appropria-
tion bill making this illegal. There was an offer made to
a group of Catholic CO's to go to England to establish a
Catholic Worker hospitality house, but passports were refused
these volunteers.[44] One intellectual venture of the CPS
was a research study program at Columbia University on war
relief and reconstruction. Fifteen men, including George
Mathues a Catholic CO, took part in this program in New York,
even though they had to pay for it out of their own pockets.[45]

In an attempt to keep the now scattered Catholic CO's
united and informed of one another and thus provide moral
support, Arthur Sheehan along with two other Catholic CO's,
Raymond Pierzchalsi and William Strube, edited the first
edition of the quarterly newspaper, The Catholic CO, in
January, 1944. It came out of the Catholic Worker office in
New York and sold not as The Catholic Worker for 1¢ a copy

but for 25¢ until it went up to 50¢ a copy in 1945. The
funds from subscriptions were used to support the publication of the newspaper and to finance the Catholic CO's in
the CPS camps. After the first edition, the publication
of the paper was assumed by the responsible hands of the
men at the Rosewood Training School. The editors who served
during the four years of the paper's existence were all
Catholic CO's, William Strube; Richard Lion, Gordon Zahn,
Ray Pierzchalsi, and Robert Ludlow. Arthur Sheehan, a staff
member of the Catholic Worker, assisted them in the work.

Until 1944, The Catholic Worker's pages had adequately
covered Catholic pacifist news. Some of the featured writings
by Americans which appeared in the paper during the 1940's
were converted into pamphlets, the three most significant of
which were: War and Conscription at the Bar of Christian
Morals by Monsignor G. Barry O'Toole, Weapons of the Spirit
by Father John J. Hugo, and Two Agitators by Ammon Hennacy.
Many other theological peace writings also appeared in The
Catholic Worker's pages.[46] There was only one article in
the newspaper on non-violent resistance during this period
which, however, clearly illustrated that there was no theological distinction made at that time between non-violent
resistance and non-resistance. The concept of non-violent
resistance had yet to be born among American Catholics.

In 1944 the editors of The Catholic CO took over the
peace writings and peace news usually covered by The Catholic
Worker. The two regular columns in The Catholic Co were "In

Passing" which contained news about the men in the camps and
a column devoted to books in review. The main feature of
each issue discussed either conscientious objection, pacifism,
or the possible alternatives for peace. All the articles
attempted to come to grips with the growing militarism in
the United States. By 1945 the atomic bomb and the withdrawal issue were discussed at length. In 1946 there was
much space given to the ACCO's withdrawal from NSBRO and the
declaration of federal Judge James E. Fee of CPS camps as
illegal. The Catholic CO also took time to protest the
National Catholic Welfare Conference's (NCWC) and the Catholic
Association for International Peace's (CAIP) ultra-nationalism
when they stated that Pope Pius XII was "not in sympathy with
a negotiated or compromising peace."[47] The NCWC was developed
to carry out policies set at the annual meeting of Catholic
bishops, to serve as a clearing house for information, to
co-ordinate Catholic organizations and efforts in various
fields, and when necessary, to represent the hierarchy's
view on national affairs. No support was given to Catholic
CO's during World War II by either group.[48]

In June, 1948, the editors discontinued The Catholic
CO. They stated their reasons in an article which appeared
in The Catholic Worker's PAX column. One reason for its dis-
continuance was the end of the war. Members of the ACCO had
very little in common except their opposition to the war;
once that ended there was little else to bind them together.
Another reason was that the editors of The Catholic CO were

radicals and pacifists as was <u>The Catholic Worker</u>. Thus,
their news would sufficiently be covered by the pages of
<u>The Catholic Worker</u>.[49]

    After the closing of the Catholic camps and the found-
ing of the paper, the next step was the withdrawal of the
ACCO from the National Service Board of Religious Objectors.
Arthur Sheehan signed the withdrawal statement written by
Gordon Zahn. The statement appeared in the January-March,
1946, issue of <u>The Catholic CO</u>. In summary, the reasons for
withdrawal were that men in traditional pacifist leadership
positions had allied themselves with the military in administering conscription in the CPS camps. The ACCO had continued
its membership in the NSBRO in hopes of working out the difficulties of the CPS and ultimately bringing a fair and honest
interpretation of the CO's status though their membership
had always been financially limited. The ACCO felt that it
at last was being honest with itself in admitting that the
CPS was a form of slavery; scarcely any good resulted from
the camp and in the end it proved a failure. Sheehan also
urged honesty on the part of the NSBRO and hoped as well for
its repudiation of the CPS. The NSBRO soon followed the
ACCO's act of repudiation.[50]

    An attempt to evaluate Catholic conscientious objec-
tion during World War II presents grave difficulties. A major
handicap is that there is no definite way of judging the
relationship and impact of Catholic faith on the individual's
decision to become a conscientious objector. Gordon Zahn in

his study on Catholic conscientious objectors during World
War II,[51] emphasized this point.

> It is hard to generalize about men holding
> essentially individual determined positions.
> The source of strength for the conscientious
> objector in World War II came from personal
> conviction that he was conforming to the true
> norms of social living as defined by the great
> humanitarian thinkers and teachers of the past.
> True he would still remain a deviant; but his
> deviation would have something of a supra-
> social encouragement behind it in the identi-
> fication with certain ideals which, for him
> at least transcended temporal and national
> considerations.[52]

Despite the difficulty, Zahn constructed five categories
which explain the theological positions of Catholic CO's.
The first was "individual" positions. This group consisted
of Christian Fronters who were scornful of the pacifism of
others and believed the United States was fighting on the
wrong side; it also included one or two CO's who traced their
objection to personal revelations of a presumably supernatural
origin. The second category included those who made no
religious references, since their position was based on a
philosophical or humanitarian ideal, and the third position
was "evangelical." These men avoided formal theological
arguments and stated their objections in terms of an antithesis
between the "spirit of war" and the "spirit of Christ." Whatever arguments were offered by the group were based upon the
unifying element they found in Redemption and the doctrine
of the Mystical Body of Christ.

Somewhat more theological was the "perfectionist" position, which was based upon a literal interpretation of the counsels of perfection as outlined in the Sermon on the Mount. Holders of this view refused to limit themselves to a just war analysis though they would agree to it. They believed the Christian was called to follow a supernatural ethic which went beyond justice to charity. This position was held mainly by the men associated with the Catholic Worker Movement. Finally, there was the "traditionalist" position; few men held this. It was based on the "just war -- unjust war" distinction developed by the writings of the great scholastics. The men who did take this position applied the traditional considerations of the just war as developed in the writings of St. Augustine, St. Thomas Aquinas, Vittoria and Suarez, Gerald Vann, O.R., G. Barry O'Toole, and Franziskus Stratmann, O.P.

The importance of Zahn's categories is that they give some indication of the relationship of Catholic faith to the personal choices of these men to be CO's, thirty-six of whom stated that their faith had no direct relationship or bearing in their decision. Though others held religious reasons, only nineteen men accepted the just war position which at that time was the only theology of war and peace that traditional American Catholicism upheld. Catholic CO's during World War II would seem to have found reasons for their positions in a tradition not encompassed in the formal or popular teaching of Catholicism.

Although there was little connection between Catholic
teaching and the individual's decision to become a CO, the
Catholic Church in the United States never denied the right
of an individual to become a conscientious objector. At the
same time the Church never articulated its support for this
right. Thus, throughout the war it remained a silent bystan-
der on the issue of conscription. The reason for this is not
hard to discover. The Church had always remained loyal to
the nation in time of war. The apparent legitimacy of World
War II in face of the evil of Nazism coupled with the official just war theory of the Church which granted the benefit
of doubt to the state in matters of war and peace only served
to justify such uncritical patriotism. Church and state were
united in a joint crusade and any official ecclesiastical
criticism was unthinkable.

During the course of the war an issue arose which
further illustrated the unofficial union of church and state.
This was the obliteration bombing of German population centers.
The American Catholic hierarchy remained silent on this question and the bombing of Cologne, Berlin, Hamburg, and Dresden
went on unnoticed. The one instance where the hierarchy did
speak out against what they called "indiscriminate" bombing
was the air attack on Rome in 1943.[53] Since Rome was the
holy city of Roman Catholicism, their statement was understandable. But their silence on the bombing of ninety other
cities in Europe pointed out the lack of any consistant position on "indiscriminate" bombing. Their own consistent posture

was to support the national crusade and only when this
threatened the holy city did a voice of protest emerge.

The bombing of German cities did elicit a response
from some segments of the Catholic community as well as
from other Americans, especially pacifists. In the process
a Catholic rationale for the immorality of obliteration
bombing emerged. The one responsible for developing this
moral protest was John C. Ford, S.J., teacher at Weston
College, who in 1944 challenged the bombing of cities as not
admissible under traditional just war criteria. By writing
a scholarly article, "The Morality of Obliteration Bombing,"
Father Ford became the only American Catholic moral theologian who addressed himself to this issue during World War
II. The basis of his argument rested on the traditional just
war criteria and not on pacifism. In the article Ford defined
obliteration bombing in the following terms:

> Obliteration bombing is the strategic bombing,
> by means of incendiaries and explosives, of
> industrial centers of population in which the
> target to be wiped out is not a definite
> factory, bridge, or similar object, but a
> large area of a whole city, comprising one-
> third to two-thirds of its whole built up
> area, and including by design the residential
> districts of workingmen and their families.[54]

Ford contended that such bombing was immoral. He based his
position in international law, the laws of humanity, and
natural law. He also pointed out that the question of obliteration bombing leads to the more general one as to the
possibility of a just modern war: "for obliteration bombing

includes the bombing of civilians, and is a necessary practice which can be called typical of total war, and if all
modern war must be total, then a condemnation of obliteration bombing would logically lead to a condemnation of all
modern war."[55] Ford, however, admitted that he did not
intend to go that far and believed that it was possible for
modern war to be waged within the limits set by the laws of
morality.[56]

Since Ford did not accept pacifism and believed that
certain wars could be just, he had to maintain that there
were some things which were inadmissible in warfare such as
the use of poisonous gas and obliteration bombing. He based
his argument against obliteration bombing on the distinction
between combatants and non-combatants and referred to the
writings of many theologians who were firmly convinced of
the distinction. One of these writers was the American
Catholic theologian, Dr. John K. Ryan, author of Modern War
and Basic Ethics which was published before the United States'
entry into World War II. In the article Ford considered
soldiers under arms as combatants. He is not clear what is
to be said of civilian munitions workers and leaves it up
to international law to decide. All the rest of the large
numbers of people living even in conditions of modern warfare
are clearly innocent non-combatants. It was the rights of
non-combatants that were violated by obliteration bombing and
thus, according to Ford, made such bombings immoral.

111

Ford concludes his article with a section on "The
Mind of the Holy See." Here, Ford cites the condemnation
of aerial bombardment of civilians by Benedict XV in World
War I, Pius XI's condemnation of the bombing of cities in
Spain during the Spanish Civil War, and Pius XII's lament of
the bombing of Rome during World War II. From such statements, Ford concludes that if words of the popes "do not
contain an implicit condemnation of obliteration bombing as
I have described it, than it is hard to see what they do
condemn."[57]

With the presentation of such a strong case condemning
obliteration bombing as immoral, Ford is careful to point
out that his article is insufficient to impose obligations
on the conscience of the individual. He states: "A clear
violation of natural law can be known to the ordinary individual soldier in a case of this kind through the definite pronouncements of the Church, or of the hierarchy, or even
through a consensus of moral theologians over a period of
time. On the question of obliteration bombing we have no
such norms."[58]

Other Catholics, besides this moral theologian, spoke
out against obliteration bombing. Father James M. Gillis in
the "Editorial Comment" in Catholic World took such a stand.
The editors of Commonweal flatly condemned obliteration bombing as murder. The Catholic Worker speaking from its pacifist
position condemned obliteration bombing and published the
statement of Most Reverend Gerald Shaugnessy, D.D., S.M. of
Seattle, the only American bishop who spoke out during World

War II on the immorality of obliteration bombing.[59] The
Catholic Worker also printed the words of Monsignor Paul
Hanley Furfey's condemnation of obliteration bombing.[60]

Thus, there were a few Catholics who protested the
United States' policy of obliteration bombing during World
War II. Most Catholics, even the CAIP, never addressed
themselves to this issue. One Catholic periodical, America,
urged precautions concerning obliteration bombing.

Perhaps if the protestations of American Catholics and
others had been stronger against the government's policy of
obliteration bombing, President Truman would have found it
more difficult to drop the atomic bomb on Hiroshima and
Nagasaki. As it was, he made the decision to drop the bombs
and one observer noted that "the general American reaction,
is one of stunned disquiet. It is not jubilant, yet it contains no real feeling of guilt."[61]

Despite the "stunned disquiet" of most Americans, some
did protest the bombing of Hiroshima and Nagasaki. Editors
of Roman Catholic publications were spurred on by the Pope's
criticism of the bombings.[62] Catholics, however, who sub-
jected the American decision to sharp attack were the same
ones who had previously challenged the policy of obliteration
bombing. Again the hard core of the opposition were the
pacifists. It is also important to note that the reasons for
their protest against the use of the atomic bomb stemmed
from the same reason for their opposition to obliteration
bombing. Gillis in the Catholic World responded to the

dropping of the atomic bombs by proclaiming, "I here and now declare that I think the use of the atomic bomb, in these circumstances, was atrocious and abominable; and that civilized peoples would reprobate and anathematize the horrible deed."[63] Dorothy Day in The Catholic Worker began her pacifist condemnation of the droppings of the atomic bomb with extreme sarcasm as she talked of the President. "He went from table to table on the cruiser which was bringing him home from the Big Three conference," she noted, "telling the great news, 'jubilant,' the newspapers said. JUBILATE DEO. We have killed 318,000 Japanese." She placed the responsibility for the atomic bomb on "scientists and captains of industry." In her typical evangelical spirit she asserted that Christ had already given his judgment of the act: "What you do unto the least of these my brethren, you do unto me."[64]

Father John J. Hugo's article, "Peace Without Victory," also appeared in the same issue of The Catholic Worker. Hugo termed the droppings of the atomic bomb "the culminating crime" and attributed it to the United States' capacity to "out-Nazi the Nazis" by using means that do not justify the end, by accepting tribal morality, and by acquiesing in obliteration bombing.

While indignation and dismay at America's use of atomic weapons held the initiative in these Catholic circles many Catholic leaders were not united behind the pacifist hard core of the discontent. This was also true among clerical

leadership of every denomination in the United States.[65]
Catholic groups who abstained from judgment on obliteration
bombing such as _America_, the Catholic hierarchy, and the
CAIP did the same in reference to the droppings of the atomic
bomb on Hiroshima and Nagasaki.

In 1947, the CAIP finally spoke out on the issue of
the atomic bomb. During the war the CAIP, like other peace
groups that were advocates of collective security, supported
the politicies of the government and focused its attention
on planning for a postwar community of nations and worked
to get the United States to adhere to international cooperation whenever peace came. When the United States helped to
build the United Nations, the CAIP made many recommendations
for a stronger United Nations. It was in this context that
the CAIP finally took a stance on the use of the atomic bomb.
It wanted a United Nations that would have "legislative
powers . . . to make effective atomic control and inspection
and general disarmament."[66] The CAIP further contended that
the use of atomic bombs was illegitimate or unjust when 1)
atomic bombing was used to break peoples' will to resist;
2) atomic total war was pursued as an end in itself; and 3)
a war was started with a shower of atomic bombs. The use of
atomic bombs was just, however, in the following situations:
1) for counter-use by a nation in a defensive war when other
means were insufficient and 2) that the United Nations may
use atomic bombs against an aggressor nation if the nation's
preparations and objective was clearly to enslave the world

or a large part of it. The CAIP concluded its statement by declaring that "the United States was obliged to stop production of the A bomb and publicly announce this due to suspicion aroused in Russia and the armaments race."[67]

Even this stance of the CAIP which did not go as far as the pacifists in its indignation at the use of the atomic bomb, it probably went beyond dominant Catholic opinion. Though there are no statistics available on exclusively Catholic public opinion, on August 8, 1945, a poll found that only ten per cent of the American population opposed the use of atomic bombs on Japanese cities, while eighty-five per cent approved.[68]

Thus, on the question of the use of the atomic bomb, American Catholics evidenced a variety of positions. The majority approved or were silent. The CAIP, the official peace organization, formulated a policy, in itself very ambivalent, two years after the war was over. For these Catholics, the just war theory still provided an ethical rationale that permitted them to support their government in war, even nuclear war. At the same time other Catholics were deriving pacifist conclusions from the just war tradition which placed them in opposition to their government. This enabled them to protest the use of the A-bomb in the same manner that it had provided them with a rationale to become CO's and to protest obliteration bombing. The pacifists, located in the Catholic Worker, provided the hard core of opposition to the government on all three issues.

One man who was fully knowledgeable of the varieties of theological thought in Catholic peace concern and who attempted to evaluate them as well as non-Catholic influences for peace was Thomas Merton. After analyzing the varieties of peace concern, Merton arrived at his own synthesis and labeled himself a "nuclear pacifist."

REFERENCES

[1] Cardinal Spellman as quoted in Wittner, Rebels . . . , p. 36.

[2] James Forest, "No longer alone: The Catholic Peace Movement," in Thomas E. Quigley (ed.), American Catholics and Vietnam (Grand Rapids, 1968), p. 144.

[3] "PAX Manifesto," located in the ACCO files at the Peace Collection, Swarthmore College, Swarthmore, Pennsylvania.

[4] The Catholic Worker, April, 1938.

[5] Dorothy Day, Loaves and Fishes (New York, 1963), p. 60.

[6] Ibid., May, 1943, p. 3. Perhaps the reading here is too positive toward Church authorities.

[7] Michael J. Ready, General Secretary of the National Catholic Welfare Conference spoke to the House Committee on Military Affairs. See Report of the Hearings anent. H. R. 10132, pp. 299-323.

[8] Barry O'Toole spoke to the House Committee on Military Affairs. See Report of the Hearings anent. H. R. 10132, pp. 353-54. He also spoke to the Senate Committee on Military Affairs. See Report of the Hearings anent. 10132, pp. 158-60.

[9] Dorothy Day spoke to the House Committee on Military Affairs. See Report of the Hearings anent. 10132, pp. 152-58. And Joseph Zarella spoke to the House Committee on Military Affairs. See Report of the Hearings anent. 10132, pp. 158-60.

[10] Leslie S. Rothenberg, The Draft and You (New York, 1968), p. 10.

[11] Ibid., p. 11.

[12] Ibid.

118

[13] Paul Comly French, We Won't Murder (New York, 1940), p. 157.

[14] "National Catholic College Poll," America, LXII (November 11, 1939), 116-19 and LXII (November 18, 1939), 144-47.

[15] Day, The Long Loneliness, p. 267.

[16] Ibid.

[17] Ibid.

[18] Ibid.

[19] "Editorial," The Catholic Worker, January, 1942.

[20] The following intellectuals appeared in The Catholic Worker's pages: The Americans, John A. Ryan, Cyprian Emmanuel, O.F.M., and Msgr. G. Barry O'Toole, the Englishman, Gerald Vann, O.P., the German, Franziskas Stratmann, O.P., and the Austrian, Dr. Johannes Udes.

[21] Gordon Zahn, "Leaven of Love and Justice," America, CXXVII (November 11, 1972), 383.

[22] Lillian Schlissel, Conscience in America (New York, 1968), p. 219.

[23] Ibid.

[24] Paul Riley, a graduate student in the Department of Religion at Temple University while doing research for Dr. Elwyn Smith on "American Catholicism and Conscientious Objection from 1776 to 1924," found only four Catholics who were CO's in World War I: Francis X. Hennessy, Christian Lellig, and Benjamin Salmon. Ammon Hennacy, a CO during World War I, later converted to Catholicism.

[25] U. S. Selective Service System, Conscientious Objection, 1950, Vol. I, pp. 53, 60, 105, 115, 117, 263, 320.

[26] National Service Board for Religious Objectors' file, Box G-76 located at Peace Collection, Swarthmore College.

[27] J. F. Powers, the noted American author of <u>Morte D'Urban</u>, is an example of such a Catholic CO.

[28] <u>The Catholic Worker</u>, April-June, 1944 and letter from Arthur Sheehan to author dated October 30, 1969.

[29] Wittner, <u>Rebels . . .</u> , p. 70.

[30] Clarence Pickett as quoted in Wittner, <u>Rebels . . .</u> , p. 70.

[31] Schlissel, <u>Conscience . . .</u> , p. 225.

[32] NSBRO's file, Box G-76, Peace Collection, Swarthmore College.

[33] <u>The Catholic Worker</u>, December, 1941.

[34] Letter from Dwight Larrowe to Miss E. S. Brenton dated July 22, 1942, for an appeal for funds. Larrowe stated that thirty-nine men were at Stoddard and that he was running the camp at $16.00 a month per man rather than the prescribed $35.00. He had spent $5,000 in the past year and needed two to three times that amount for the next year. This letter is located in the ACCO file at Peace Collection, Swarthmore College.

[35] Day, <u>Loaves and Fishes</u>, p. 64.

[36] Interview with Richard Leonard of LaSalle College, Philadelphia, Pennsylvania, a Catholic CO at Stoddard, Warner, and Rosewood, on Tuesday, November 4, 1969.

[37] Theodore Pojar, Robert Lindorfer, and Francis Bates were three such Catholic CO's. See <u>The Catholic Worker</u>, May, 1942.

[38] Arthur Sheehan of the Catholic Worker in New York City visited Paul Comley French, director of NSBRO, in Washington, D.C. French told him to visit the American Friends CPS camp at Cooperstown which had a budget of $50,000 a year. Sheehan believed that the Catholic Worker would run a camp for $15,000 annually. Archbishop John T. McNicholas of the diocese of Cincinnati gave $300 and the American Civil Liberties Union gave $500. Four other bishops helped financially: Karl J. Alter, Bishop of Toledo, Ohio; Francis J. Beckman, Bishop of Dubuque, Iowa; John B. Peterson, Bishop of

Manchester; and Gerald Shaughnessy, S.M., Bishop of Seattle, Washington. Other sources of revenue came in small donations of $25.00 or less.

[39]The Catholic Worker, May, 1943.

[40]Day, Loaves and Fishes, p. 64.

[41]Telephone conversation between Arthur Sheehan and the author on October 21, 1969, Mr. Sheehan indicated that the decision to close the CPS camp at Warner was not simply a matter of finances as Wittner in Rebels . . . contends.

[42]NSBRO's file, Box A-44 at the Swarthmore Peace Library.

[43]Wittner, Rebels . . . , p. 60.

[44]Memorandum in the files of the ACCO box at Swarthmore Peace Library.

[45]George Matthues, "CO's Studying War Relief, Urge Feed Europe New," The Catholic Worker, March, 1943.

[46]Monsignor G. Barry O'Toole taught in the philosophy department at The Catholic University of America and Father John J. Hugo was a promising young theologian. Ammon Hennacy later became one of the leading figures in the Catholic Worker Movement and wrote his famous book, The Autobiography of a Catholic Anarchist.

[47]The Catholic CO, October, 1944, p. 1. This newspaper is available at the Catholic Worker in New York City and is also on microfilm at the University of San Francisco.

[48]The only effort made by the CAIP in support of Catholic CO's during World War II was the publication in 1941 of a pamphlet, The Morality of Conscientious Objection to War written by Cyprian Emmanuel, O.F.M.

[49]The Catholic Worker, June, 1948.

[50]Mulford Q. Sibley and Philip E. Jacob, Conscription of Conscience (New York, 1952), p. 468-75.

[51] Gordon Zahn, <u>A Descriptive Study of the Sociological Backgrounds of CO's in CPS during World War II</u>, (Ph.D. dissertation, The Catholic University of America, 1953).

[52] Gordon Zahn, <u>War, Conscience and Dissent</u> (New York, 1967), p. 152.

[53] Thomas T. McAvoy, <u>The History of the Catholic Church in the United States</u>, (Notre Dame, 1969), p. 436.

[54] John Courtney Ford, S.J., "Morality of Obliteration Bombing," <u>Theological Studies</u>, V (September, 1944), 267.

[55] <u>Idem</u>.

[56] <u>Idem</u>.

[57] <u>Ibid</u>., p. 305.

[58] <u>Ibid</u>., pp. 268-69.

[59] <u>Ibid</u>., p. 271.

[60] <u>The Catholic Worker</u>, October, 1944. See also, Paul H. Furfey, "Bombing of Non-Combatants Is Murder," <u>Catholic CO</u>, (July-September, 1945, 3-4) and <u>The Mystery of Iniquity</u>, (Milwaukee, 1944), pp. 165-66.

[61] "Atomic Bomb," <u>Commonweal</u>, XLIII (August 31, 1945), 468.

[62] "Atomic Bomb," excerpt from <u>Osservatore Romano</u>, August 10, 1945, in <u>Tablet</u>, August 18, 1945, p. 78.

[63] J. M. Gillis, "Editorial Comment," <u>Catholic World</u>, CLXVI (September, 1945), 449-50.

[64] <u>The Catholic Worker</u>, September, 1945.

[65] Wittner, <u>Rebels . . .</u> , pp. 126-28.

[66] AMU, CAIP Collection, "Summary of CAIP Committee Work-End of War to 1952," p. 21.

[67] _Idem._

[68] Wittner, _Rebels . . ._ , pp. 128-29.

CHAPTER IV

THE THOUGHT OF THOMAS MERTON AND THE CROSSROADS OF PEACE

After World War II, the Cold War between the Soviet Union and the United States permeated every aspect of American life. The peace movement retreated in face of the issues raised by the Cold War, such as the fear of communism, the arms race, and defensive security. The loyalty-security mania of the early fifties developed a McCarthyism that was the domestic counterpart of the American foreign policy of the Cold War.[1] Ironically, they were the very forces the peace movement sought to restrain. The remnants of the movement continued their struggle against war by formulating alternatives to American military policies and by serving as prophets of non-violence.

The American Catholic aspect of the peace movement faced the same forces. After World War II, the Catholic peace movement for the most part was represented by the relatively few Catholic conscientious objectors who had performed alternative service and their even fewer supporters. "Basically, it dissolved completely until nothing remained to show for it but the Catholic Worker, its principal benefactor throughout the war period.[2] For the most part, Catholic Worker pacifists returned to their roots of social justice concerns and administered the corporal works of mercy to the poor. The

pacifist witness remained, however, as Dorothy Day and other
Workers attempted to extend their pacifism into performing
symbolic actions of non-violent resistance during the fifties.
The other Catholic peace organization, the CAIP, had not
been part of the very small American Catholic peace movement
during the war because it had supported the United States'
involvement in World War II. During and after the war, the
CAIP kept its committees functioning and centered its energies within the United Nations in hope of formulating policies for international peace. During the nadir of the fifties,
there remained at best a small scattering of Catholic individuals who did what they could to keep the peace witness alive.
Needless to say, these few Catholics as well as the barely
surviving peace movement in America failed to awaken the
public.

Beginning in the late fifties, a renaissance of the
American peace movement occurred when attention was focused
upon thermo-nuclear weapons. The immediate cause for this
was the atmospheric testing of the hydrogen bomb. As the
nuclear testing increased, Americans began to re-examine the
nature of war in light of the development of thermonuclear
weapons. Despite the sudden commotion at the obliteration
of Hiroshima and Nagasaki, the American people had never
truly appreciated the possibility of their wholesale slaughter
until the Soviet Union detonated a series of hydrogen bombs
during the middle and late fifties. Although the Soviet
breakthrough in thermonuclear weaponry spurred an acceleration

of the American "defense effort," it also cut the other way.
Prominent political and military leaders now began to talk
about the impossibility of victory in a war that rendered
survival unlikely.[3]

Catholic concern for peace in face of thermonuclear
warfare arouse once again from the CAIP and the Catholic
Worker. The CAIP invoked the just war tradition and attempted
mainly through the tactic of lobbying in the United Nations
to establish a criteria for the use of nuclear weapons.
Rooted in pacifism, the Catholic Worker condemned the use
of nuclear weapons and in practice were nuclear pacifists.
In its attempt to prevent the use of such weapons, however,
the Catholic Worker extended its pacifism to include a wider
variety of non-violent tactics. In face of thermonuclear
warfare, Catholic Worker pacifism was changing and what was
becoming more important during the 1950's was not the traditional style of pacifism, but the tactics of non-violent
resistance.

These three positions of the just war, pacifism and
non-violent resistance challenged one another for the position
of the most viable alternative in a nuclear age. Though
members of the CAIP clung to the just war tradition, the
Catholic Worker contended that the nuclear age had revealed
as never before the bankruptcy of the just war theory. At
the same time they realized that pacifism was also an inadequate rationale and they began to turn increasingly to non-
violent resistance.

This shift in action, though very limited and seemingly insignificant in the fifties, had its impact on Catholic thought as well. None of these Catholic activists were attempting to provide an intellectual rationale for what was going on. In fact, no Catholic in the fifties was attempting to explain what was happening to the Catholic peace movement during this period.

It was not until non-violent resistance achieved some success and notoriety that individuals attempted to relate its significance to Catholic teaching. The Catholic who best accomplished this task was Thomas Merton. From the vantage point of the sixties, he was able to look back and articulate the intellectual shift that was taking place within the Catholic peace movement.

The decade of the fifties was an important intersection for the movement, a crossroads of peace. The theological rationales of the just war and pacifism were beginning their demise and the new ethic of non-violent resistance was being born in the American peace movement. The sixties would complete the process and witness the blossoming of non-violent resistance. Thomas Merton stood at this crossroads and related the significance of the changes taking place.

Thomas Merton was born in Praedes, France on January 31, 1915. Six years later his Quaker mother died. While spending most of his time studying in France or England, he frequently accompanied his father, who traveled widely throughout Europe in quest of ideas for his paintings.

In 1934, after attending Cambridge for one year, Merton came to the United States and completed his formal education at Columbia University obtaining an M.A. degree in English. The religious and mystical elements of the writings of William Blake and the advice of a Hindu monk to read St. Augustine and the Early Church Fathers had a strong influence on Merton's move toward Catholicism.

After years of wide and varied experiences,[4] Merton became a convert to Catholicism, and was baptized in 1938 at Corpus Christi Church in New York City. In The Seven Story Mountain,[5] an autobiographical account of his spiritual pilgrimage, he wrote that he had been converted from "rank savage paganism, from the spiritual level of a cannibal or of an ancient Roman, to the living faith."

Within two years of his baptism, Merton decided that he wanted to become a priest. His desire to do so was initially frustrated when his application to the Franciscan Order was rejected. Accepting this decision, he went to teach in a small Franciscan men's college, St. Bonaventure located in Olean, New York. While teaching there, the conviction grew in him that he would dedicate himself to the contemplative life and in 1942 he applied to and was eventually accepted into the Trappist Abbey of Gethsemani in Kentucky.

While making this decision, Merton was faced with the draft. He decided to register as a non-combatant conscientious objector, but was rejected for health reasons. Later he was recalled for the draft and passed the physical examination.

128

Before he was drafted, he entered the monastery. Merton's
concern for the individual in face of totalitarianism in
World War II was also evident in the book he wrote during
this period, Journal of My Escape From the Nazis.[6] This book
was finally published in 1968 under the title My Argument
with the Gestapo.

Thomas Merton's writings extended over a period of
thirty years, and Merton himself divided them into three
periods. The writings of the first period, from his conversion in 1938 to his ordination in 1949 were ascetic, intran-
sigeant and somewhat apocalyptic in outlook. Written in his
"first fervor" days they represented a rigid, arbitrary
separation between God and the world. The second period
extending from 1949 to 1959 was mainly one of transition in
which Merton began to try to discover ways to integrate God
and the world. Readings in depth psychology, Zen Buddhism,
and existentialism greatly influenced him and led him to
develop a positive view of man which he combined with the
theological doctrine of the incarnation. The integration,
however, did not appear until the third period beginning in
1959, when he increasingly focused on contemporary social
issues.

Merton's writings, as he acknowledged, reveal two con-
flicting facets of his thought: one ascetic, conservative,
traditional, and monastic; the other radical, independent and
somewhat akin to the hippies of the "counter-culture."[7] His
literary works seem to have fit best in The Catholic Worker

as well as small literary magazines; the publishing house,
New Directions,[8] printed all his works.

It was during the third period that Merton wrote on
peace. Like Catholic peace activists, he first addressed
the social justice issues of poverty and race. The international issue of the Cold War and the much discussed issues
of the Christian-Marxist dialogue provided the background
which eventually led him to address himself to the issues of
war and peace.

In his first essay on peace, "The Pasternak Affair,"
in Disputed Questions (1960) Merton established the context
for his subsequent writings on this issue. In this essay he
suggests that man has lost all hope of freedom in his present
social structure. The structures, he felt, were diminishing
the value of the individual. Merton contended that God alone
and no other person or group, not even the official government,
had the right to extend a superior force over the individual.
He urged man not to abdicate his own judgment in order to be
accepted by the establishment. He goes on to say that he is
tired of a world that cannot appreciate a man such as Boris
Pasternak. He then suggests that the world will improve only
if there is more willingness on the part of man to respond to
Christ. For Merton, Christ is the only redeeming element
that can bring civilization to its intended form. Unless
modern man responds to Christ's invitation to bring about the
necessary revolution, the world will continue at its present
rate and drift farther and farther away from its goal. Merton

leaves the reader with the question: "Do we have the courage
to do so?" Belief in Christ, an emphasis on the individual,
a love-hate relationship with the world, and a revolution
that would be achieved only at the eschaton or the second
coming of Christ would characterize all of his subsequent
writings on peace.

Merton's identify was inextricabally connected with
being a monk. Accused of being "stranded in the medieval-
garde," his monastic commitment served both as his limitation
and his strength. Merton viewed the origin of monasticism as
a form of protest to the wedding of the Church and State which
occurred under Constantine. Monastic withdrawal from the
world as a means to reach union with God emerged as a life-
style that would stand over against the existing social
order.[9] Speaking out from this monastic tradition, he became
one of the most impressive and influential spokesmen in the
Catholic peace movement. Since Catholics respected the monk
as a man who had made great sacrifices to reach union with God,
Merton's peace writings attracted a far wider audience than
the writings of other members of the Catholic Left. He also
provided the dimension of contemplation which Catholic peace
activists would seek to cultivate in themselves to clarify
and bring meaning to their actions.

The focal point of his contemplation was his belief in
the eschatological dimension of the Judeo-Christian vision of
a "new heaven and a new earth." According to Merton, the
ultimate triumph of the vision would be achieved in the eschaton,

the second coming of Jesus Christ. This belief became known
to Catholic participants in the peace movement as the long
view. Its sources were the more mystical and exchatalogical
doctrine of the New Testament and the writings of the Early
Church Fathers. As the threat of a nuclear holocaust became
more immediate with the advance of the Cold War between the
Soviet Union and the United States, Merton's eschatological
vision assumed a new significance to his readers.

The long view accounted for Merton's unique contribution to the Catholic peace movement. It was not what he did
but what he wrote that accounts for his significance. As a
result, an internal anaylsis of Merton's thought is crucial
for an understanding of Catholicism's relationship to the
American peace movement. His writing mirrors the basic theological rationales that were used by peace activists in
America from World War II through the war in Vietnam. During
these years, Catholic peace activists used terms such as just
war, pacifism, nuclear pacifism, and non-violent resistance
to explain the reason for their actions, but few of these
activists were articulate enough or knowledgeable enough of
Catholic theology to develop a rationale for their actions.
None were able to explain theologically the significance of
their positions within the Catholic tradition of peace.

Through his writings, Merton clarified the varieties
of Catholic peace concern that emerged during World War II
and he defined the theological positions of the just war theory
and pacifism in light of their historical antecedents. With

this clarification Merton was able to point out the inade-
quacies of both traditions and develop a theological framework
for nuclear pacifism. He was also able to combine the new
ethic of non-violence which emerged in the American peace
movement after World War II with Catholic eschatology. All
of this pointed toward a new theology of peace.

Though Merton was not a systematic theologian, nor an
original thinker in terms of developing a theology of peace,
he is the only Catholic writer whose expansive study of the
question of peace considered the full variety of approaches.[10]
In his writings he provides an appreciation of the problems
and contradictions of the various approaches and above all,
he points out the limits of any ideology of peace.

Merton provides the theological dimension necessary
for a complete understanding of the impact of the American
Catholic peace movement. Peace activists never provided this
dimension themselves. A study of Merton's thought provides
the theological categories and points out the theological
shifts necessary to evaluate the full implications of the
impact of peace action on Catholic thought and teaching on
peace.

Thomas Merton saw the Cold War, the ideological, national
and military struggle between the communist and free worlds,
as the most serious threat to international security after
World War II.[11] The threats were so great because both the
United States and the Soviet Union possessed nuclear weapons.
He opposed the extreme nationalism of both the United States

and the Soviet Union for fear that technological knowledge
would trigger a nuclear war. Merton's most explicit response
to this struggle was written in a "Letter to Pablo Antonio
Cundra Concerning Giants:"

> The two great powers are like sorcerer's
> apprentices, spending billions of dollars on
> space exploration and nuclear weapons while
> failing to feed, clothe, and shelter two-
> thirds of the human race. They are like the
> twins Gog and Magog in the book of Ezechiel,
> each with great power and little sanity,
> each telling lies with great conviction. . ..
> If a citizen is not properly classified, Gog
> shoots him, while Magog deprives him of a
> home, a job, a seat on the bus. In both,
> life and death depend on everything except
> who you are.[12]

Merton opposed the Cold War between Gog and Magog primarily because he feared that an escalation into a nuclear
confrontation would destroy the world. He believed that there
was no effective control over the use of nuclear weapons and
the Cold War was releasing forces that would eventually lead
the great powers into national suicide.

Merton was one of the first theologians to see that
the Cold War threat of nuclear war and destruction had warped
traditional Christian ethics. He held that both the traditional Catholic doctrine of the just war and conventional
pacifism were inadequate in the nuclear age. He also contended
that the only posture that was both reasonable and Christian
in the face of nuclear warfare was nuclear pacifism. Such a
position meant that a Catholic would condemn the use of nuclear
weapons by any nation under any circumstances and would refuse
to participate in any aspect of a nuclear war.

To arrive at this ethical stance, Merton first pointed
out the inadequacy of the traditional just war theory held by
Catholics when applied to nuclear warfare. He first located
the beginnings of the development of the just war tradition
in early Christianity. The Father of all modern Christian
thought on war and the adapter of the pagan just war criteria
to Christianity, as Merton stated, is "for better or worse"
St. Augustine. By the fourth century, according to Merton,
the question of war and peace had become far more complex
for the Christian because of the conversion of Constantine
and his transformation of the Roman Empire from persecutor
of Christians to defender of Christendom.[13] According to
Merton, Augustine explains this new Chruch-State relationship
in a time of war by stating that every society seeks peace and
may have to wage war to preserve peace. Since the Christian
lives in the earthly city and participates in its benefits
he is bound to share society's responsibilities even if that
means going to war. Christians may participate in war, or
may abstain from participation, but their motives are different from those of the pagan. The Christian is waging war
to establish peace and his defense of the earthly city is
secondary to his fulfillment of the divine will. So the
Christian, concludes Augustine, is justified by the interior
motive: the love of peace to be safeguarded by force.
Augustine, as Merton said, imposed many limits on the
Christian soldier and these were not entirely unrealistic
in a less destructive age. Yet, Merton concluded his essay

with the following analysis: "The twofold weakness of the
Augustinian theory is its stress on a subjective purity of
intention which can be doctored an manipulated with apparent
'sincerity' and the tendency to pessimism about human nature
and the world, now used as a JUSTIFICATION for recourse to
violence."[14]

The logical arguments for the just war were expounded
by St. Thomas Aquinas and his commentators and disciples down
to the present day.[15] Merton, himself, a neo-Thomist, believed
that nuclear weapons had altered the nature of war by bringing
instant death to millions of noncombatants and had consequently altered the traditional Catholic doctrine of the just
war. He feared that the just war tradition which had sanctioned Christian participation in the atrocities of Dresden
and Hiroshima might be used as an excuse to tolerate a nuclear
exchange of fire.[16]

The contention that there can be no religious justification for a policy of all-out nuclear aggression led Merton
to look at the teachings of other contemporary theologians as
a second source for his analysis of the just war. He recognized and confessed that especially in the Church in America,
there existed a strong and articulate body of theological
opinion in favor of nuclear deterrance as necessary to an
"adequate posture of defense." Father John Courtney Murray,
S.J., was the leading spokesman for this view.[17] Merton
sarcastically attacked Murray's position that nuclear warfare
could ever be defensive or limited. He described Murray's

position in the following manner: "He takes his stand on the natural law and on the traditional Just War theory. He believes that defensive wars may be necessary and they ought to be fought with conventional weapons or with small nuclear bombs . . . it is adequate on paper, but the 20 kiloton bomb dropped on Hiroshima would be small according to Father Murray."[18] Merton also cited one of Murray's footnotes which seemed to indicate that a pre-emptive strike could be regarded as "defensive." "One wonders," Merton conjectured, "if this does not after all tend to validate morally everything that goes on at Cape Canavaral or Los Alamos."[19]

Merton concluded his criticism of defenders of nuclear warfare by again affirming that nuclear warfare is always total and offensive. "In our age," he wrote, "there is essentially a new kind of war and one in which the necessary conditions for a 'Just War' are extremely difficult to maintain. A war of total annihilation simply cannot be considered a 'Just War' no matter how good the causes for which it is undertaken."[20]

The third and final source to which Merton looked for direction in his analysis of the just war was the writings of the popes. He was disturbed that none of the popes had formally condemned the use of nuclear weapons, and in various articles he tried to explain this neglect, not only to his readers but also to himself. His writings reflect his own ambiguous feelings on the matter. Merton once explained that the popes had not formally condemned the use of hydrogen

bombs because to condemn a specific weapon would leave some
critics free to make the pope appear to be approving other
kinds of weapons.[21]   Another time he explained that the popes
had not condemned nuclear weapons because the weapons condemned themselves.

In relation to the popes, Merton's strongest argument
against nuclear bombs, like that of Father Ford's argument
against obliteration bombing, was that the popes' statements
of condemnation of certain aspects of war, before the dis-
covery of nuclear power, satisfied the need for a formal
condemnation of nuclear war. Merton's last evidence for this
position was Pope Pius XII's statement that a weapon is immoral
when it becomes so destructive that it cannot be controlled.
He believed that Popes Pius XII, John XXIII and Paul VI, had
said in so many words that the new means of warfare, especially
nuclear weapons, have altered the traditional Catholic norms
of morality and created a new kind of war in which the concept
of just war is irrelevant. Thus, Merton believed that the
testimony of history on the just war is clear and that the
attempt to subject the irrationality of war to the rule of
reason alone fails miserably. He quotes Pope John XXIII from
Pacem in Terris as making clear that the key to the meaning
of peace lay not in

> a casuistical treatment of the problem of
> nuclear war but in profound and optimistic
> Christian spirit with which the Pope lays
> bare the deepest roots of peace, roots which
> man himself has the mission to cultivate.
> (This necessitates a free commitment to the

ethic of Christianity which goes beyond
logic to the spiritual and mystical rooted
in deep and simple love for God which is
also love for His creation and for God's
child: man.)[22]

To make such a commitment, Merton declared himself a nuclear

pacifist. Though he qualified the just war criteria in terms

of nuclear warfare, he could never totally reject it for two

reasons which he himself admitted: First he believed that a

Christian could never be forbidden to fight and secondly he

refused to admit that a war could never be just.[23] For these

reasons, he could never claim to be a total pacifist, only a

nuclear pacifist.

By refusing to totally reject the just war theory and

by limiting his pacifism, Merton came into open disagreement

with the leading Catholic pacifist, Dorothy Day. Merton wrote

for The Catholic Worker in June, 1967, an article entitled,

"The Shotgun in the Backyard Shelter." It was a response to

an essay that had appeared in Commonweal. The author of the

Commonweal article advanced the argument that in a case where

a possessor of a backyard shelter was confronted by a less

provident neighbor and his family during a nuclear attack, it

would be licit for him to defend his shelter against the

intruder at the point of a gun. Merton's response was not

concerned with the correctness or error of the article's

theology. He was willing to grant that one did have the

right to kill someone if there was no other way to protect

his family and himself. What Merton objected to was seeing

the issue completely in these terms. He held that it was

unchristian since it gave the impression that every man was
for himself -- such an attitude was wrong on a purely natural
level and disastrous even to the political interests of the
United States. Because of her pacifism, Dorothy Day took
issue with Merton on theological grounds. She held that a
Christian should not take the life of another even in self-
defense.[24] Beyond this single incident, there is little
evidence of any other disagreement between Merton, the
nuclear pacifist, and Day, the total pacifist.

In defending his qualified position on pacifism,
Merton contended that he could not call himself a pacifist
since pacifism depended solely upon the conscience of the
individual Christian and had no inherent social orientation.
He also believed that "the religious ambiguities in the term
'pacifism' gave it implications that were somewhat less than
Catholic." A pacifist who believes in peace as an article
of his faith, warned Merton, will result in "contending that
Christians who are not pacifists are apostates from Christianity."[25]

He also rejected the unqualified label of pacifist
because of the misconception and naïveté unfortunately associated with the term. The noxious reputation which is
attached to pacifists in America is the result, he believed,
not only of ignorance, but also of the lack of any distinctions between different types of pacifists. To speak of
pacifism inevitably gives people an excuse for justifying
their own bellicosity. Such discussions too often imply

that there is the theoretical acceptability of either alternative: pacifism or bellicism. For Merton there was no alternative. It was not a question of some "ideal" or "cause," but of basic human justice.[26]

In an article published in 1968[27] Merton explained the carricature of the pacifist held by the majority of people by explicating the character Bloom in Ulysses. For Merton, Bloom is not an authentic pacifist, though most critiques of Ulysses portray him as such. He rejects Bloom as an authentic pacifist because his is a merely temperamental passivity before justice. Merton is restless even with his own pacifism when it cannot confront the realities of political and social life. To those who base their stance of total pacifism on the Gospel, Merton replies: "Jesus did not call men to be pacifists but to be peacemakers."

The final argument Merton gives for the rejection of unqualified pacifism relates to his concern for the oppressed people of the world. He affirmed the right of an individual to resort to violence to restore rights wrongfully denied or to re-establish an order necessary for decent human existence. Merton lamented the hidden violence which masquerades as just authority in oppressive and highly organized societies. "Those who in some way or other concur in the oppression -- and perhaps profit by it -- are exercising violence even though they may be preaching pacifism. And their supposedly peaceful laws, which maintain this spurious kind of order are in fact instruments of violence and oppression."[28] His position

on this point can be summarized in his statement, "if the
oppressed try to resist by force -- which is their right --
theology has no business preaching non-violence to them.
Mere blind destruction is, of course, futile and immoral:
but who are we to condemn a desperation we have helped to
cause!"[29]

In the final analysis, for Merton the ethical philosophy
of pacifism was as inadequate as the doctrine of the just war
in reference to nuclear weapons. Thus, he urged his readers
to adopt a position of nuclear pacifism. Such a position
meant that a Catholic would accept the tradition of the just
war except where nuclear weapons were involved, since a
nuclear war could never be just.

The war in Vietnam caused Merton to shift the emphasis
in his writings on peace away from nuclear warfare to limited
warfare. All of the distinctions made by him pertaining to
nuclear pacifism, the just war, and pacifism seemed ultimately
to disappear[30] when he considered the issue of limited warfare in reference to the war in Vietnam. Though Merton had
contended that a limited nuclear war could never be just,
he had also contended that a limited war without nuclear
weapons could be just. This distinction became tenuous in
Merton's writings, when he stated that even limited wars
(however just) presented an almost certain danger of all-out
nuclear war.[31] Thus, it became highly questionable for Merton
if any war could be just.

Having already demonstrated the inadequacy of the
traditional just war doctrine and pacifism in Catholic
theology, there was no need for Merton to attempt to apply
to Vietnam the rigid and sterile categories of the theological discipline. As a result the Vietnam war forced him to
search for a new ethic of peace.

The essential evil of the United States in Vietnam,
Merton said, was "the total commitment to violence in utter
disregard for the rights of individuals the war had come to
represent."[32] He felt that the American choice of "limited
warfare" saved it from being charged with genocide. He did
see, however, a psychological parallel between American action
in Vietnam and the Indian wars of extermination which he set
forth in an article entitled, "Ishi: A Meditation."[33]

For Merton, Vietnam was a symbol of the eschatological
moment when a nuclear holocaust could result. He wrote in
his Preface to the Vietnam edition of No Man Is an Island,
"The war in Vietnam is a bell tolling for the whole world,
warning the whole world that war may spread everywhere and
violent death may spread over the entire earth."[34]

But the Vietnam war had further implications for Merton.
It led him to search for a new theology of peace that would
speak against the United States' unleashing of a campaign
of destruction upon Vietnam and the utter disregard for the
rights of individuals involved. Referring to Vietnam, Merton
contended that "a problem arises not when the theology admits
that force can be necessary but when it does so in a way that

implicitly favors the claims of the powerful and self-seeking
establishment against the common good of mankind or against
the rights of the oppressed."[35]

Merton looked to the doctrine of non-violence as a
means that would provide a new social ethic to meet the moral
problems of the nuclear age and replace the inadequate traditional Catholic doctrine of the just war. He also hoped that
non-violence would aid pacifists in advancing themselves
beyond a mere position of conscience to one that would speak
more effectively to the problems of the world.

In striving to realize his hopes, Merton again looked
to tradition by first turning to Sacred Scripture and the
writings of the Early Church Fathers.

Merton begins with Jesus and affirms that, neither
blessed nor forbidden by Jesus, war belongs to the world outside the Kingdom which He came to establish. It is the
Apocalypse, according to Merton, which presents the eschatological view of peace in its symbolic description of the
critical struggle of the nascent Church with the powers of
the world. War in the Apocalypse is the "Rider of the Red
Horse" who, Merton states, is to prepare the destruction of
the civil power structure. Merton asserts that the Holy
Roman Empire was clearly understood by the early Christians
to possess a demonic power, and this is evident in the
Apocalypse where "the battle was non-violent and spiritual,
and its success depended on the clear understanding of the
totally new and unexpected dimensions in which it was to be

fought."[32] There is no indication whatever in the Apocalypse, concludes Merton, that "the Christ would be willing to fight and die to maintain the 'power of the beast,' in other words to engage in a power-struggle for the benefit of the Emperor and of his power."[37]

In his consideration of the early Church Fathers, Merton emphasises the writings of Origen, the author of Contra Celsus. Origen denied that the early Christians were violent revolutionaries, or that they intended to bring about the overthrow of the empire by force. Origen, himself, did not believe in the need of war because the time would come for all men to be united in the Logos, though this fulfillment most probably awaits the second coming of Christ. Origen believed that human society had been radically transformed by the Incarnation, and that, among other things, Christians, who desired the good of all men, should be united against war, in obedience to Christ. Because Christians are a "royal priesthood," they did more by their prayers to preserve peace than they could by force of arms.

Using this eschatological doctrine of the New Testament and the early Church Fathers as sources, Merton calls for a new theology of peace based on these sources in place of the Just War criteria.

At this point, what we have in Merton is the presentation of the Christian myth which provides a vision of the future without any attention to specific means for its achievement. This presentation lacks any consideration of institutional

involvement in the shaping of the future. Too, since Merton
contends that the New Testament says nothing about politics,
these sources, as interpreted by Merton, have definite limitations. Such institutional involvement in the political
process is a pertinent question today, especially with the
contemporary development of a theology of peace. Merton
claims that the whole Christian thrust against evil is summed
up in the phrase "nonresistance," then how does one allow for
what Merton in other writings refers to as non-violent
resistance?

Merton's eschatological vision as applied to human
institutions presupposed the existence of a Christian state
which he claims has never existed. All extant ages, according to Merton, have been pre-Christian or post-Christian.
Such a view implies that the Christian ethic has nothing to
do with the political process. Realizing this contradiction,
Merton modified his position by accepting the position of
Karl Rahner who states:

> Thus the political action of the Christian does
> not become confused with projects centered
> around an official and clericalist "party line,"
> nor is it inevitably associated with the propa-
> gation of a dogmatic message which the rest of
> the world is not disposed to hear without
> challenging it. But on the other hand, this
> Christian action is concretely ordered to advanc-
> ing the work of Redemption and deepening the
> penetration of grace into the realm of society
> and nature. . .. It is the "action of Chris-
> tians but not action of the Church".38

Accepting Christ's Sermon on the Mount as the basis for ethics,
Merton links the Beatitudes with natural law in his attempt to

justify man's political action. He states that "the Beatitudes indeed convey a profound existential understanding
of the dynamic of the Kingdom of God . . . a dynamism of
patient and secret growth. . . . This is not merely a matter
of blind and arbitrary faith. The early history of the Church,
the record of apostles and martyrs remains to testify to this
inherent and mysterious dynamism of the ecclesial 'event' in
the world of history and time."[39]

Merton, rooted in a Catholic tradition which looks not
only to the New Testament but also to its doctrine or natural
law for its principles, realized that the Church adopted the
natural law from pagan philosophy and made it a basis for
much of its doctrine and practices. Thus, the natural law
became the basis for Christian doctrine concerning the social
order. Merton stated: "Once the Law of Christ has been pro-
mulgated, it is no longer possible to isolate the natural law
in a sphere of its own. The natural law itself acquires a
Christian perspective from the Sermon on the Mount. It has
an aim higher than the mere avoidance of brutality, savagery,
and sin. It becomes obligatory for the Christian to orientate
all his conduct according to the law of love and to make use
of non-violent means of persuasion whenever it is humanly
possible. He must do this out of generous love both for his
neighbor and for the truth.[40] This is exactly what the Catholic doctrine of a just war attempted to do.

Thus, Merton was able to move in his theology from the
passive resistance of Christ's crucifixion to the justification

of a more active resistance by attempting to replace the
inadequate just war and pacifist doctrines with Christian
non-violent resistance. Though Merton does not see the
political as an area of direct concern, he affirms theological principles which a socially concerned individual can
embrace. After World War II many Americans involved in the
peace movement advocated and tried such means. Among Catholic
peace activists, Catholic Workers alone moved into the study
and practice of Gandhian non-violence. Merton added very
little in his writings to the traditional concept of Gandhian
non-violence. What he did do was show the compatability of
these means with the Catholic faith.

According to Merton, Gandhi attempted to provide a
means that would involve human beings in the decision-making
process and in the discipline of meaningful participation.
It would enable participants to correct the evils of the
existing social order without demanding the participants to
engage in and become part of the evil social structure they
were attempting to correct. Thus, the means of Gandhian
non-violent resistance, unlike passive resistance, does provide a dynamic for social change. Gandhian non-violence was
consistant with the Catholic faith, according to Merton,
because it rested on the Gospel principle of willingness to
endure suffering rather than to inflict it upon another and
also because its primary goal was truth. Thus, the question
of effectiveness in the political realm of the here and now
is not the primary goal.

Merton takes Gandhian non-violent resistance and adds
the eschatological dimension which provides for the ultimate
triumph of truth and love only with the second coming of
Christ. It seems, according to Merton, that if enough individuals make a free commitment to the love ethic of Christian
non-violence, a new earth would exist and the problem of
force-dominated politics would cease. The ethic of Christian
non-violent resistance, he hoped, would replace the doctrine
of the just war for Catholics and provide the basis for a new
theology of peace.

This new ethic of non-violence reconciled with the concepts of eschatology and individual responsibility constitute
the unique positive contribution of Merton's writings on
peace. Merton, himself, pointed out his own limitations in
attempting such an integration. Aware of his lack of political astuteness and removed from participation in direct
action[41] in his monastery, he contended that he was not
primarily concerned with the tactical strategy of building
a peace movement. He also acknowledged that he could not
develop what he termed a "systematic theology of love," which,
in crisis situations might support actions of resistance.
Merton admits, that at best, he was only examining "principles
and cases which help an individual to see the unacceptable
ambiguities of a theology of 'might makes right' masquerading
as a Christian theology of love."[42] He was certain, however,
that the new ethic required a development of a more optimistic
view of man. This optimistic view was needed to replace the

negative view of man which provided the touchstone upon which the doctrine of the just war was based.

Merton also believed that man's power of global self-destruction in the Eschatological Age was forcing man into a confrontation with the depths of his spiritual self. In Faith and Violence Merton states that he is writing from a Christian view of man, "a concept, which is held in common by all the religions which can be called 'higher' or 'mystical.' This posture views man as spiritual, or self-transcending being."[43] Thus, Merton's Christian belief in man's capacity for transcendence, which could make him one with his fellowmen and one with God, is the unquestioned presupposition on which he bases his hopeful view of man.[44] This hope found repeated expression in Merton's writings on the war-peace issues. He held that if man consciously grasped the truth of his plight, no matter how desperate, he could make good use of his freedom to transcend the injustice he suffered. Thus, the second presupposition of Merton's optimistic view of man is his belief that man has the capacity to assume personal responsibility. The crucial question for man was not "What is going to happen to us?"; but a more existential question, "What are we going to do?" Because man is capable of acting. Merton wrote, "'the supreme obligation' of every Christian taking precedence over absolutely everything else is to work for the abolition of war and thereby to do his best to preserve humanity from the threat of total annihilation."[45] Merton's urgency can be accounted

for by his identification of the age as "nuclear" and his
insistance on the eschatological perspective of any attempt
to define the role of the Christian.

In order for the individual to be a Christian in America
during the nuclear era, Merton contends that each individual
must first recognize the predominant myths operative in his
country. He portrayed America as a "sick nation" where
"people are fed on myths" and "are stuffed up to their eyes
with illusions" so that "they can't think straight." The two
great American myths blinding man, Merton asserts, are that
"force is the only alternative" and that "power is the only
basis for human relationships."[46] These myths predominant
during the Cold War are supported and reinforced by mass media
according to Merton, and they cultivate a "state of mind"
which prevents man from grasping the plight of his present
situation. This "state of mind," he warns, has taken over
the role of morality and conscience and will, and rationalized
its prejudices with convenient religious and ethical formulas
to condone what has occurred in the United States since World
War II.[47] This "state of mind" increases the enslavement of
men and the possibilities of personal destruction, because as
Merton points out, the massive power structures are the only
benefactors. As a result, the power structures within that
nation exploit the individual and ultimately conscript him
into warfare.

After asserting that the individual personality is in
great danger in America of being swallowed up by the Leviathan

State, Merton urges individual Christians to look upon the
acts and demands of their nation's leaders with intense
suspicion and recognition that there is a high probability
of jeopardy to their personal spiritual responsibilities
and well being if they obey such leadership. Merton insinu-
ates in his writings that authority in America is suspect.
The reason he gives is that it seeks to compel obedience
by increasingly resorting to external force or to the law
of fear. Though Merton documents this position by a reference
to Pope John XXIII, he gives no concrete examples. "When
authority ignores natural law, human dignity, human rights,
and the moral order established by God," he concludes, "it
undermines its own foundation and loses its claim to be
obeyed."[48]

Merton sees this sickness which infects the State
reflected in the Church in America, especially in its stands
on the issues of war and peace. In his view this sickness
accounts for the ambiguity of so many Catholics on the war
question, or worse the frank belligerency of the majority
of them. Merton laments the failure of his Church to inspire
its members to oppose America's militaristic ethos and the
arms race, even though it is clear that he does not see the
Church as an effective agent for social change. His hope for
change rests on the actions of individuals and he views
spirituality as the basic dynamic in human behavior for
durable social change.

Merton holds that the "state of mind" which exists in "sick" America threatens not only the spiritual basis of society but also the democratic process itself. If such a "state of mind" continues in the majority of American people, he feared that America would become the equivalent of Nazi Germany or Totalitarian Russia. He compares the spiritually sterile man in America to Adolph Eichman. In Raids on the Unspeakable, Merton notes that Eichman was considered to be a "sane" man even though he felt no guilt at the extermination of the Jews. The refusal of Eichman and men like him to accept the imperatives of personal responsibility and oppose Hitler, made a Nazi Germany possible.

In contrast to Eichmann, Merton in Faith and Violence celebrates such responsible individuals as Alfred Delp, Max Josef Metzger, Franz Jägerstätter, Dietrich Bonhoffer, and Simone Weil, whom he considers authentic Christians. These people defied the totalitarian power of the rulers of Nazi Germany by their acts of resistance and for Merton their non-violent resistance was a measure of their faith.

Hence, the problem for the individual in America is how to transform his present "state of mind" into a new consciousness that will result in human liberation and a capacity to act responsibly in face of totalitarian power. Without realizing it, Mertin gives some impetus and direction to such a process. He insists that man be properly informed, not only about the situation in which he finds himself, but also about non-violent resistance; and that man must exercise his right to protest or resist. Both of these demand the recognition of individual conscience. Merton stresses the need for individual conscience to be based on spiritual principles for the process to succeed. He believes that modern man must assume a spiritual posture; such a posture would give man a critical perspective and enable him to demythologize the warfare mentality and to stand over against the destructive uses of force and power by the State and society. The means of non-violence would still enable the individual Christian to have a direct relevance to the State and society, by trying to discover the way to a new policy.

Merton realistically recognizes the central role of fear operative in man which inhibits such a transformation of consciousness. In an article "Fear the Root of All War" Merton writes that one of the major obstacles of achieving peace is fear, not so much "the fear men have of one another as the fear they have of everything. It is not merely that they do not trust one another; they do not even trust themselves. . . . They cannot trust anything, because they have ceased to believe in God."[49]

Merton's insistence on a spiritual base as a prerequisite seemingly contradicts some of the statements in his writings on peace. In the latter, the only prerequisite for the end of war and the unity of man is the human dimension. In the essay, "Nhat Hanh Is My Brother," Merton points to the over-arching nature of the concept of human solidarity. Nhat, a Vietnamese, deplores war, as does Merton, and for the same reasons: human reasons -- reasons of sanity, justice, and love. They are both poets and both existentialists. Merton states,

> I have far more in common with Nhat than I
> have with many Americans, and I do not hesi-
> tate to say it. It is vitally important that
> such bonds be admitted. They are the bonds of
> a new solidarity and a new brotherhood which
> is beginning to be evident on all the five
> continents and which cuts across all political,
> religious and cultural lines to unite young men
> and women in every country in something that is
> more concrete than an ideal and more alive than
> a program. This unity of the young is the only
> hope of the world.[50]

Also, in the essay "Taking Sides on Vietnam," Merton says, "the side I take is, then, the side of the people who are sick of war and want peace in order to rebuild their country."[51]

And finally, in what is perhaps one of Merton's most famous statements on the entire issue of peace, first written in a letter to James Forest, later reprinted and widely circulated by A. J. Muste, the same human dimension is paramount.

> It seems to me of course that the most basic
> problem is not political, it is a-political
> and human. One of the most important things
> to do is to keep cutting deliberately through
> political lines and barriers and emphasizing
> the fact that these are largely fabrications
> and that there is another dimension, a genuine
> reality, totally opposed to the fictions of
> politics, the human dimension which politics
> pretends to abrogate entirely to themselves.
> Is this possible? I am accused of being too
> ready to doubt the possibility, though I am
> as ready as anyone to put some hope in it.
> At least we must try to hope in that, otherwise

all is over. But politics as they now stand
are hopeless. Hence the desirability of a
manifestly non-political witness, non-
alligned, non-labeled, fighting for the
reality of man and his rights and needs in
the nuclear world in some measure against
all the alignments.

In most of Merton's writings, however, the contradiction between spiritual and human is more apparent than real
because his definition of the "spiritual" or "religious"
dimension always presupposes the human which it seeks to
elevate or perfect. The distinction between human and
spiritual motivation is most apparent when Merton addresses
himself to the eschatological dimension. For him, the inner
change in man and the consequent change in the social order
which the reign of justice and love demands, is inextricably
bound up with the Second Coming of Christ or the Eschaton.
Only at that time will each man have undergone the inner
change which he considers a prerequisite for the revolution
of society and the reign of justice and peace. His insistence
on the inseparable association of personal and social change,
and the role of non-violence in both, is articulated in the
following passage: "Never was it more necessary to understand the importance of genuine non-violence as a power for
real change because it is aimed not so much at revolution
as conversion."[52]

This insistence on the prerequisite of personal conversion and Merton's long view which places all of his writings
on war and peace within the Catholic tradition and the second
coming of Christ affects his concept of revolution. The

revolution which Merton calls for cannot be realized until
the Second Coming of Christ when all creation will be ful-
filled, therefore, revolution is impossible to achieve in
human history. Yet, because of Merton's optimistic view of
man, where the individual is capable of transcendence and
of acting responsibly, the revolution can be realized in
human history to the extent that individuals are willing to
let Jesus Christ and His Spirit work through them.

In his writings on peace, Merton turns toward Gandhian
non-violence as a way for the individual believer to trans-
late his Christian belief concerning peace into life-style
and behavior that will realize, at least partially, the
revolution. Merton recognizes non-violence as a viable way
for the individual to use his reason, religious faith, and
courageous spirit of self-sacrifice to resist evil and
injustice and to give meaning once again to the ideals of
Christianity and democracy.[53]

Merton's optimistic view of man enables him to make
great demands on the individual. As Merton sees it, the
crucial link between Christianity and non-violence as espoused
by Gandhi is faith in the meaning of the Cross and the redemp-
tive death of Jesus who instead of using force against his
accusers, took all the evil upon himself and overcame the
evil by suffering. Merton sees this stance as a basic
Christian pattern; but a realistic theology that

> will, give a new practical emphasis to it.
> Instead of preaching the Cross for others and
> advising them to suffer patiently, the violence

which we sweetly impose on them, with the aid
of armies and police, we might conceivably
recognize the right of the less fortunate to
use force, and study more seriously the
practice of non-violence and humane methods
on our own part when perhaps, as it happens,
we possess the most stupendous arsenal of
power the world has ever known.[54]

Merton's major contribution was to integrate Gandhian
non-violence into Christianity. In the pamphlet, _Blessed are
the Meek: The Christian Roots of Non-Violence_, he sets forth
a list of seven criteria as touchstones for a relative
honesty in the practice of Christian non-violence. These
coincide with many of the points made by him in all of his
writings on the war-peace issues. They call for a transformation of the present state of the world by an individual who
is free from all association with unjust use of power, who
stands in solidarity with the poor and underpriviledged, who
is free of self-righteous blindness, who avoids the fetish of
immediate visible results, who is concerned with manifesting,
not obscuring the truth, and who grounds his action in
Christian hope. Merton says that power can never be the
hallmark of Christians. Rather the "key to non-violence is
the willingness of the non-violent resister to suffer a
certain amount of accidental evil in order to bring about a
change of mind in the oppressor and awaken him to personal
openness and to dialogue."

It is evident from his writings on peace that Merton
repeatedly stresses that the burden and responsibility is
with the individual. He assures the reader of his own

conviction that "the witness of genuine non-violence has been
incontestable."[55] He also points out that "the non-violent
ideal does not contain in itself all the answers to all our
questions. These will have to be met and worked out amid
the risks and anguish of day to day politics. But they can
never be worked out if non-violence is never taken seriously.[56]
Finally, Merton offers the peacemaker a bleak promise: "It
is the 'men of good will,' the men who have made their poor
efforts to do something about peace, who will in the end be
the most mercilessly reviled, crushed, and destroyed as
victims of universal self-hate of man which they have unfortunately only increased by the failure of their good intentions."[57]

Thus, Merton's notion of non-violence affects both the
individual and society, for it demands that the ends and means
of an individual's action be compatible. Though his work on
war-peace issues begins with conscience seen in the light of
the history of moral law as both social and individual, both
rationale and "beyond reason," he argues that when conscience
assumes the compatible means offered by non-violent resistence,
the individual is able to preserve his own integrity and at
the same time act with relevance and effectiveness in bringing
about social change. The Christian who has embraced the means
of non-violent resistance, according to Merton, will provide
an alternative to, rather than a cooption into, the means of
interest group democracy or power politics. He also believes
that Christian non-violence can open the road to a new policy,

more in keeping with the self-interest of the individual and
the good of society as a whole.

Merton's primary concern with the role of the Christian
against the massive power of the state and his own solitary
life as a monk did not enable him to address himself to the
question of individuals joining together in building a movement. He believed that "Christianity is against all mass
movements, for they are intrinsically detrimental to man's
well-being. . . . Leaders of movements place their trust in
money or technology rather than God."[58] His opposition to
them extended from Nazism to Communism and even in a modified
way to the peace movement in latter years. He believed that
mass movements mentally portrays man not as a real person,
but as a part of a group; it labels people who are part of
the group as friends and others outside the group as enemies.
Jesus, according to Merton, was mistaken for the enemy and
was killed because he did not conform to the pattern of
behavior dictated by the dominant group of his day.[59] Merton
in no way promises an effective and successful revolution in
terms of human history. He offers only the hope that individuals will bring about "a new heaven and a new earth." He
assures such individuals of Christ's promise of suffering
and death and ultimate resurrection.

Thomas Merton's writings on the issues of war and
peace can be faulted in many areas. He becomes dogmatic when
he relies solely on the statements of popes or leading historical figures for support; there is little scholarly rigor and

discipline in his expoundings; he tends to be flamboyant in his choice of literary illusions or references by converting events into "pseudo events;" his writings are often filled with warnings of doom and total nuclear destruction; he does not face the considerations of the practical and pragmatic imperatives confronting an individual and mass movements outside the monastery; he often seems to escape problems by attempting to resolve them by reverting to "transcendence" or eschatology as the answer; and finally he never develops a systematic theology of peace, he rather invited people to "experiment in truth," with non-violence. Despite all of this, Merton's writing on peace did become a source of support to the action of prophetic individuals who embraced Christian non-violence in America during the sixties.

Merton did make a difference by emphasizing the special Catholic theological dimension in peacemaking. He asked each of his readers not to consider the peace movement as simply another of several new ideologies in a never-ending cycle for power. Rather, he wanted each individual to see peacemaking and non-violent resistance as a completely new way of life, a life that would liberate man from the logic of power and power relationships. He also called upon individual Christians to serve the community of all mankind, a service that was radical in so far as its aim was to replace a dominative society of force with a society dominated by love. His long view, based on faith, assured the revolution.

Merton is significant to the Catholic peace movement for the theology that he wrote. His writing offers the best analysis of the changes in Catholic thought that occurred after World War II until his death in 1968. It is difficult to ascertain the impact of Merton on the Catholic peace movement. It varied from individual to individual. The two brothers who led the Catholic peace movement in the sixties illustrate this point. Philip Berrigan contends that Merton did not influence him in his concern for peace.[60] Daniel Berrigan, on the other hand, contends that Merton was one of the major influences in his thought on peace. Daniel Berrigan also laments his death because Merton alone provided a "long view" of peace and there is no one else of his stature to provide that dimension.[61]

Though it has not been documented, it would not be an overstatement to say that every Catholic peace activist of the sixties read Merton's writings on peace either before or after their involvement. The same could be said for many non-Catholics who were involved in peace activities against the war in Vietnam. Some Catholic peace activists would disagree or go beyond what Merton wrote and advocated for peace; nevertheless, Merton remained a source of support to these people because of their common concern for peace.

It is not as difficult to ascertain the impact of the American Catholic peace movement on Merton's thought. His friendship and respect for Dorothy Day and the Catholic Worker Movement had a great influence. James Forest, a young Worker,

kept Merton informed of what peace activists were doing
through an extensive correspondence that lasted ten years.
James Douglas, a young theologian and main lobbyist of the
Catholic peace group, PAX, at the Second Vatican Council
kept Merton informed of events and relied heavily on Merton's
theological judgments. Daniel Berrigan, too, wrote to Merton
of events and a close relationship developed. They shared
their theological insights of what was happening in the peace
movement in their letters. It was the life and action of
these peace activists that provided much of the motivation
and knowledge of events necessary for Merton's theological
reflection and writing. It was in them that Merton found a
source of hope for peace, and in return he was the only
Catholic who attempted to develop through his writings a
theological rationale for their involvement in the peace
movement. He did this because he viewed a concern for peace
as central to the life of a Christian.

It was during the nadir of the fifties that national
policies and economic practices were formulated which evoked
the resurgence of the American peace movement. It was also
during this same period that the tactics of non-violent
resistance were being applied and developed by the remnant
of peace activists as they attempted to bring their varied
messages of peace to their nation in response to the threat
of nuclear warfare and to their church at the Second Vatican
Council.

REFERENCES

[1] Wittner, _Rebels . . ._ , p. 213.

[2] Gordon C. Zahn, "The Future of the Catholic Peace Movement," _Commonweal_, XCIX (December 28, 1973), 338.

[3] Wittner, _Rebels . . ._ , p. 254.

[4] For an excellent personality sketch of Merton see: James Forest, "The Gift of Merton," _Commonweal_, XXXVIII (January 19, 1968), 465-6. For an excellent account of Merton's wide range of interests see: "In Memory of Thomas Merton," _Continuum_, VII (Summer, 1969).

[5] The original unexpurgated manuscript of _The Seven Story Mountain_ is located in the Boston College library.

[6] Merton wrote three books during this period. At least one of the other two manuscripts was destroyed by Merton himself before he entered the monastery. Letter to author from Naomi Burton Stone dated November 12, 1971.

[7] In a letter to a personal friend, Merton said that he was conservative like Camus and Gandhi-in the sense of consciously keeping alive the continuity with a past wisdom stated in contemporary terms.

[8] These two paragraphs are a paraphrasing of a letter written by Thomas Merton to a student working on her master's thesis in order to assist her in organizing his writings. This letter written by Thomas Merton is dated June 17, 1968.

[9] In November, 1964, Merton directed a "retreat" -- the first in a series that would lead to efforts for peace -- on the "Spiritual Roots of Protest." Six of the men in attendance were later to be in prison for "crimes" of resistance. They were Revs. Daniel and Philip Berrigan, Rev. Robert Cunnane, James Forest, Thomas Cornell and John Peter Grady. Two other participants were Protestant Peace Leaders, A. J. Muste and John Howard Yoder.

163

[10]Merton had established a wide circle of correspondents on the peace issue which crossed professional, racial, and credal lines. For a more comprehensive list refer to Merton's "Cold War Letters" which were never published because of censorship but are available in mimeographed copies.

[11]For the best account of Merton's writings on the Cold War and Marxism see: James Thomas Baker, Thomas Merton, Social Critic, (Kentucky, 1971), pp. 66-97.

[12]For accounts of Merton's use of Gog and Magog see: Ibid., pp. 70-89 and Gordon C. Zahn, Introduction, in Thomas Merton on Peace, (New York, 1971).

[13]Merton felt that very little was actually known about what really took place in the thinking of the Church at this time, the time when he believed "Christiandom went into business." It should be clarified at this point that many sources that have been used in this article are not available for direct and identified quotation because of legal restrictions included by Merton himself in the documents establishing the Merton legacy. Where such items are used, their contents will be paraphrased. Direct references will be made where it is possible to do so.

[14]Thomas Merton, Seeds of Destruction, (New York, 1964), p. 151.

[15]The just war criteria is not solely a Catholic doctrine. The foremost contemporary exponent of it in the United States is the Presbyterian, Paul Ramsey.

[16]Zahn, in his Introduction, Thomas Merton on Peace, contends that Merton resorted to using classical imagery to tone the origins of such thinking of Christians, i.e., Christ was looked upon as the Prometheus figure: force and power were idealized.

[17]John Courtney Murray used the just war doctrine as the basis for his defense of selective conscientious objection when he served on the President's Commission on Selective Service in 1967.

[18]Thomas P. McDonnell (ed.), A Thomas Merton Reader, (New York, 1962), p. 291.

165

[19] Ibid., p. 295.

[20] Ibid., p. 288.

[21] Thomas Merton, Breakthrough to Peace, (New York, 52), p. 108.

[22] Merton, Seeds of Destruction, p. 129.

[23] Ibid., p. 90.

[24] Interview with James Forest, December 3, 1972.

[25] Merton, Seeds of Destruction, p. 91.

[26] Thomas Merton, "Peace and Revolution: A Footnote om Ulysses," Peace, IV (Fall/Winter, 1968/69).

[27] Idem.

[28] Merton, Seeds of Destruction, p. 123.

[29] Thomas Merton, Faith and Violence, (Indiana, 1968), 8. It is interesting to note that the Catholic peace tivists are often admonished for refusing to criticize the e of violence by "revolutionary" groups or to impose res- ictions upon others whose leadership they do not share.

[30] Zahn in his Introduction, Thomas Merton on Peace, duces and dismisses Merton's qualification of pacifism as rely a matter of semantics.

[31] It was only the uprising in Hungary in 1956 that rton would cite as an actual situation where the waging war was just on the part of the people to defend themselves.

[32] Thomas Merton, "Vietnam: An Overwhelming Atrocity," omas Merton on Peace, p. 195.

[33] Zahn, Thomas Merton on Peace.

[34] Thomas Merton, "Preface to Vietnamese Translation of Man Is an Island," Thomas Merton on Peace, p. 64.

[35] Merton, Seeds of Destruction, p. 146.

[36] Merton, Seeds of Destruction, p. 132.

[37] Idem.

[38] Ibid., p. 136.

[39] Merton, "Blessed are the Meek: The Christian Roots of Non-Violence," Thomas Merton On Peace, p. 210.

[40] Merton was plagued by the contradiction between politics and the New Testament and by 1968 in a letter to a friend, he said that he was interested in any insights on the problem, but would leave the area alone. Merton expressed the fact that he felt himself moving into a kind of "post-political eschatology" which he could not articulate. In another letter written in 1967, Merton hinted that appeals to politics lacked firmness and to accept politics as a religious area of reality would only contribute in the end to the slide into "technical totalism." What he called for was a radical rethinking of politics.

[41] By 1965 in personal letters Merton was contending that he was apolitical and was asking for information on how others were dealing with the issue of politics and the Gospel. This does not mean that Merton was not interested in concrete actions for peace. He had been a non-combatant objector in W.W. II, was a long standing member of the Catholic Worker, joined the Fellowship of Reconciliation, and lent his name as sponsor in 1962 to the American PAX Association and in 1964 to the Catholic Peace Fellowship. He even desired to become personally involved in the "Peace Hostage Exchange" project. He praised and supported the demonstrations of civil disobedience protesting the New York air raid tests, praised the San Francisco to Moscow Peace March, The Golden Rule, Phoenix, and Everyman projects, and counseled young men seeking conscientious objection status during the Vietnam War. However, he had reservations about the tactic of draft card burning and draft file destruction and was most upset by the self-immolation of Roger LaPorte, a young member of the Catholic Peace Fellowship. Merton advocated most strongly the need for pastoral and educational work in the area of peace. For details on these specific actions refer to Zahn, Introduction, Thomas Merton on Peace.

[42] Merton, Faith and Violence, p. 7.

167

43 *Ibid*., p. 111.

44 Merton's existentialism differs from the existentialism of a man like Camus. For Camus, truth and compassion
are the only valid human postures but in an absurd universe
there is no certainty that they will prevail. Merton is
with Camus all the way but sees his religious belief taking
him further still. Truth and compassion will prevail,
according to Merton, because they are of God. For more of
Merton's writing on Camus refer to: Thomas Merton, "Terror
and the Absurd," *Motive*, XXIX (February, 1969), 5-15.

45 Zahn, Introduction, *Thomas Merton on Peace*, p. xii.

46 Thomas Merton, "The Christian in World Crisis,"
Thomas Merton on Peace, p. 25.

47 Thomas Merton, *Life and Holiness*, (New York, 1963),
p. 114.

48 Merton, *Seeds of Destruction*, p. 122.

49 Many participants in the Catholic ultra-resistance
hold that the main value of the draft-board action is
theraputic in relation to how it taught them to handle or
channel their fear.

50 Merton, *Faith and Violence*, p. 108.

51 *Ibid*., p. 110.

52 Merton, "Peace and Revolution . . . ," p. 10.

53 Thomas Merton, Preface to Piere Regamey, *Non-Violence
and the Christian Conscience*, (London, 1966), pp. 12-14.

54 Merton, *Faith and Violence*, p. 10.

55 Merton, Preface, *Non-Violence and the Christian
Conscience*, p. 13.

56 *Ibid*., p. 14.

168

57 Thomas Merton, <u>New Seeds of Contemplation</u>, (Connecticut, 1969), p. 115.

58 Thomas Merton, <u>Disputed Questions</u>, (New York, 1960), p. 115.

59 Thomas Merton, "Christianity and Mass Movements," <u>Cross Currents</u>, XIV (Summer, 1969), 203-4.

60 Interview with Philip Berrigan, February 4, 1970.

61 Letter from Daniel Berrigan to author dated June 12, 1969.

CHAPTER V

FROM WORLD WAR II TO VATICAN II:
THE RISE OF NON-VIOLENT RESISTANCE AND
THE DECLINE OF THE JUST WAR DOCTRINE

After World War II, the CAIP and the Catholic Worker
continued to survive as Catholic groups concerned about the
issue of peace. They both maintained the zeal with which
they adhered to their traditional theories of the just war
and pacifism. If there was any difference in the two groups,
it was that after the victory of the United States in World
War II, the CAIP had emerged all the more confident of its
just war position while the Catholic Worker sought a way to
strengthen its pacifism. After all, pacifism had failed to
deter nations from their violent course.

Though the CAIP had sanctioned the United States'
declaration of World War II, it devoted its energies, once
the war was underway, to working for a just and lasting peace
based on Pope Pius XII's "Five Peace Points." It also worked
hard for the establishing of the United Nations in hopes of
strengthening American Catholic's concepts of internationalism.
Because of the CAIP's ambiguous relationship with the NCWC,
the Association at least tacitly supported the NCWC's efforts
in building up the Armed Service Chaplaincy and War Relief
Services during the war.[1] After the war, the CAIP, like many
non-pacifist peace groups in America held observer status
within the United Nations.[2]

Until the 1950's the CAIP's work for peace at the
United Nations was directly linked with the NCWC. Miss Rita
Schaefer, former secretary of the CAIP, served as the representative of both groups in a consultant position at the
United Nations.[3] Her main effort during this period was
spent on drafting the International Covenant on Human Rights.
Other Catholic groups which supported her efforts were the
National Catholic Conference of Women and the National Federation of Catholic College Students all of which were affiliated
with the NCWC in America. The Sword of the Spirit, a periodical of Catholic peace groups in London and The British Society
for International Understanding[4] also collaborated with her
on this project. Besides promoting human rights, the CAIP
did its best to help establish a sound world organization
for peace.

Though the CAIP always aimed at combating nationalism
and building cooperation among nations for peace, it was
particularly unsuccessful at both after World War II. The
temper of the Cold War in America pervaded the CAIP's efforts.
Because of pronouncements by government leaders in America
against communism and also the Pope's condemnation of
atheistic communism, the CAIP was very conscious of the need
to combat it. This attitude pervaded the CAIP's work in
America and at the United Nations. The fear of communism
was most evident in the Association's policy toward China.
On the one hand, it worked toward bringing the China question
into the open at the United Nations. At the same time it
went on record as opposed to Communist China's entrance into

the world organization.[5] The CAIP also viewed the Korean War as an example of communist aggression.[6]

During the Post-World War II period, the CAIP was also represented at the State Department's "off-the-record" meetings. These sessions focused on topics related to issues at the United Nations such as Germany, Point IV, the agenda of the Economic and Social Council, and the agenda of the General Assembly. Discussions also centered on general questions about American foreign policy, the Korean situation, and technical assistance to the underdeveloped nations of the world.[7]

In 1955 Monsignor George Higgins was appointed head of the Department of Social Action in the NCWC and automatically was named Executive Secretary of the CAIP. Higgins like Ryan and McGowan before him was mainly concerned with the problems of labor[8] and had very little grasp of international affairs.[9] The direction of the CAIP immediately after World War II changed little under his direction. The Association continued to play an indirect role in the process of formulating public policy by functioning as a Catholic lobbyist group or as invited observers at the United Nations and the State Department. The committee system still served as the core unit of the Association. The publication of policy statements, pamphlet reports and a monthly newsletter, CAIP News, served as the chief means of carrying out the Association's program. Under the directorship of Higgins, the CAIP became almost undistinguishable from the NCWC. The aim of

the CAIP, as always, was to make known to its Catholic con-
stituency the "official" position of the Catholic Church on
the issues of war and peace.[10]

The most significant group in the CAIP from 1958
through the Second Vatican Council was the Arms Control subcommittee of the International Law and Juridical Institutions
Committee.

Key members were Rev. Edward A. Conway, S.J., member
of the Advisory Committee to the United States Arms Control
and Disarmament Agency; Dr. Alain C. Enthoven, Deputy Assistant
Secretary of Defense for Systems Analysis; Dr. Charles M.
Herzfeld, Deputy Director, Advanced Research Projects Agency,
Department of Defense; Dr. William J. Nagle, Director,
External Research, Department of State; editor: Morality and
Modern Warfare; Dr. John E. Moriarity, Department of State;
Colonel (ret.) U. S. Air Force; formerly with Weapons Systems
Evaluation Group, Department of Defense; Dr. James E. Dougherty,
St. Joseph's College; Assistant Director Foreign Policy
Research Institute, University of Pennsylvania; currently
professor at the National War College in Washington (1964-65);
Dr. William V. O'Brien, Professor of International Law and
Chairman of the Institute of World Policy, Georgetown University; author of a number of books and articles on the legal
and moral aspects of modern war, active reserve officer in
the United States Army.[11] It was this committee of active
laymen who wrote the CAIP statements on modern warfare and
delivered lectures, sponsored symposiums, and compiled literature on the topic.

In 1960 Dr. Nagle edited a book for the CAIP called, Morality and Modern Warfare on the state of the question of nuclear weapons. Nagle admits in the Introduction that the selections in the book indicate the failure of the Christian community to come to terms with the event of Hiroshima. He attempts to account for the absence of nuclear pacifism and the persistance of the just war criteria in the writings of American Catholics by stating, "[The contributors to the book] are citizens of the nation that has the major responsibility for the defense of the free world. The question here is not one of patriotism but responsibility."[12]

Nagle is also careful to point out the noticeable difference between his Morality and Modern Warfare and a book published a year earlier in Britain on the same topic. In the British book, Morals and Missiles: Catholic Essays on the Problem of War Today,[13] its tone is strongly pacifist. Nevertheless, Nagle concludes his introductory essay with a defense of the just war tradition by quoting the address of Bishop John J. Wright of the Diocese of Pittsburgh at the 1958 CAIP meeting. Wright said, "It is unfortunately not yet possible for honest theologians to deny that justice may require of us duties from which charity would prefer to shrink."[14]

Several contributors of the book were members of the Arms Control Subcommittee of the CAIP, James E. Dougherty, John K. Moriarity, and William J. O'Brien. All the contributors except for the pacifist, Gordon Zahn, Ph.D.,[15] a

member of the Sociology Department of Loyola University of
Chicago, were just war theorists who were employed by the
United States government either in the Defense or State
Departments.

In 1962 the CAIP and the Adult Education Centers of
the Archdiocese of Chicago co-sponsored a two-day convention
in Chicago on "Christian Conscience and Modern Warfare."[16]
Most of the speakers were members of the CAIP and contributors
to Nagle's book: John K. Moriarity, James E. Dougherty,
Rev. Edward A. Conway, S.J., and William Nagle. Gordon Zahn
was also present to represent the pacifist viewpoint. The
most significant address of the conference was delivered by
Rev. Thomas C. Donohue, S.J., Project Director of the Center
for Peace Research at Creighton University, Omaha.

Father Donahue noted in a factual analysis what Catholic
moralists in the United States had been saying about nuclear
warfare. He based much of his analysis on the scholarship
of the men represented in <u>Morality and Modern Warfare</u>. He
divided American Catholic views on nuclear warfare into the
following seven major categories:

> The first theme is that of the theologians
> who have an <u>apocalyptic</u> preoccupation, seeing
> the most important element of our age as a race
> to extinction. They believe we are unable to
> prevent the doom that is sure to encompass us.

> The second approach is that of <u>prevention</u>.
> These moralists say we simply have to prevent
> a major war because it just doesn't make sense
> to destroy ourselves. No one can win a nuclear
> war, they believe.

The third theme centers around the idea
of justification. This school of thought
among the moralists holds that we are unable
today to justify a war under present circumstances and that the principle of justifying
a defense war is inapplicable here.

Theme number four is that of innocence.
It notes that too many innocents (non-combatants,
civilians) would be killed in any kind of
nuclear warfare. Indeed, one writer feels the [17]
old theory of a just war is intrinsically altered.

The fifth theme stresses the idea of public
responsibility and raises many questions about
what the government can do morally in a situation when force is required if that force is
nuclear.

Theme number six is concerned with problems
of policy. It discusses the morality of certain
aspects of foreign policy and matters such as
the use of war as an instrument of policy.

And, finally, among the moralists who have
been writing and speaking on the Christian conscience in a nuclear world, one group lays stress
on the use of deterrents. Many of them seem to
feel that the emphasis on counterforce seems
praiseworthy, but they realize there are grave
difficulties involved in the use of effective
deterrents for if the deterrents fail to deter,
mass destruction on both sides will result.[18]

Thus, in the United States, "the Catholic view" in
relationship to the pertinent question of nuclear warfare
had not even been located in 1962. Unlike Nagle, Father
Donahue did not defend just war theorists, rather, he pointed
out that "American Catholics are not even agreed on two or
three major positions of what moral theologians have been
saying."[19] By noting the absence of any agreement on a moral
criteria for nuclear warfare at the conference, he uninten-
tionally launched a frontal assault upon the whole Catholic

tradition of just war in moral theology in relation to modern
warfare.

Despite these results, the CAIP continued to hold firm
to the normative position of the just war criteria. The next
year, in 1963 the CAIP with the Adult Education Centers again
co-sponsored a conference on "Peace and World Order" with
emphases on Pacem in Terris, the peace encyclical written by
Pope John XXIII, the role of the United Nations, and the
moral and political implications of the Cold War. Within
such a context, the just war criteria remained the underlying
pre-supposition that prevaded the talks at the conference.

By the Second Vatican Council there was no doubt that
the CAIP held as strongly as ever to the just war theory.
Neither World War II nor the possibility of nuclear warfare
had raised any serious doubts as to the validity of this
normative position within their Catholic concern for peace.
The small liberal membership of the Association, with their
key positions in the church, in universities, the state
department, the defense department, and the military, believed
that they had done much to apply Catholic moral teaching to
contemporary events had served them well in their efforts
toward establishing international peace. The CAIP believed
that they could look back on the period after World War II
and point to the many accomplishments of which they had been
a part. The United Nations, the first international organization chartered to promote world peace and understanding had
been established. Communism had been deterred by the

non-admittance of the People's Republic of China into the
United Nations and the Korean War had prevented the extension of communism within that country. Above all the CAIP
had established a just criteria that limited the possibilities of a nuclear war.

Just as the CAIP had continued to apply its just war
ethic after World War II, so too did the Catholic Worker
Movement attempt to continue its pacifist witness. There
were two distinct phases with the Catholic Worker after the
war. The first phase was from 1948 to 1955 when the writings
of Robert Ludlow intellectually dominated the movement's
pacifism. After 1955 the actions of Ammon Hennacy dominated
not only the thought but also the actions of Catholic Worker
pacifism. It was Ammon Hennacy that moved the Worker into
non-violent resistance.

Robert Ludlow had been raised in Scranton, Pennsylvania,
and had become a Catholic through reading the works of the
English convert, John Henry Newman. Employed in some non-
descript laboring job there, he delighted at the opportunity
to leave Scranton by taking a job in the library at Catholic
University. The prospect of remaining there seemed exceed-
ingly dull to him and after six months he left to join the
Catholic Worker at Mott Street in New York City. Before he
could settle in at the House he had to confront the prospect
of fighting in World War II. He chose not to do so and as a
conscientious objector he took his place along with other
Catholic CO's at the Rosewood Training School in Maryland.

After the war was over, and he was free to do as he chose,
he returned to Mott Street to remain with the Workers for a
decade.[20]

During this time he wrote on a variety of subjects,
but tended to concentrate on pacifism, anarchism, and psychia-
try and mental dysfunction. The historian, William Miller
claims that "Ludlow's contributions to The Catholic Worker
in this era helped much to make it a distinguished paper."[21]
John Cogley has also described Ludlow as "the predominant
intellectual figure of the movement" during this period.
Cogley singles out Ludlow along with John J. Hugo and Ammon
Hennacy as the main figures who partially reshaped the movement. The reason for the word "partically," Cogley explains,
is that "the abiding imprint of the movement has always been
that of Miss Day herself, whose genius it has been to cut
through all kinds of distractions, abstractions and intellectual complexities to get at the heart of Christianity itself."[22]

Ludlow's emphasis on the intellectual rather than the
activist dimensions of pacifism greatly shaped the kind of
peace testimony of the Catholic Worker. It was through writing
rather than through action that the Catholic Worker maintained
its position of militant bearers of Catholic pacifism in the
post-World War II era. Ludlow's writing on pacifism was
featured in the "PAX" column of the newspaper. One of his
main themes was that the Christian pacifist would be considered
abnormal or psychotic because of the growing irrationality
of modern society which was becoming fragmented by a rapidly

expanding technology. This theme increased in significance when President Truman announced that he was sanctioning the testing of the hydrogen bomb. Ludlow's response to the announcement was that "'The whole thing has become unreal and fantastic.' If nothing else would bring man to 'the conclusion that absolute pacifism is the only answer,' this development certainly should. 'We live in a world of hate and we can only oppose it by going to the opposite extreme.'"[23]

In the "PAX" column Ludlow also wrote an occasional report on Catholic conscientious objectors. Once, he thought it necessary to make clear that Catholic Worker CO's had nothing to do with Coughlinite CO's. In his opinion there were none that were not anti-Semitic; thus, they were not true pacifists. This return to the past as a source of keeping the issue of pacifism alive during the post-World War II period was also reflected in April, 1948, when the paper carried again the full text of Father Hugo's "The Immorality of Conscription." Seventy-five thousand additional copies were printed for handout distribution. This was The Catholic Worker's way of combating the increasing talk in America of establishing Universal Military Training.

The increasing talk of war with Russia amidst the frightfulness of bomb testing also led Dorothy Day to a re-emphasis of those positions she had taken during the war. On the thirteenth anniversary of The Catholic Worker, she wrote a passionate denunciation of war. In the article she applied her pacifism of World War II to the threat of nuclear war.

180

Miss Day also spent much of her time attempting to counteract the increase of anti-communist sentiment that was mounting to produce the Cold War. Along with Robert Ludlow and Irene Naughton, she published a statement on anti-Communism:

> Although we disagree with our Marxist brothers
> on the question of the means to use to achieve
> social justice, rejecting atheism and materia-
> lism in Marxist thought, we respect their
> freedom as a minority group in this country. . . .
> We protest the imprisonment of our Communist
> brothers and extend our sympathy and admiration
> for having followed their conscience even in
> persecution.[24]

The Catholic Worker pages were filled during this period with opposition to the anti-Communist Smith and McCarran acts and with horror at the trial of Julius and Ethel Rosenberg and co-defendent Morton Sobell. The writings reflected a concern of mounting anti-Communism among Catholics. In June, 1953, as the Rosenbergs who were found guilty and were awaiting their execution, a despondent Ludlow revealed these concerns:

> It is not a just age we live in. It is an age
> where guilt by association is fast becoming the
> accepted method of judging. . . . And our
> patriotic Catholics and our wretched publica-
> tions do not see this as the leaders of the
> Church in France did not see it before the
> Revolution and as the leaders in Spain did not
> see it. And when they do see it (of course
> they never really do) then they will envision
> themselves as the innocent victims of devils. . . .
> May all Catholics, in union with the Supreme
> Pontiff who has already asked that clemency be
> granted the Rosenbergs, send one last plea that
> these lives be spared.[25]

The pages of <u>The Catholic Worker</u> reveal an attempt on
the part of the movement to keep pacifism alive. In doing
so atomic testing is condemned as well as anti-Communist
hysteria. Constant references to pacifist actions of the
past in their writings, however, emphasizes the low ebb of
the movement's peace witness. Never was inactivity in terms
of direct action to affirm their spiritual values and combat
evil so absent in their pacifist witness as during this
decade. The extent of the demise of action by Catholic pacifists becomes all the more evident when viewed in comparison
with what was happening in the broader American peace movement, especially from 1946 to 1950.

The American peace movement had had a long-term interest
in Gandhian non-violent resistance. It was not applied in
the United States, however, until young pacifists during World
War II found the tactics of non-violent resistance most use-
ful in dealing with the injustices in American race relations,
the CPS camps, and the prisons. The use of these tactics to
correct injustice achieved the greatest success when performed
by the pacifist non-cooperators in the prisons.[26]

After the war was over many of the CO's who had been
in the CPS camps and prisons held new ideas about the functions of a peacemaker gained from their experiments with non-
violent resistance. For a time a split occurred between
traditional pacifists and this young generation which were
termed radical pacifists. The two oldest pacifists groups
in the United States, Fellowship of Reconciliation (FOR) and

War Resisters League (WRL) revealed this split. In 1946,
however, the radical pacifists who had joined the Congress
of Racial Equality that had been begun by FOR sponsored the
first Freedom Ride. This was a definite victory for the
radical pacifists, for the Freedom Ride was a tactic of non-
violent resistance. In June, 1947, the executive committee
of the WRL adopted a resolution declaring that it would
"adopt its literature and activities to the promotion of
political, economic, social revolution by non-violent means.
Though the radical pacifists had greatly influenced these
traditional pacifist groups, they still attempted to form
their own peace organizations.

The first peace organization of any size and permanence
which they created was Peacemakers. The focus of the new
group was war resistance. The most unique of their programs
was the non-payment of taxes to protest war. Though not so
unique when recalling the actions of Henry David Thoreau over
a century ago, it was unique in so far as tax resistance was
not just an individual act but an action performed by a group
of people in opposition to war.[27]

Radical and traditional pacifists alike joined in an
attempt to secure amnesty for CO's imprisoned during World
War II. They also cooperated in the struggle against the
proposal of President Truman to continue compulsory military
training into the post-war era. The opposition of the radical
pacifists against conscription again applied the tactics of
non-violent resistance in this area. In February, 1947, five

pacifists burned draft cards in San Francisco's Union Square.
A meeting in a New York gathering of about two hundred and
fifty persons the same month witnessed the burning of sixty-
three draft cards. All of this activity, however, was soon
to come to an end.[28]

By 1950 three policies of the United States government
brought an end to the American peace movement. The first,
was the heightening of the Cold War; the second, was President
Truman's announced continuation of tests on the hydrogen bomb,
and finally, the outbreak of fighting in Korea. The Korean
war dealt the final blow to the fragile post-war peace movement because world government organizations almost universally
accepted the American role in the conflict. By 1950 only
despair remained among the peace remnant.

Beginning in 1957 the American peace movement underwent a revival. The immediate innitiator of the renaissance
was the atmospheric testing of the hydrogen bomb with the
health hazards attached to nuclear "fallout." Around this
issue the National Committee for a Sane Nuclear Policy developed.
In 1957 they ran their first ad in the November 15 issue of
the New York Times. The group was open to pacifists and non-
pacifists alike. By 1958 the group had 120 chapters representing approximately 25,000 Americans.[29]

The onset of the nuclear testing issue also caused a
renaissance among the radical pacifists. In June, 1957, a
small group of pacifists committed to non-violent resistance
organized an ad hoc committee, Non-Violent Action against

Nuclear Weapons. In 1958 it was reorganized as the Committee
for Non-Violent Action (CNVA). Perhaps the most successful
project of the CNVA was the 1958 voyage of the Golden Rule.
The main idea was to sail a vessel of protest into a bomb-
test area.[30] CNVA also sponsored other actions and became
most noted for its peace walks throughout the world. It
seemed a tragic commentary on the American peace movement
that it could only achieve significant expression when the
development of weaponry had reached the point of representing
mankind's final thrust toward annihilation.

Ammon Hennacy, a native American radical from the
Midwest and throughout the United States, began his "one-
man revolution" in 1950 just when most peace action was
receding into oblivion. His motivation came from his own
vision; the end of which was the paradise of the anarchist
where oppression, injustice, and violence were all resolved
in a community of free men. The object of his crusade was
the state and his aim was to live apart from any aspect of an
institutional life that contributed to the power of the state
to do harm to man. He had refused to serve in World War I
because as a Socialist he would have nothing to do with a
capitalist war. In World War II he was a Christian anarchist
and would not serve the government.[31]

Hennacy also wrote his own autobiography, The Book of
Ammon,[32] and subtitled it, The Autobiography of an Unique
American Rebel. Dorothy Day is quoted on the back cover of
the book jacket as stating that "The Story of his prison days

will rank with the great writings of the world about prisons."
The book reveals his thought and action of what he terms
his "one-man revolution."

The reason that Hennacy's one-man revolution merged
with the Catholic Worker Movement was not because of any deep
reflection, but because he admired Dorothy Day and got what
he called a "crush" on her.[33] It was because of her that he
gave seven years of his life to the Catholic Worker and was
baptized a Catholic. It must be pointed out that within the
movement he found individuals who shared many of his same
concerns. The vision of Peter Maurin dominated the movement;
yet, it had always been open to the visions of others. Gandhian non-violent resistance had long been a matter of concern
with the Catholic Worker. The movement had always advocated
and practiced fasting, picketing, and leafleting as means to
correct the evils of social injustice. It had resisted the
payment of taxes from its inception and had also advocated
resistance to conscription. What Hennacy brought to the
Worker was the breezy self-confidence of a fighter who possessed a self-discipline and bravery that made him appear
invincible. With these personal characteristics he lead the
Catholic Worker Movement into a new level of pacifist activism that was labeled non-violent resistance. His emphasis
was on civil disobedience. Thus, he gave focus to a concern
that was, after World War II, increasingly central to the
movement -- opposition to war.

Hennacy had begun his one-man revolution in 1950 in
Phoenix, Arizona.[34] He fasted and picketed the tax office
for five days to protest tax money being spent on bombs and
troops in Korea and in penance for the dropping of the bomb
on Hiroshima. When he joined the Catholic Worker he continued
to perform this action adding an additional day for each year
since the tragedy had occurred. In 1954, he experimented
with an idea he had for a variation of this action. The
experiment led the Catholic Worker Movement into the most
widely publicized action of non-violent resistance to have
occurred in the United States. The focus of the resistance
was New York City's air raid drill, which according to the
Civil Defense Act, required that all take shelter for at
least ten minutes during a sham air raid.

In 1954 Ammon Hennacy, Dorothy Day and a few other
Catholic Workers refused to take shelter during the drill.
The event occurred in City Hall Park in New York. On June 15,
1955, Ammon Hennacy, Dorothy Day and five other Catholic
Workers were joined by twenty-three others, who were mainly
members of the WRL and the FOR. Key members of these organizations: David Dellinger, Bayard Rustin, and Jim Peck joined
them in their act of civil disobedience. The following year
they repeated their performance. After their demonstration
this time; they were sentenced to five days in jail. Every
year thereafter, a dozen or more practicers of non-violent
resistance had appeared, committed civil disobedience, and
served prison sentences for it. A. J. Muste, America's most

acclaimed peace activist, expressed their attitude when he
told the Director of Civil Defense in New York that, "Civil
defense, after all, is an integral part of the total preparation for nuclear war. We, on the other hand, are convinced
that the only way to a secure defense is for people to refuse
to participate in any way in the preparations for war."[35] In
response to an article in the Village Voice and a letter in
the New York Post, several newcomers arrived to take part in
the 1959 demonstration in addition to the usual contingent.
When they suggested broadening the 1960 demonstration, the
regulars, mostly CNVA activists, agreed and organized the
Civil Defense Protest Committee to spread the word.

On May 3, 1960, approximately 2000 students and adults
throughout New York City resisted the yearly drill.[36] Ten
minutes before the sirens were scheduled to blow, about 500
persons assembled in the park, with many more arriving all
the time. Among those present were writers Nat Hentoff,
Dwight Macdonald, Norman Mailer, and Kay Boyle. It was the
largest direct action demonstration against nuclear warfare.
Radio and television covered the event well. Lengthy articles
in The Village Voice, Nation, Commonweal, New York World
Telegram, and the New York Post gave it added publicity. It
marked a new departure in the type of strategy the American
peace movement would use in the 1960's.[37]

It also marked a new spirit of cooperation among
Catholics with other peace groups in the United States. The
Catholic Worker, Peacemakers, WRL, FOR, and CNVA all practiced

the more radical response of non-violent direct action.
These groups also joined with the National Committee for a
Sane Nuclear Policy (SANE) in advocating unilateral disarma-
ment.[38] Karl Meyer, a tax-resister and member of the Catholic
Worker in Chicago joined the San Francisco to Moscow Walk for
Peace sponsored by the CNVA. Dorothy Day helped to lay the
plans for the CNVA Polaris Action, a Gandhian assault on
submarines bearing nuclear-tipped missiles stationed in the
town of New London, Connecticut. Catholic Workers also
participated in the first General Strike for Peace begun in
January, 1962, and in many sit-ins and vigils held at the
Atomic Energy Commission's Office in New York. Fall-out
shelters were also picketed.[39] Nuclear warfare was the focus
of all of these actions. It was not until after the election
of President Johnson in 1964 and the escalation of the war in
Vietnam that the focus of the peace movement's efforts shifted
away from nuclear warfare to the draft.

During these years with the Catholic Worker, Ammon
Hennacy had not limited his activity to New York City. He
often took his anniversary of Hiroshima demonstration to various
parts of the United States. In 1957 he went to Las Vegas
because the Atomic Energy Commission was conducting a series
of nuclear tests there; in 1958 he was in the nation's capital;
and in 1959 he took his one-man revolution to Florida to protest another government installation. One of the last episodes
in the confrontation that Hennacy had with the federal government in his role as a member of the Catholic Worker was going
"over the fence," as he called it at the Omaha missile base.

This act of going "over the fence" had cost other
pacifists six months in jail, one of whom had been a Catholic
Worker from Chicago, Karl Meyer. He had participated in this
act of non-violent resistance because while he was running
the St. Stephen House in Chicago, the construction of missile
sites and the continued testing of atom bombs had struck him
as hideous madness that required the most desperate resistance. Hennacy, very attracted to the action, wanted to
perform it himself. He was also given six months for his
act of civil disobedience. He served his term in Sandstone,
Minnesota's federal penitentiary. He left Sandstone in January,
1960. His spirit was undaunted and by June of the same year
he, Hugh Madden, and Charlie Butterworth of the New York
Catholic Worker house joined a group of pacifists walking from
New York to New London, Connecticut, to picket the plant that
had built the atomic-missile-carrying submarine, Polaris. That
fall he picketed for the last time as a member of the New York
Catholic Worker group. With leaflets and signs asking the
public to cease cooperating with any more civil defense drills
he and his friends kept a daily vigil from noon until 2 p.m.
in front of the civil defense office at Forty-sixth Street
and Lexington Avenue.[40]

On January 2, 1961, he went to Salt Lake City and from
then until his death on January 14, 1970, it served as his
home. Though he had left the Catholic Worker in New York
City, he did not desert his work. He continued as usual to
write his column for The Catholic Worker, calling it "Joe

Hill House," the name of his own house of hospitality. The
name honored the IWW songwriter who was executed in the state
of Utah in 1915.[41]

Ammon Hennacy had done more than just keep the issue
of peace alive in the Catholic Worker. By his undaunted
actions of non-violent resistance, he had opened for the
movement an entirely new thrust to their pacifism. Catholic
Workers were now much clearer about their pacifism than they
had been before World War II. Well aware of the non-violent
resistance of Mahatma Gandhi in India and Danilo Dolci in
Italy, Ammon Hennacy had shown Catholic Workers the way to
apply these tactics to the issue of peace in America. The
radical pacifists in the American peace movement immediately
after World War II had already begun to perform such actions.
Catholic Workers would begin to collaborate with them as never
before after the peace movement's revival in 1957. In fact,
the collaboration worked both ways as seen in the participation of the broader peace movement in the non-violent resistance to air raid drills. Ammon Hennacy led the Catholic Worker
in this direction and as a result, he was the movement's hero
during his seven year stay.

Peace was not the only issue, however, that concerned
the Catholic Worker Movement. Under Miss Day's direction
concern for the poor and oppressed remained a priority as well
as the issues of civil rights and labor. Her vision was Peter
Maurin's vision and the Catholic Worker would always be concerned about the multitude of evils that needed correction.

Her aim was to bring the spirit into all of these areas. One of the main values of non-violent resistance to Catholic Workers was that its tactic would be applied to many areas of concern. Also, as a group they were not ready to abandon in their acceptance of non-violent resistance, the basic corporal works of mercy. Miss Day best describes the difference between the peace movement and the Catholic Worker when she described the difference between Ammon Hennacy and Peter Maurin. "Ammon is deep and narrow, but Peter was so broad that he took in all the life of man, body, soul and mind."[42]

By the early sixties it became clear to many Catholic Workers that the peace issue was of such significance that a Catholic group solely dedicated to peace should be formed. Catholic Workers confronted with multiple ills to be corrected were diverting their energies into many areas, civil rights especially at this time was consuming much of its time.

In 1962 at a round-table discussion in the Catholic Worker house on Chrystie Street in New York, there was talk of forming a Catholic group solely dedicated to peace. The reason for this was that many of the Catholic Workers had diverted their energies not into peace, but into the civil right's movement. In 1962 at a round-table discussion in the Catholic Worker house on Chrystie Street in New York one idea put forth at the meeting was to re-activate PAX; the other possibility was to form a Catholic Peace Fellowship (CPF) under the auspices of FOR. The CPF idea was rejected because of the old Catholic suspicion of Protestants. As one

Catholic Worker editor put it at the time, "All they want to
do is use you."[43] Despite the level of cooperation that had
been achieved among peace groups during the fifties, Catholic
Workers had struggled hard to achieve their own identity.
Self-consciously Catholic, yet critical of the existing militaristic and capitalistic American system, they often had to
avert the encroachments of other groups, even of other Catholic
groups. Stressing autonomy, the idea of reactivating PAX was
adopted.

Eileen Egan, a life-long Catholic Worker and close
friend of Dorothy Day, was mainly responsible for the organization. Despite her relationship with the Catholic Worker Movement, she still maintained an executive position of the Catholic
Relief Services and was the author of the book, The Works of
Peace. PAX in America was affiliated with the PAX in England
whose most prominent member was Archbishop Thomas D. Roberts.
The Archbishop also stressed the need for autonomy. He told
the group to be sure to keep PAX totally free of hierarchical
control, especially financially. He pointed to the CAIP as
an example of what happens if autonomy is not maintained.[44]

Because of financial difficulties, PAX grew slowly,[45]
but has succeeded in issuing a valuable quarterly magazine,
Peace, begun in 1963 under the editorship of Eileen Egan. PAX
also observes an annual peace Mass on August 9 in commemora-
tion of Hiroshima, sponsors an annual conference at the
Catholic Worker Farm in Tivoli, New York, as well as conducts
monthly meetings in a room above the Paraclete Book store in
Manhattan.

Founders of PAX proclaimed no official position though they themselves were pacifists. Emphasis on the individual as the one who applies the tradition and teaching of the Church on issues of war and peace pervaded all of their statements. Ironically, PAX devoted most of its energies not to individuals directly but to lobbying for peace within the institutional Church.

The main reason for PAX's emphasis on the institutional Church was that in the same year of its founding, 1962, more than 2,400 bishops from every continent in the world assembled in Rome for the solemn opening of the Second Vatican Council. Three years previously, January 25, 1959, Pope John XXIII had announced that he would convene the Council. The proposed agenda for the meeting touched on many issues confronting the Church in the last half of the twentieth century and included in these topics was the issue of peace. This topic came up for debate in 1964 when the Council Fathers were composing what was ultimately to be one of the more significant documents, The Pastoral Constitution on the Church in the Modern World. The drafts, proposals, amendments, and debates on the issue of peace centered on Schema 13 of the document during the third and fourth sessions of the Council held in 1964 and 1965.

Prior to convening Vatican II, Pope John XXIII had issued his world renowned encyclical on peace, Pacem in Terris. It was to set the tone for discussion of the issue at the Council. What John XXIII did in his encyclical was to call

for a new attitude toward peace based on the universal father-
hood and the entire family of mankind. He explicitly expressed
a hatred of nationalism, repudiated force because it violated
the dignity of man, and rejected fear in favor of mutual
trust, truth and suffering love as the basis for international
cooperation. An emphasis on non-violence in his writing
transcended the old moral categories of the just war and
pacifism; yet, he never explicitly rejected either. Thus,
the door was wide open on the issue of peace when the Council
convened.

At the Council these two positions of the just war and
pacifism, especially pacifism's new emphasis on nuclear warfare and non-violent resistance, collided at the Second
Vatican Council. By 1964 the Cold War, the possibility of
a nuclear holocaust, and the Pope's encyclical on peace, had
suggested to a number of bishops throughout the world that a
just war was no longer possible.

Thomas Merton sent an "Open Letter"[46] to the hierarchy
at the Second Vatican Council in 1964. The letter focused on
two aspects which he considered to be crucial to the issue
of peace in the nuclear age. According to Merton, the moral
problems involved in the use of nuclear weapons and the right
of a Catholic to be a conscientious objector to war had to be
faced by the bishops gathered in Rome. He did not believe
that the writings of Popes Pius XII and John XXIII had already
implicitly condemned nuclear weapons and affirmed individual
conscience.[47] In his opinion, it was now up to the council

to make these points explicit. Significantly, Merton's letter pin-pointed the two main areas of debate that would emerge at the Council

The first draft of Schema 13 presented at the Third Session of the Council condemned total war, and the condemnation was accepted without debate. The draft, however, also contained a similar condemnation of the use of nuclear weapons.[48] It was on this point that debate flourished in St. Peter's, Rome. In order to understand what part the American peace groups had in determining the final statements of Vatican II on the issues of war and peace, it is necessary to clarify their different approaches to the great debate on peace in the Church.

In 1963, Harry W. Flannery was President of the CAIP and he worked closely with the CAIP's subcommittee on Arms Control. Flannery, a firm believer in the just war, urged the members of the subcommittee to prepare a statement to be sent to the bishops at Vatican II. In a letter to a CAIP member concerning nuclear warfare, Flannery said,

> No subject is of more importance today, as you well know, and I am pleased to hear that you are planning to try to get something out of the Council. The European pacifist influence in Rome may need to be offset. Here, too, we need to speak out because of the formation of PAX. Like all extremists, they may have most persistent, devoted and possibly persuasive adherents.[49]

Six active Catholic laymen, Dr. Alain C. Enthoven, Dr. Charles M. Herzfeld, Dr. William J. Nagle, Dr. John E. Moriarity,

Dr. James E. Dougherty and Dr. William V. O'Brien, all members of the subcommittee on Arms Control of the International Law and Juridical Order Committee of the CAIP prepared a critique of the nuclear war passages in the Schema.

The critique was not a formal CAIP statement since the Committee believed that there was not time nor any need for it to go through the necessary procedures. On August 5, 1964, a copy was sent to Bishop John J. Wright of the Diocese of Pittsburgh. Catholic pacifist lobbyists at the Council referred to it as the "secret memorandum." Essentially, the statement declared "the right to have recourse to war in extreme cases is justified by the present defective state of international society, law, and organization."[50] The just war ethic pervaded the entire statement.

Because of the CAIP's close relationship with, and by the 1960's its total financial dependency on, the NCWC, it is clear that the CAIP statement on nuclear war did not basically conflict with the beliefs of the American hierarchy. Members of the CAIP saw no need to go to Rome to lobby for acceptance of their critique of Schema 13. William V. O'Brien in a memorandum, "Morality, Nuclear War, and the Schema on the Church in the Modern World,"[51] written in October, 1964, perceptively gave the reasons why the Council could not condemn nuclear warfare and would therefore accept the recommendations submitted by the CAIP. His main reason was not the threat of communism but the age old form of nationalism peculiar to American Catholics known as "Americanism"[52] --

if Catholics did not obey their lawfully elected leaders they
would be considered disloyal Americans. O'Brien writes, "if
the Council were to adopt such a schema (the condemnation of
nuclear weapons), it would place close to fifty million
American Catholics in an awesome dilemma as to whether to
listen to the solemn findings of a Vatican Council or to the
hitherto accepted assurances of their government that America's
nuclear deterrent is the foundation for international stability and the <u>sine qua non</u> of the defense of the United
States."[53] Thus, the only action taken by the CAIP in reference to the Second Vatican Council was to prepare and send to
Rome a critique of the nuclear war passages in Schema 13.

The pacifist branch of the American Catholic peace
movement, however, took a more direct approach. In 1964
some members of the Catholic Worker and PAX went to Rome in
hopes of encouraging the Council Fathers to condemn nuclear
weapons and affirm the right of conscientious objection.
There were two types of peace witness offered by these American Catholics at the Council. The first type consisted of a
group of women headed by Dorothy Day[54] who fasted and prayed
and discussed the issues with the members of the hierarchy.
This type of witness was intensely personal and spiritual.
The other type of witness consisted of three members of PAX
who self-consciously performed the tasks of a political lobby.
Eileen Egan, Gordon Zahn, and James Douglas,[55] a young lay
theologian and close friend of Thomas Merton, were tireless
in their efforts to produce a positive statement in condemnation

of nuclear warfare. They worked simultaneously on two issues
in Schema 13, nuclear weapons and conscientious objection.
Both issues involved a different theological emphasis. The
strongest argument against the use of nuclear weapons was
that of nuclear pacifism which was based on the just war ethic.
The issue of conscientious objection depended upon the individual conscience and its strongest argument was based on the
pacifist ethic.

On these two issues, it was the work of James Douglas
that accounts for the major American contribution to the final
statements at Vatican II. James Douglas was both a theologian and a lobbyist. He worked hard at locating members of
the hierarchy throughout the world that were already sympathetic
to these two positions. He had also done his homework as a
theologian and had well drafted arguments for the positions.
On the issue of nuclear warfare he attempted to show the
hierarchy exactly how to condemn it within their own traditional framework of the just war ethic. Douglas, greatly
influenced by Thomas Merton, believed that the just war categories were inadequate in face of the present world crisis,
yet he attempted to use the theory with which the Council
Fathers were most familiar. At the same time, Douglas also
tried to move the Council Fathers toward a new ethic of peace
based on the Gospel, the rights of man, and non-violence.

At the end of the third session, Bishop John Taylor,
the American bishop of Stockholm, Sweden[56] submitted an intervention on Schema 13 that Douglas had prepared.[57] Taylor's
statement began with a reference from Thomas Merton:

Thomas Merton, one of the most profound
mystical theologians of our times, has written
that total nuclear war would be a sin of mankind only to the crucifixion of Christ. Modern
means of war threaten the very existence of
man. Moreover, the Council has a sacred duty
to respond with all its moral power to this
threat of mankind's self-destruction.[58]

The intervention changed the technical term "uncontrollability"
to the moral term "indiscriminant" based on the rights of
non-combatants, supported conscientious objection and pleaded
for non-violence. Copies of Bishop Taylor's statement were
also distributed by the peace lobby to twenty-five Council
Fathers, some of whom used sections of it for their own
interventions.

After debate on the floor and written interventions
were made on the first draft of Schema 13 during the third
session, the text was revised and again presented to the
Council for discussion in its fourth session in 1965. In
article 98, titled "Modern warfare, and in particular so-called
'total' war," the term "indiscriminant" was used rather than
"controllability." This was a definite achievement for the
peace lobby. Philip Hannan, the Auxiliary Bishop of Washington, D.C., however, challenged Schema 13's revised text,
with the support of nine bishops, three of whom were also
Americans; Francis Cardinal Spellman of New York, Bishop
Patrick O'Boyle of Washington, D.C., and Lawrence Cardinal
Sheehan of Baltimore.[59] The challenge claimed that total war
had never been condemned in such a manner by "recent popes,"
as the final draft of the Schema stated. Bishop Hannan also

wanted to keep the term "controllability." The Council
voted against the challenge and accepted the revision.
Article 98 in its final form reads as follows:

> All these considerations compel us to
> undertake an evaluation of war with an entirely
> new attitude. The men of our time must realize
> that they will have to give a somber reckoning
> of their deeds of war for the course of the
> future will depend greatly on the decisions
> they make today.
>
> With these truths in mind, this most Holy
> Synod makes its own the condemnations of total
> war already pronounced by recent popes, and
> issues the following declaration:
>
> Any act of war aimed indiscriminately at
> the destruction of entire cities or extensive
> areas along with their population is a crime
> against God and man himself. It merits
> unequivocal and unhesitating condemnation.[60]

The exact role of the American hierarchy in the revision of Schema 13 is not clear. After the third session,
Dr. Gordon Zahn in the March, 1965, issue of _Ramparts_ charged
that some American bishops were circulating a "secret" memorandum and trying to block the condemnation of the use of
atomic weapons by the Second Vatican Council. Certainly
Bishop Hannan's statements in both sessions and the circulated CAIP critique (secret or not) give some weight to Zahn's
charges.

Monsignor George Higgins of the CAIP, the NCWC, and a
Council consultant issued a NCWC news release on February 22,
1965, refuting Zahn's charges. Higgins release first berrated
Zahn as a pacifist for having an "infuriating holier-than-thou
attitude" and for writing an "outrageously superficial

article." Higgins claimed in his article "that the American
bishops, with few exceptions, have never even seen the so-
called 'secret' memorandum referred to . . . and are certainly
not carrying on a concentrated effort, either singly or col-
lectively to block condemnation."

Higgins' position is supported by several events which
occurred during the fourth session. First, was the absence
of a CAIP lobby in Rome. Second, before Bishop Hannan spoke
during the fourth session, there were efforts on the part of
other members of the American hierarchy to modify his speech.
At the annual NCWC meeting in Rome Hannan had introduced the
topic of nuclear warfare, but Joseph Cardinal Ritter, who was
presiding, ruled him out of order and encouraged those interested to stay for discussion after the meeting. Several
bishops did remain and tried to persuade Bishop Hannan to
modify his position but they were unsuccessful.[61]

The last significant event that supports Higgins argument was the intervention submitted by Joseph Cardinal Ritter
at the Council. During the fourth session three British
prelates, Abbot Christopher Butler and Bishops Gordon Wheeler
and Charles Grant had spoken against a clause in Schema 13
which upheld nuclear weapons as a deterrant. Ritter then
submitted a written intervention asking that the very possession of total-war arms be clearly condemned. Peace
lobbyists conjectured that Cardinal Ritter delivered the
intervention in writing rather than raising the issue on the

floor because he feared provoking a scandalous opposition
from some of the more nationalistic American bishops.[62]

Cardinal Ritter represented clearly a very different
position from Bishop Hannan at the Council. The degree of
diversity among the American Council Fathers is unknown. The
fact that there was a compromise position on the part of the
bishops on the issue of deterrance illustrated that there was
diversity among all Council Fathers from around the world.
The final Constitution did not make an "absolute condemnation
of the possession of arms which involve the intention or
grave peril of total war,"[63] as Cardinal Ritter suggested.
Nor did the final Constitution affirm the possession of such
arms as the more nationalist bishops would prefer. Instead,
the Constitution remained silent on the morality of deterrance
since it would not pass judgment on the intention of nations
in possession of nuclear weapons.

The Council Fathers did not transcend the just war
criteria because they would not deny the underling fundamental
presupposition of the just war theory -- a nation's right to
self-defense. The Pastoral Constitution on the Church in the
Modern World proclaimed that:

> As long as the danger of war remains and there
> is no competent and sufficiently powerful
> authority at the international level, govern-
> ments cannot be denied the right to legitimate
> defense once every means of peaceful settlement
> has been exhausted.[64]

Since that right remained even in a nuclear age, the just war
was rejected in the end only in the execution of indiscriminate

acts of bombing whether by nuclear weapons or traditional methods of warfare. By not explicitly condemning both the intention and execution of modern methods of warfare, the Council failed to draw explicit conclusions on deterrance and military defense. Bishop Hannan feared, as had the CAIP technical experts' critique, that if the Council had acted otherwise, Schema 13 would have meant a wholesale withdrawal of Catholic support from every nuclear arsenal in the world. The Council did provide norms on modern warfare, but logical objection and national loyalties could still subject them to the priorities of nations.

The peace lobby was more successful in the Council's explicit affirmation of the right to conscientious objection. The thrust for such a provision had come from Archbishop Roberts who spoke at both sessions.[65] After the third session Thomas Merton wrote to Archbishop George Flahiff of Winnipeg suggesting ways of strengthening the provision on conscientious objection. Merton urged that the right to be a conscientious objector had to apply to all wars, not just Vietnam and that it should not be expressed negatively. Merton suggested that the provision in the draft be changed from "encouraging the consciences of the faithful to submit to the decision of authority in cases of doubt," to a "positive statement using the words of Pacem in Terris, 'Those who are morally convinced of the necessity of non-violent conflict resolution, and who reject war as a solution which will hardly be reasonable in our time.'" He concluded his letter with a plea to get away

from the idea of pacifist to the real truth of Christian
resistance to evil on a non-violent basis.[66]

The only American objection on the floor of the Council
to a provision on conscientious objection came from Francis
Cardinal Spellman, the head of the Military Ordinate for the
United States armed forces and in effect the bishop of Catholics in the services. Cardinal Spellman asked for a provision
in Schema 13 which would make military service obligatory.
In a speech before the assembled Council Fathers he said,
"the responsibility for judging the necessity of drafting
men for service belongs to civil authorities and individuals
cannot refuse their obedience to the state."[67] It is note-
worthy that Cardinal Spellman praised the rest of the revised
draft on Schema 13 and only objected on this issue.

The final text on conscientious objection adopted by
the Council clearly upheld the rights and duties of individual
conscience and recommended legal provisions for those who
resist military commands. The final text also dropped the
negative statement which presumed the duty of a person to obey
lawful authority until its injustice was clearly manifest.[68]

The peace lobbyists at Vatican II wanted to shut the
door on the scholastic just war doctrine as a viable ethic
for modern warfare. They hoped to do it with a condemnation
of nuclear weapons and the affirmation of the right of conscientious objection. They were most successful in achieving
the latter and the Council's final statements on modern warfare were the result of a series of compromises.

Indeed, the door was partially shut on the just war.[69] The development of nuclear warfare and the Cold War had sufficiently influenced the Council Fathers to attempt to reevaluate the traditional normative ethic in which they had been trained, but the attempt did not result in the development of a new ethic on the issues of war and peace. This incapacity on the part of the entire assembly had already been experienced by the peace activists themselves, by individual members of the hierarchy, and by theologians throughout the world who had previously made the same attempt. At best, the Council Fathers opened the way for a new ethic of peace based on their affirmation of the dignity of man, the Gospels, and non-violence.[70] Thus, the very small parts played by all of these participants at the Council who desired to see the condemnation of nuclear warfare were only partially successful. The new ethic was yet to be born.

The role of the American hierarchy in working towards the condemnation of nuclear warfare was almost non-existent except for the intervention of Joseph Cardinal Ritter. The statements of other members of the hierarchy throughout the world, particularly of the bishops from England and the solemn and clear condemnation of all nuclear warfare by Patriarch Maximos of Antioch did more for the partial successes achieved on the issue than did the actions of any American. Viewed in these terms, the work of PAX, particularly its representative, James Douglas pales in significance. Yet, he was able to do a great deal and was listened to by many members of the hierarchy considering the fact that he was not a member of the hierarchy nor did he possess any power other than the moral power of his message of peace.

After the Second Vatican Council, the just war tradition was no longer normative for Catholics. Instead those concerned about peace were affirmed in their rights to be conscientious objectors and were encouraged to work toward the development of a new ethic of peace. The escalation of the war in Vietnam intensified the issues of war and peace and Catholics for the first time would be a significant part of the American peace movement.

REFERENCES

[1]
On December 11, 1939, Archbishop Francis Spellman was appointed Bishop of the Armed Forces of the United States and Father John F. O'Hara, C.S.C., the President of Notre Dame, made his auxiliary on January 15, 1940. In 1940 The Catholic Directory listed a total of 367 priests as members of the Military Ordinate in the United States. By September 2, 1945, there were 5,379 Catholic priests associated with the chaplaincy and after 1945 "many would remain in them because there was no returning of the armed forces to the states before the war."

In 1940 The National Catholic Community Service composed of the Administrative Board of the NCWC and the Military Vicar was formed to cooperate with the United Service Organization in charge of relief services for the Armed Forces. The bishops announced that $200,000 had been raised for the relief of suffering peoples abroad and that the Bishops' Committee on Polish Relief had raised $347,332.60 for their work. See Thomas T. McAvoy, C.S.C., A History of the Catholic Church in the United States, (Notre Dame, 1969), pp. 430-37.

[2]
Other peace groups were the Carnegie Endowment for International Peace, Women's Action Committee for Lasting Peace, and the pacifist group, Women's International League for Peace and Freedom. AMU, CAIP Collection, Memorandum entitled "Organizations to be Represented at Paris," dated July 9, 1948.

[3]
Miss Rita Schaefer represented not only the NCWC and the CAIP, but also the National Catholic Conference of Women. AMU, CAIP Collection.

[4]
John Eppstein, author of The Catholic Tradition of the Law of Nations was director and editor of the British Society for International Understanding. AMU, CAIP Collection, Letter dated April 13, 1948, John Eppstein to Miss Rita Schaefer.

[5]
AMU, CAIP Collection, "Summary of CAIP Committee Work, 1927 to 1952," 25.

[6]
AMU, CAIP Collection, "Catholic Association for International Peace, Annual Report, June 30, 1949-June 30, 1950," 2.

207

[7] AMU, CAIP Collection, "Catholic Association for International Peace, Annual Report, June 30, 1949-June 30, 1950," 5.

[8] In 1962 George Meany received the CAIP's Annual Peace Award.

[9] Letter dated August 17, 1972, George N. Shuster to author.

[10] AMU, CAIP Collection, untitled typed memorandum by Harry W. Flannery.

[11] James Douglas Collection (JDC), copy of CAIP critique and cover letter dated August 5, 1964, William V. O'Brien to Most Rev. John J. Wright, D.D.

[12] William Nagle, (ed.), Morality and Modern Warfare, (Maryland, 1960), pp. 6-7.

[13] Charles S. Thompson, (ed.), Morals and Missiles: Catholic Essays on the Problem of War Today, (London, 1959). This book includes essays by Cannon F. H. Drinkwater, Dom Bede Griffiths, O.S.B., Christopher Hollis, Sir Compton Mackenzie, Archbishop Thomas D. Roberts, S.J., Father Franziskus Stratmann, O.P., and E. I. Watkin.

[14] Nagle, Morality and Modern Warfare, p. 7.

[15] In 1962 Thomas Merton edited Breakthrough to Peace: Twelve Views on the Threat of Thermonuclear Extermination. In the Introduction, Merton admits that he edited the book to counter the written and spoken statements of nuclear "realists." Unable to find American Catholics with such a position besides Gordon Zahn, Merton drew on American writers, "faithful to the Judeo-Christian tradition on which our civilization was built." Merton was inspired to take such action by the influence of Walter Stein in Britain who edited in 1961, Nuclear Weapons and Christian Conscience.

[16] In July, 1961, the Institute of World Polity at Georgetown University published the papers presented at the Second Annual Conference on Christian Political and Social Thought. The topic of the conference was "Christian Ethics and Nuclear Warfare." Dr. William V. O'Brien was one of the editors of the compendium. The conference noted that much of

what had been accomplished through the centuries by way of
the just war providing limits to warfare collapsed in the
nuclear age and that technically "aggressive" modern war
became unjustifiable as Pius XII said in his Christmas
address of 1944.

[17]John C. Ford, "The Hydrogen Bombing of Cities,"
Morality and Modern Warfare, bases his argument against the
use of nuclear weapons as he did in his arguments against
obliteration bombing on the rights of non-combatants. This
position is adopted by the Second Vatican Council.

[18]Donald J. Thorman, "The Christian's Conscience and
Nuclear Warfare," New City, (November 15, 1962), reprint
found in AMU, CAIP Collection. This is a condemnation of
the definitions of the major approaches given in this chapter.

[19]"The moral or political principles on which our most
critical decisions are to be made may, in themselves, be
relatively simple, but the assumptions on which they are based
are immensely complicated. It is not difficult to appeal to
traditional norms of justice and law, and apply them to our
present situation in such a way as to come up with logical
and plausible conclusions. But the very plausibility of the
conclusions tends to be the most dangerous things about them,
if we forget that they may be based on premises which we
take to be axiomatic and which, in fact have been invalidated
by recent developments of weapons technology. ... There is
a very serious danger that our most critical decisions may
turn out to be no decisions at all, but only the end of a
vicious circle of conjectures and gratuitous assumptions in
which we unconsciously make the argument come out in favor
of our own theory, our own favorite policy." Thomas Merton,
Breakthrough to Peace . . . , p. 13.

[20]Miller, Harsh and Dreadful . . . , p. 219.

[21]Ibid., p. 220.

[22]John Cogley, "A Harsh and Dreadful Love," America,
CXXVII, (November 11, 1972), 395.

[23]Miller, Harsh and Dreadful . . . , p. 225.

[24]The Catholic Worker as quoted in Ibid., p. 229.

[25]Ibid., p. 234.

[26]Wittner, Rebels . . . , pp. 62-96. He gives a detailed account of the acts of non-violent resistance performed by the radical pacifists during the war.

[27]Ibid., pp. 156-57.

[28]Ibid., p. 163.

[29]Ibid., p. 244.

[30]Ibid., pp. 154-55; 247-48.

[31]Miller, Harsh and Dreadful . . . , p. 279.

[32]Ammon Hennacy, The Autobiography of a Catholic Anarchist, (New York, 1954). Edition used by author.

[33]Miller, Harsh and Dreadful . . . , p. 267.

[34]A spur to Hennacy's decision was a two week fast in Glen Gardner, New Jersey, begun by Dave Dellinger and others, against the sending of troops to Korea. Hennacy wrote to Dellinger that he too would fast, but was unsympathetic to Dellinger's World Citizen emphasis. See Hennacy, Autobiography . . . , p. 163.

[35]A. J. Muste as quoted in Wittner, Rebels. . . , p. 265. Wittner gives a very detailed description of the demonstration and the author has borrowed heavily from it.

[36]The Catholic Worker, June, 1960. A similar event occurred in London's Trafalgar Square where 75,000 people turned out in support of unilateral disarmament of nuclear weapons.

[37]Ibid., April, 1960.

[38]Ibid., January, 1963.

[39]Ibid., January, 1962. Jean Morton, Nelson Barr, Bob Kaye, Charles Butterworth, Elin Paulson, Mark Samara, Carol Kramer, and Jim Forest were Catholic Worker participants. Thomas Merton wrote a letter of support which was published in the same issue.

[40] Miller, Harsh and Dreadful . . . , pp. 283-301. A chapter entitled, "Hennacy at the Catholic Worker," from which this information was obtained.

[41] Ibid., pp. 300-01. Much of Miller's information on why Hennacy left is obtained from Dorothy Day's chapter on Hennacy in Loaves and Fishes.

[42] Dorothy Day as quoted in Ibid., p. 266.

[43] Forest, "No Longer Alone . . . ," p. 146.

[44] Address given by Archbishop T. D. Roberts, S.J. to a small group at Pendle Hill, Pennsylvania (a Quaker center), Fall, 1970, attended by author.

[45] Sponsors of American PAX included: Rev. Thomas Merton, Edward Rice, Rev. Marion Casey, Professor Gordon Zahn, Rev. Robert Hovda, Dorothy Day, Rev. Robert McDole, Anne Taillefer, Rev. Robert Fox, Helen Iswolsky, Rosemary Sheed, Dorothy Dohen, and Arthur Sheehan.

[46] JDC, Letter dated August 13, 1965, Thomas Merton to Archbishop George Flahiff states that Merton sent a copy of the letter to Commonweal for publication but it was rejected.

[47] Thomas Merton, "In Acceptance of the PAX Medal, 1963," Thomas Merton on Peace, pp. 257-58.

[48] The original text in the first draft read as follows: "Although after all helps to peaceful discussion have been exhausted, it may not be illicit, when one's rights have been unjustly trammeled, to defend those rights against such unjust aggression by violence and force, nevertheless, the use of arms, especially nuclear weapons whose effects are greater than can be imagined and therefore cannot be reasonably regulated by men, exceeds all just proportion and therefore must be judged most wicked before God and man." See Floyd Anderson, (ed.), The Council Daybook, Session III, (Washington, 1966), p. 243.

[49] AMU, CAIP Collection, Letter dated March 14, 1963, Harry W. Flannery to Victor C. Ferkiss.

[50] JDC, copy of CAIP critique, p. 2 of Alternative Text section.

[51]AMU, CAIP Collection.

[52]Ellis, American Catholicism, pp. 120-22.

[53]AMU, CAIP Collection, Memorandum, "Morality, Nuclear War, and The Schema on the Church in the Modern World."

[54]A text of a leaflet issued to explain the purpose of the fast is found in "Appeal to Rome," Reconciliation Quarterly, (Fourth Quarter, 1965), 612-14.

[55]James Douglas attained an M.A. degree in theology at Bellarmine College during which time he became friends with Thomas Merton. After lobbying at the Council, he wrote The Non-Violent Cross. In 1969 he was co-director of the Program in Non-Violence at the University of Notre Dame. In 1971 he wrote his second book, Resistance and Contemplation. And in 1972 after returning to the University of Hawaii to teach, he was arrested for the destruction of files on technological warfare.

[56]The intervention was also signed by Archbishop George Flahiff of Winnepeg and English Bishops Gordon Wheeler and Charles Grant. Copy of intervention in JDC.

[57]James Douglas based much of the final version of the text on the suggestions of Philip Sharper, another member of PAX. Douglas had also consulted many theologians on the wording of the intervention. Fathers Bernard Haring, Yves Congar and Gregory Baum expressed virtually complete agreement with the text. Father Karl Rahner was reluctant to condemn the concept of a total war deterrent for mainly political reasons and Father Charles Davis wanted more on the responsibilities of the heads of states rather than the emphasis on conscientious objection. JDC, Letter dated November 28, 1964, James Douglas to Philip Sharper.

[58]JDC, "Intervention of Bishop John Taylor (Stockholm, Sweden)."

[59]JDC, Copy of Challenge dated 2nd December 1965.

[60]Pastoral Constitution on the Church in the Modern World, (National Catholic Welfare Conference), pp. 87-88. All quotations from the Constitution used here are taken from the NCWC translation.

[61] JDC, Letter dated, February 2, 1966, Donald Quinn to James Douglas. Donald Quinn is editor of the St. Louis Review, the official newspaper of the Archdiocese of St. Louis.

[62] Douglas, The Non-Violent Cross, p. 117.

[63] Ibid., p. 118. For a complete text of Cardinal Ritter's intervention, pp. 118-19.

[64] Pastoral Constitution . . . , p. 87.

[65] In the third session intervention, Archbishop Roberts called attention to the fact that Catholics have been denied this right. In the fourth session he devoted his intervention to the case of Franz Jägerstätter. See Gordon Zahn, In Solitary Witness: The Life and Death of Franz Jagerstatter, (New York, 1964). Copies of both interventions are in the JDC.

[66] JDC, Letter dated August 13, 1965, Thomas Merton to Archbishop Flahiff.

[67] The Council Daybook, p. 37.

[68] Pastoral Constitution . . . , p. 86.

[69] Again, See "War," The New Catholic Encyclopedia, or footnote 86 in Chapter I, p. 57 in this text.

[70] The Council mentions the use of non-violent resistance as an alternative to war: "We cannot fail to praise those who renounce the use of violence in the vindication of their rights and who resort to methods of defense which are otherwise available to weaker parties too, provided this can be done without injury to the rights and duties of others or of the community itself. Pastoral Constitution . . . , p. 85. Douglas in The Non-Violent Cross, p. 134, attributes the inclusion of this reference to non-violence to the tireless lobbying at the Council of Jean and Hildegard Goss-Mayr of the International Fellowship of Reconciliation.

CHAPTER VI

THE CATHOLIC PEACE MOVEMENT IN THE 1960's

In less than a year after the adoption of Schema 13 at
the Second Vatican Council, Pope Paul VI undertook a series
of pilgrimages for peace. The climax of the pilgrimage
occurred on October 5, 1965, when the Pope addressed the
General Assembly of the United Nations on the twentieth
anniversary of the foundation of this world institution for
peace and for collaboration between the peoples of the entire
world. In his address, Pope Paul VI extended and confirmed
the teachings of the great peace encyclical, Pacem in Terris
and the new approach to the issues of war and peace stated
in the pastoral directives of the Second Vatican Council.

The Pope's message at the United Nations reached its
highest point in the statement: "No more war, war never
again! Peace, it is peace that must guide the destinies of
peoples and of all mankind."[1] The Pope elaborated on this
point by stating:

> If you wish to be brothers, let the arms fall
> from your hands. One can not love while holding
> offensive arms. Those armaments, especially those
> terrible arms, which modern science has given you,
> long before they produce victims and ruins, nourish
> bad feelings, create nightmares, distrust and somber
> resolutions. They demand enormous expenditures,
> they obstruct projects of union and useful col-
> laboration. They falsify the psychology of peoples.
> As long as man remains that weak, changeable and
> ever wicked being that he often shows himself to
> be, defensive arms will unfortunately, be necessary.[2]

214

As the first pope in history to come to the United States, Paul VI brought the message of peace close to the forty-six million American Catholics. His message, like that of the Council, called for a new approach to the issues of war and peace. Yet, the right to possess defensive weapons was maintained in his plea for peace.

The peace messages of Pope John XXIII, the Second Vatican Council and Pope Paul VI's address to the United Nations inevitably resulted in a need for a re-definition of the proper relationship between Church and State. As the war in Vietnam escalated in the 1960's, some members of the Catholic Church in America reflected this new emphasis on peace by increasing their opposition to war. Changes in the Church on the issues of war and peace were least perceptible in the American Catholic hierarchy. The American hierarchy, like the entire hierarchy at the Second Vatican Council, had refused to explicitly condemn the use of nuclear weapons.

The Cold War with its emphasis on communist aggression and military defense continued to pervade the attitude of the American hierarchy on war and peace issues in the 1960's. The threat of a nuclear holocaust, however, diminished in proportion to the escalation of the war in Vietnam. It became evident after the election of 1964 that President Lyndon B. Johnson would continue the escalation of the war. He defined the war, however, as "limited" and its escalation excluded the use of nuclear weapons in favor of an air war of obliteration bombing conducted with new electronic and bio-chemical

methods. Official leadership in the Church characteristically
continued to obey the state's lawfully constituted authority
on the issues of war and peace. Just as the American Catholic
hierarchy had refused to condemn the use of nuclear weapons,
so too, would it refuse to condemn as immoral the war in
Vietnam by the United States Government.

It was the issue of the draft and individual conscience
and not the issue of the war itself that became the focal
point of change in the teaching of the Church in America. The
right of an individual Catholic to become a conscientious
objector to the Vietnam war provided the vehicle for change.
The church in support of conscience was able to come into
conflict with the state's policy of conscription without coming into total conflict with the state's policy on the war in
Vietnam.

In June, 1966, the National Conference of Catholic
Bishops passed a resolution on peace. The statement which
appeared in the New York Times, contended that the United
States' presence in Vietnam could be justified.[3]

In July, 1966, Lawrence Cardinal Sheehan issued a
pastoral letter, "Vietnam, Patriotism and Individual Conscience," which was to be read aloud at all masses celebrated
in the Archdiocese of Baltimore. Since this was to be the
first official pronouncement by a prominent Catholic ecclesi-
astic to give any indication of moral misgivings or reservations regarding the war in Vietnam, it received widespread
attention in the American press when it first appeared. The

pastoral letter presented a restrained and carefully balanced set of reminders of the traditional limits to be observed in warfare and a cautious endorsement of conscientious objection.

Less than two months later, the Cardinal explicitly repudiated what he described as attempts "to interpret my pastoral as a condemnation of American presence in Vietnam."[4] In a letter to the National Commander of the Catholic War Victims, he made his position clear. "Our presence in Vietnam and the reasons which have prompted us to involve ourselves there are honorable. The alternative of the withdrawal could well have catastrophic results under the present circumstances."[5] So determined was he to correct the "distortions" he protested that the printed copies of the original text distributed by the Baltimore chancery also include the full text of his subsequent clarification.[6]

The other statement during this period by an individual member of the hierarchy against the war was that of the late Richard Cardinal Cushing of the Archdiocese of Boston who in his 1967 Christmas message pleaded: "For God's sake we must bring this war to an end."[7] Yet, this Cardinal could not be persuaded the following year to lend support to efforts to put the National Conference on record in support of selective conscientious objection.

There was only one American prelate prior to 1969 who spoke out consistently in opposition to the war in Vietnam. He was Bishop James Shannon of the Diocese of St. Paul. It was mainly due to his persistence that the bishops took a stand

in support of conscientious objection in 1968. It was also
the frustration which this bishop experienced on the Vietnam
issue that partially accounts for his resignation from the
hierarchy.[8]

While these messages were being delivered, other individual members of the hierarchy were speaking out in support
of the Vietnam War. Most notable were Archbishop John Lucey,
who as a young priest had worked zealously to build the CAIP
and the late Francis Cardinal Spellman. Cardinal Spellman's
annual Christmas messages to the American troops received
wide publicity. The Cardinal of the Archdiocese of New York
conceived of the war in Vietnam as "a war for civilization"[9]
and undauntedly endorsed the principle of "my country right
or wrong."[10]

Because of diverse views on the war in Vietnam among
the American hierarchy itself, joint statements on the war
were few and when made reflected a compromise position. In
the April, 1967, bishop's meeting there was no mention of the
Vietnam War. In November, 1967, the National Conference
praised the Johnson administration for "repeated" efforts to
negotiate peace, and in April, 1968, it endorsed Johnson's
decision to limit the bombing in North Vietnam. Finally, in
November, 1968, the National Conference issued the important
pastoral letter on Human Life in Our Day which not only
endorsed the principle of conscientious objection but also
recommended that the conscription law be changed to admit
selective conscientious objection.[11] In order to understand

why the American hierarchy issued such a joint-statement on conscientious objection, it is necessary to trace the development of the Catholic peace groups and note the actions of their individual members during the 1960's.

Because of the pastoral directives of the Second Vatican Council, it became clear to American Catholics concerned about peace, and by 1964 especially concerned about the war in Vietnam, that there were two avenues of approach: one approach was to declare the immorality of war based on the use of means such as the bombing of centers of population which had its roots in the just war criteria and the second, was the right of a Catholic to be a conscientious objector. The second was rooted in the issue of individual conscience and amenable to both pacifists and just war traditionalists. Since, individuals were powerless to alter directly the means of warfare employed by the military in Vietnam, the focus for organizing protest to the war became the draft. On the issue of the draft, individuals could assume personal responsibility and visibly take a stand to reflect their moral commitment. Thus, for American Catholics who wanted to do something to stop the war and still be consistent with the teachings of their Church, there emerged many individuals who could reflect their commitment on this issue. The draft became the main organizing tool for Catholic peace activists as well as the entire American peace movement during the 1960's.

Since for more than thirty years the Catholic Worker Movement was virtually the only Catholic group that provided

support to Catholic conscientious objectors or seriously
sought to challenge the hierarchy's traditional enlistment
in America's military efforts, it was natural for them to
be in the forefront on the draft issue. By the Second Vatican
Council, the Catholic Worker had moved to a position of cooperation with other pacifist peace groups. It had also
advanced from the simple fundamentalist pacifism of Christianity's earliest days and the form of non-resistance characterized by CO's during World War II to non-violent resistance
with an emphasis on the activist imperative reflected in the
acts of civil disobedience during the Civil Defense Alerts
in New York City in the 1950's. Symbolic acts of non-violent
resistance against the draft in the 1960's enabled the intense
personalism and moral commitment of Catholic Workers to witness against the war in Vietnam. An emphasis on peace
pervaded the energies of the Catholic Worker Movement after
1964. Other issues such as poverty, labor, and civil rights
receded into the background. Houses of Hospitality, farming
communes, and the paper, however, continued to flourish.
Despite the emphasis on peace in the movement and their
formation of PAX in 1962, a new Catholic group, solely committed to peace was formed: the Catholic Peace Fellowship,
(CPF).

One reason for the formation of the new group was the
emphasis of PAX. Having formed the backbone of the American
peace lobby at the Second Vatican Council, it continued to
focus on institutional change for peace in America. Eileen

Egan, friend and traveling companion of Dorothy Day, was mainly responsible for the organization. She directed the energies of the small group increasingly toward achieving institutional changes in the Roman Catholic Church in America on the issue of the draft.

The idea of the CPF was much more within the tradition of the Catholic Worker. In 1964, Fathers Daniel and Philip Berrigan asked three Catholic Workers, James Forest, Thomas Cornell, and Martin Corbin[12] to work with them in forming the new peace group. Though the Catholic Worker did not conceive the idea for the formation of the group, it was from its membership that the Fathers Berrigan secured their personnel.

Another reason for the formation of the group was the extent of cooperation between Catholics and other peace groups in America by the 1960's. The CPF was the first Catholic peace group to exist under the auspices of an interdenominational organization, the Fellowship of Reconciliation (FOR). FOR desired the formation of an arm of its pacifist organization to address American Catholics and thus provided the CPF with financial support and office space at 336 Lafayette Street in New York City.

The CPF based its thought on the issues of war and peace on the belief in life: "War has been the way of life of the majority of mankind throughout history, and we only deceive ourselves if we think it is not just as much the life of our times, the impulse of much of our economy, and the preoccupation of our politics. But war is not life, nor even a necessary part of life."[13] The founders viewed their job as that of educating Catholics and any one else interested in this belief.

As an educational agency, the CPF hoped to address itself to many areas of concern, including building interest in and opposition to the war in Vietnam, raising medical relief for victims on all sides of the tragedy of war, and providing draft information and counseling services.

Self-consciously Catholic, the founders of the CPF also wanted to develop a "theology of peace" with an emphasis on the principles and techniques of non-violent resistance and, out of the Second Vatican Council, a "vision of a Church that is peacemaking to its very core."[14]

From Vatican II until 1968, the Catholic Worker, the CPF, and PAX were united in their desires for peace and to stop the war in Vietnam. The issue of the draft was the focal point of their energies. These groups, however, differed in their strategy and tactics.

The Catholic Worker Movement in support of traditional non-violent resistance reached a high point in their actions ten days after Pope Paul VI had spoken at the United Nations. On October 15, 1965, a young Catholic Worker named David Miller stepped to the front of a platform and said, "I believe the napalming of villages is an immoral act. I hope this will be a significant political act, so here goes." And then he burned his draft card.[15]

Destroying draft cards was nothing new to the American anti-war protest movement, nor was it the first such act performed by a Catholic Worker. At a series of nationwide demonstrations on February 2, 1947, some four or five hundred Americans either publicly destroyed their draft cards or mailed them to President Truman.[16] At a rally in Washington Square at the end of the Second Worldwide General Strike for Peace in November, 1963, Tom Cornell, who was then an associate editor of The Catholic Worker destroyed his draft card along with twenty-five others. He and Chris Kearns, also a Catholic Worker, led a draft card burning at an anti-conscription rally in Union Square on Armed Forces Day, May 16, 1964. This rally was sponsored by the War Resisters League, the Student Peace Union, the Committee for Non-Violent Action, and the Catholic Worker.[17]

Again in 1965, a nationwide coordinated National Assembly of Unrepresented Peoples was held from August 6th to August 9th. Life magazine ran a long article on the demonstrations. This article contained a picture of a Chris Kearns dropping his draft card into a flaming cooking pot. In direct reaction to the picture, Representative Mendel Rivers of the House Armed Services Subcommittee rammed a bill through Congress that made draft card burning a crime punishable by $10,000 fine and/or five years imprisonment. President Johnson signed the bill into law on August 31st.[18]

Thus, David Miller's action on October 15th became a test-case for the act. Miller had joined the Catholic Worker

the previous June following his graduation with a degree in
sociology from LeMoyne College. Miller's action had great
visibility since it took place at the largest nationwide
anti-war rally to date in New York City. David Miller
appeared on the program not as a representative of the
Catholic Worker but of draft non-cooperators. And James Peck
of the War Resisters League introduced him. Three days later
Miller was arrested.

At a rally on November 6, 1965, in front of the Federal
Court House in New York City where 150,000 people had gathered
to protest the Vietnam War, five more men burned their draft
cards. Dorothy Day and A. J. Muste introduced the men. Three
of the five were members of the Catholic Worker Movement.
They were James Wilson, Roy Fisher and Tom Cornell.

Tom Cornell as spokesman for the group prefaced his
statement by citing the futility of previous protests and the
continuing escalation of the war. He claimed that the Rivers'
Bill which outlawed the burning of draft cards was merely an
attempt to stifle protest. He summed up the reason for his
course of action by quoting a letter from Karl Meyer to his
draft board which was printed in the October, 1965, issue of
The Catholic Worker. Meyer was a Catholic Worker from the
Midwest who was known for his witness of draft and tax resistance. Cornell added to Meyer's words: "The grave crime, we
are told, is not the destruction of life but the destruction
of a piece of paper."[19] These five men were also arrested.

Miller went to trial on February 9, 1966, claiming
that the act of burning a draft card was "symbolic speech"

and thus guaranteed by the first Amendment. He was found
guilty and a unanimous Court of Appeals later upheld the
conviction.[20]

Of the five draft card burners who participated in the
November 6th rally, one, Jim Peck pleaded guilty and received
a two year sentence.[21] The other four pleaded not guilty
and based their case on freedom of speech as had Miller.
They too were found guilty and served six months sentences.[22]

After these acts of civil disobedience and resistance
in October and November, 1965, many others followed the path
of the Catholic Workers. Thus, the draft resistance movement, later known as "The Resistance" was born. Since over
3,500 draft cards had been publicly destroyed in various
ways,[23] the Rivers' law was unenforceable and the movement
proved to be a success.

There were other young men in America, however, who
did not choose the path of resistance to protest the draft
during the war in Vietnam. They preferred to register their
dissent against the war within the laws of American society.
PAX was one Catholic group which attempted to help these young
men. The PAX group of the 1960's was very different from
the first PAX group in America during World War II. The
first PAX group attempted to aid Catholic conscientious
objectors who were sent to Civilian Public Service camps.
These camps had been declared illegal after World War II
and a two year alternative service policy replaced the old
system for conscientious objectors (CO's). The Selective

Service law of 1940, however, had not basically changed by
the 1960's in so far as the privilege of conscientious objector status was concerned. Only a total pacifist who professed
belief in a "Supreme Being" and who based his position on
"religious training and belief" could qualify as a CO. The
aim of the new PAX group was to change church and state
institutions in their position on conscientious objection.

The Supreme Court in the U. S. v. Seeger Case in 1965
extended the privilege of CO status to include as "religious"
certain beliefs even further removed from conventional religion and thus identified conscientious beliefs with religion.[24]
Congress's response was to omit the Supreme Being clause
from the 1967 Draft Act. The Seegar decision aided many
young men who were not identified with an official church in
applying for CO status. It did not aid those, however, who
were only opposed to some wars. The Supreme Court did not
alter the requirement of total pacifism for the granting of
the privilege.

The Seegar decision also aroused the hopes of just war
theorists that the courts or Congress would extend the privilege of CO's to selective conscientious objectors (SCO). The
rationale for SCO was advanced by three politically sophisticated
theologians -- John Courtney Murray, Ralph Potter, and Paul
Ramsey.

The Catholic case for SCO was developed by John Courtney
Murray, S.J. of Woodstock, Maryland, who died on August 16,
1967. Murray had served on the President's Advisory Commission

on Selective Service.[25]   In 1967, Murray undertook to advocate that "the revised statute should extend the provisions
of the present statute to include not only the absolute pacifist but also the relative pacifist; that the grounds for the
status of conscientious objector should be not only religious
or non-religiously motivated opposition (Seegar decision) to
participation in war in all forms, but also similarly motivated opposition to participation in particular wars."[26]

    This position was rejected by the majority of the Com-
mission. No Presidential recommendation was made to Congress
on the issue and there was evidence that Congress was not
sympathetic to the position of selective objector. Also, as
of 1968, there was no indication on the part of Congress or
the courts that either would extend CO to SCO.[27]   At the time
of his death, Murray believed that the issue was not satis-
factorily settled and that it should be kept before the
country. One of his last acts was to lend his support to the
"official" Catholic peace group, the CAIP in planning their
1967 conference on the topic of "Selective Conscientious
Objection." The prestige of Murray as a theologian and the
fact that he believed the Vietnam War to be justifiable
meant that his position on SCO would carry great influence
among the just war believers in the Catholic community. This
was to be especially true among the hierarchy.[28]

    After the Second Vatican Council, PAX's desire to
effect change in church and state institutions on the draft
resulted in the development of a strategy that would include

both pacifists and just war traditionalists. The tactic was
the pioneering of a Rights of Conscience Campaign. The campaign had a two-fold purpose: "1) to have the Bishops of
the United States issue a clarifying statement that a
Catholic had the right to be a conscientious objector and
further to be one on the grounds of the traditional Catholic
teaching of the just war which makes 'selective conscientious
objection' a valid Catholic position and 2) to change the
draft law so that those who follow the just war tradition
should not be discriminated against when they claim the
right of conscientious objection."[29]

In order to achieve these goals, PAX published a book,
The War That Is Forbidden: Peace Beyond Vatican II which was
sent free to every bishop in the United States. The organiza-
tion sent two memoranda to every bishop before the Selective
Service Law was extended in 1967. PAX even inserted in
Commonweal magazine a paid announcement on the Rights of
Conscience Campaign and gathered signatures from a wide range
of supporters, including theologians, educators, writers, and
seven Catholic bishops. The book, the memorandum and the
Commonweal statement were also sent to every member of Congress.
One Congressman, Donald Edwards of California, read the PAX
statement into the Congressional Record urging that Congress
take into account the validity of its arguments.[30] Despite
the efforts of PAX, Congress remained unfavorable to SCO.

PAX was much more successful, however, in effecting
change in the institutional church. The strategy of unity

pacifists and just war traditionalists in their campaign served as a way of bringing the institutional church to action in support of CO and SCO.

The one Catholic peace group which adopted the same position as PAX was the CAIP. Though the Association would not work directly with the "too pacifist" PAX, it did work in its own way to help bring about the same desired change in the institutional church. PAX realized this would happen when it devised its strategy. It also knew that the CAIP was a dying organization after the Second Vatican Council and that it did not have the resources to wage a campaign. Since the CAIP was the only "official" peace organization in the church, PAX rightly assessed the need for its support to effect any change in the institutional church.

By the 1960's the CAIP had been totally absorbed into the NCWC. Monsignor George Higgins, executive secretary of the CAIP by virtue of his position as director of the Social Action Department for the NCWC managed to keep the CAIP alive by issuing a monthly newsletter, CAIP News, and maintaining its annual conferences. The NCWC had refused to allot suffi- cient funds for a full-time CAIP staff.[31] In 1967 the reor- ganization of the NCWC into the United States Catholic Conference (USCC) brought along with its new name a Commission for World Justice and Peace. The USCC announced that the duties of the new commission duplicated the work of the CAIP. Because of the CAIP's total dependence after World War II on the NCWC, it had no choice but to relinquish its duties to

the Commission for World Justice and Peace. Thus, the CAIP,
the first American Catholic peace organization, ceased to
exist in 1968.[32]

In 1967 and 1968, Patrick McDermott, S.J., one of the
members of the new commission, worked diligently in securing
a statement from the American bishops on sonscientious objection. McDermott, a friend of both pacifists and just war
theorists, wrote the drafts for and did the organizing among
the American hierarchy on the issue. Finally, in the
pastoral letter, Human Life in Our Day (1968), the National
Council of Catholic Bishops not only endorsed the principle
of conscientious objection but further recommended that the
conscription law be changed to admit selective conscientious
objection.[33]

The success of PAX as a pressure group on the institutional church must be applauded. PAX's choice of the Human
Rights Campaign pin-pointed the possibilities and limits of
the institutional church on the issue of the draft. It
failed, however, to change the position of the government on
SCO. Yet, it must be remembered that even after the institutional church recommended such a change, there was still no
response on the part of the government. PAX, the CAIP, the
Commission for World Justice and Peace, and the American
hierarchy attempted to reform America; none of them fundamentally challenged the draft much less the American system.

The value of the PAX campaign was that it affirmed the
supremacy of the individual's conscience over the state in

matters of war and peace. It also provided a way for the
state to grant a privilege rather than persecute opposition
on an individual level. The support of Catholics on this
issue did not necessitate, as in the case of Murray, that
they challenge the right of the state to set policy on issues
of war and peace. Thus, by 1968, the American Catholic hierarchy affirmed the right of individual conscience in both CO
and SCO cases. The tragedy was that they could not go one
step further and condemn the actions of the United States
Government as immoral in the war in Vietnam. The reason was
the inherent limitation of the just war theory. The theory
always gave the benefit of doubt in matters of war and peace
to the state and the burden of proof always fell to the
individual.

Unlike PAX, the CPF remained more within the Catholic
Worker tradition. Basically pacifist, the CPF from 1964 to
1968 directly challenged the church and state from outside
the existing institutions. Their aim was to stop the war in
Vietnam and the focal point of their energies was the draft.
The center for the CPF was New York City. Here the CPF
operated a speakers' bureau, a tape and film library, a
publication program and a production of a bi-monthly CPF
Bulletin. It was also the center for collaboration with other
peace groups in organizing demonstrations and "beg-ins"
against the war in New York City. Plans were made for national
campaigns too. The main work of the group on a day to day
basis was the providing of free draft counseling for as high
as one hundred conscientious objectors a week.[34]

Other CPF groups were found in major cities throughout the United States. Each group was autonomous, but could
draw on the resources of the New York group. Activities
of each CPF group varied greatly and there was no serious
attempt made to coordinate these groups. Some groups devoted
their energies solely to draft counseling, others to organizing demonstrations either against the government or the church.
The Washington chapter made an effort to influence the American bishops before their fall National Conference in 1966.
The group received most attention when they placed an ad in
The National Catholic Reporter:

                    When is A
                      BISHOPS'
                    meeting a
                      HAPP
                       EN
                      ING?
                    maybe when
              Pentecost first occurred
                  maybe when John
          called a Council maybe when our Bishops
       show they are bothered by the same things we are
       The rightness of continuing massive civilian casulties
       in north and south Vietnam -- the draft -- conscientious
       objectors to unjust wars going to prison -- plans for
       universal training -- laws against showing love of enemy.
       As Christians and Americans these things bother us. We
       ask for some concern, some sharing of our difficulties.
       In the problem of war, we ask that Bishops go as far
       as Paul VI and call for an immediate end of the fighting
       "even at the expense of some inconvenience or loss."[35]

The bishops, however, issued a statement that hedged on the
war, saying it could be justified. They also made no mention
of other war and peace issues in 1966 such as conscientious
objection to particular wars, conscription, or efforts to
provide medical relief to areas of the world labeled "enemy"
by the government.

The New York City CPF issued a statement on the issue
of medical aid in 1967 when The National Catholic Reporter
and the New York Times revealed[36] that the Catholic Relief
Service provided material assistance to members of the South
Vietnamese Popular Forces, yet refused assistance to war
victims in North Vietnam. The CPF asked Catholics in their
statement to withhold contributions to Catholic Relief Services and to send their money to Caritas Internationalis,
the Vatican's relief-coordinating body that provided material
assistance to the North Vietnamese Red Cross as well as
participating in relief efforts in the South. Since Eileen
Egan of PAX worked for Catholic Relief Services, she resented
the embarrassment caused her by Catholic pacifist friends in
the CPF.[37] All of these efforts obtained publicity and gave
visibility to those American Catholics who opposed the war
in Vietnam. The most significant aspect of the CPF was that
it served as a transition period for its founders. Of the
five original founders one was to return full-time to the
Catholic Worker, one was to go to jail for burning his draft
card, and three were to go to jail for destroying draft files.
The act of destroying draft files marked a new departure in
the level of resistance performed by Americans against the
United States government.

During the 1960's a viable Catholic peace movement
existed for the first time in America. Unlike the scattering
of individual Catholics supported only by the Catholic Worker
in World War II, the war in Vietnam brought forth enough

awareness of broad common objectives to justify the use of
the term movement to describe their opposition. The increase
in numbers, level of commitment, and accomplishments describe
a Catholic peace movement in the 1960's that was not on the-
fringe, but was a significant part of the entire American
peace movement.

Three Catholic groups, the Catholic Worker, PAX, and
the CPF formed the backbone of the Catholic peace movement
until 1968. In their attempts to stop the war in Vietnam,
they focused their energies on the draft. Members of the
Catholic Worker, by burning their draft cards, spearheaded
the most extreme individual resistance. The CPF offered the
most personal response by providing draft counseling. And
PAX functioned as a pressure group to secure an institutional
pronouncement by the Catholic Church in support of CO and SCO.

The CAIP, would not oppose the war in Vietnam any
more than it had opposed World War II. Yet, it did support
the right of a Catholic to be a CO or an SCO. The work of
the CAIP and PAX resulted in 1968 in the Catholic Church in
America's official statement of support for CO's and SCO's.

The impact of these events was reflected in the increase
of the number of Catholic conscientious objectors. Although
there are no accurate records of the number of Catholics who
resisted the draft, records do exist for the number of Catholic CO's who received CO classification from the United States
Government. From September, 1967, to November, 1968, 2.8 per
cent of men classified for alternative service as CO's were

Catholic; between November, 1968, and September, 1969, the percentage of Catholic CO's rose to 7.8 per cent.[38] The percentage of Catholics who declared themselves CO's was larger than that of any other single denomination. Thus, the Vietnam years, witnessed large numbers of young Catholics seeking and gaining the CO classification while others went to prison for refusing to register, burning their draft cards, and other forms of activist resistance.

Even more remarkable was the extent to which Catholics who, for reason of sex or age, were not subject to the draft but, nevertheless, found ways to register opposition to the war -- marching and demonstrating; refusing to pay telephone and other taxes; and engaging in overt civil disobedience. Though there is no way to document the extent of Catholic participation in such actions, and it may have represented only a small segment of the total Catholic population, its visibility made it a phenomenon unique in modern Church history.

The obvious failure of the American Catholic peace movement as well as of the entire American peace movement was that by 1968 it had not stopped the escalation of the war in Vietnam. Nor was it successful in extending the government's position on CO to SCO. Other failures on the part of the American Catholic peace movement were that it could not secure a statement from the institutional church that would condemn the war in Vietnam as immoral. Nor could it totally eradicate the fear of communism and the desire for a strong military

defense on the part of most American Catholics. And finally,
it could not develop a new theology of peace sufficiently
adequate to replace the traditional just war ethic.

Despite these failures, large numbers of American
Catholics for the first time in their nation's history joined
with other Americans to protest the policies of their govern-
ment at a time of war. On May 17, 1968, nine Catholics
exhibited a more daring level of commitment to their opposi-
tion by destroying draft files at Catonsville, Maryland.
The action began what was to become known as the Catholic
Left in the American press. Fathers Daniel and Philip
Berrigan provided its leadership and under their direction,
Catholics moved into the vanguard of resistance to the war in
Vietnam.

REFERENCES

[1]"Address of Pope Paul VI to the General Assembly of the United Nations," Catholic Mind, LXIII (November, 1965), 7.

[2]Ibid., 8-9.

[3]Gordon C. Zahn, "The Scandal of Silence," Commonweal, XCV (October 22, 1971), 80. This is an excellent article that evaluates and criticizes the memorandum by the Office for Information of the USCC concerning the position the American hierarchy has taken on the war in Indochina. This section on the hierarchy is based on the memorandum and Zahn's article.

[4]Idem.

[5]Idem.

[6]Idem. The CPF, immediately issued a reprint of the text for sale at 5¢ per copy, since it went to press before the clarification that part is missing.

[7]Idem.

[8]Bishop Shannon's name is never mentioned in the memorandum issued by the USCC.

[9]James Forest, "No longer alone . . . ," p. 147.

[10]Zahn, "The Scandal of Silence," 81.

[11]Ibid., 82. Also, "Human Life in the Family of Nations, Guidelines from the American Bishop's Pastoral," reprint from PAX.

[12]Dorothy Day was asked by the author about Daniel Berrigan and his role in The Catholic Worker. Dorothy replied that she hardly knew Dan. All she knew was that he dedicated a book to her, invited her to speak at LeMoyne College and took all her men away from the Catholic Worker into the peace movement. Interview occurred at a rally at St. Ignatius Church in Baltimore two days before the opening of the trial of the Catonsville Nine, 1969.

238

[13] The Catholic Peace Fellowship, membership pamphlet.

[14] Idem.

[15] Catherine Swann, "Burning a Draft Card," The Catholic Worker, November, 1965. For this section on burning draft cards, most of the factual data is taken from John L. LeBrun who completed his doctoral dissertation in American Studies at Case Western Reserve University. His title is "The Role of the Catholic Worker Movement in American Pacifism, 1933-1972," (unpublished).

[16] Michael Ferber and Staughten Lynd, The Resistance (Boston, 1971), pp. 3-4, 9-10; and Dwight MacDonald, "Why Destroy Draft Cards?" The Catholic Worker, November, 1965.

[17] Edward Forand, "Christie Street," The Catholic Worker, December, 1962.

[18] The New York Times, August 11, 1965, 14 and September 1, 1965, 17.

[19] Tom Cornell, "Life and Death on the Streets of New York," The Catholic Worker, November, 1965; Cornell, "Not the Smallest Grain," in Ferber and Lynd, The Resistance, pp. 39-40. Cornell's statement printed in full as "Why I am Burning My Draft Card," Commonweal, LXXIII (November 19, 1965), 205.

[20] Schlessel, Conscience . . . , "United States v. Miller, District and Circuit Court Decisions, 1965-66," pp. 275-84.

[21] The complete statement was printed in The Catholic Worker, March, 1966. See also Jim Wilson, "Chrystie Street," The Catholic Worker, March, 1966 and The New York Times, January 12, 1966, 8 and March 5, 1966, 21.

[22] "Draft Card Burners Convicted," The Catholic Worker, December, 1966; "CPF Head Found Guilty in Draft Card Case," Fellowship, XXXII (October, 1966), 1; "CPF Head Appeals Six-Month Sentence," Fellowship, XXXIII (February, 1967, 3; and The New York Times, October 25, 1966, 11 and July 19, 1967, 42.

[23] James Forest, "In Time of War," in Delivered into Resistance, ed. The Catonsville Nine-Milwaukee Fourteen Defense Committee, (New Haven, 1969), pp. 5-7. There is no way to document this with accuracy.

239

24U. S. v. Seeger, 380 U. S. 163 (1965).

25For a complete transcript of the report of the
President's Advisory Commission on Selective Service, "In
Pursuit of Equity: Who serves when not all serve?" Washington,
1967, see, "John Courtney Murray, S.J., Collection," located
in the Archives of Woodstock College, New York.

26John Courtney Murray, S.J. Selective Conscientious
Objection, Indiana: Our Sunday Visitor, 1968, 5.

27John A. Rohr, Prophets Without Honor: Public Policy
and the Selective Conscientious Objector (New York, 1971).
Rohr more explicitly than any other writer points out the
limitations of the just-unjust war theory. According to him,
the SCO cannot base his position on the just war theory since
it places all responsibility for war on the state and the
individual bears no responsibility. Therefore, the individual
has no obligation to become a SCO; he is free in conscience
to comply with the state since the just war theory has made
it the decision maker for all individual consciences. He
also considers the three cases which were presented for SCO
before the Supreme Court during the 1970-71 term: Negre V.
Larsen, U. S. v. Gillette, and U. S. v. McFadden. None of
the cases were successful.

28Interview with Patrick McDermott, S.J., June 21, 1971.

29"Catholic Conscience and the Draft," Peace, V (Special
Draft Issue with n.d.), 31. PAX did a brief summary of their
activities in the campaign.

30Idem.

31AMA, "CAIP Collection," Msgr. Higgins made an unsuccessful attempt to secure foundation funding for the CAIP from
1963 to 1965. See letter dated September 27, 1963, Richard
M. Catalano, assistant to Higgins to Mr. Howard G. Kurtz of
the Ford Foundation; Letters dated December 16, 1964, Charles
J. McNeill to William E. Moran, Jr., President of the CAIP
and to Msgr. G. Higgins. There are also letters expressing
discontent with the committees, for example, letter dated
January 15, 1964, Alba Zizzamia to Rev. James L. Vizzard on
the defunct Cultural Relations Committee and letters to Rev.
James L. Vizzard dated November 15, 1963 from William Glade,
November 11, 1963 from Rev. T. J. McDonagh, and (n.d.) from
Charles F. Johnson on dissatisfaction with the Economic Life
Committee.

240

32 Interview with Patrick McDermott, S.J., June 21, 1971.

33 Idem.

34 Forest, "No longer alone . . . ," p. 146.

35 As quoted in Ibid., p. 147.

36 Idem.

37 Interview with James Forest, December 3, 1972.

38 "1970: A Year of Concern for all CO's," The Reporter for Conscience's Sake, XXVII (January, 1970), 2. This coincides with the report dated May 11, 1970 sent to author from the NSBRO which gives the number of Catholic CO's as of February, 1966 as 17, as of November, 1968 as 69, and as of September, 1969 as 175.

CHAPTER VII

THE BERRIGAN BROTHERS AND THE CATHOLIC LEFT

On May 17, 1968, nine men and women entered Local
Board No. 33 at Catonsville, Maryland. The group seized the
Selective Service records and burned them outside the building with napalm. They had manufactured the napalm themselves,
following a recipe in the Special Forces Handbook published
by the United States Government. Within a few minutes the
local police arrived and heard Father Daniel Berrigan, S.J.,
lead his companions in praying the Our Father as a thanks-
giving for the completed action. The police waited until the
end of the prayer, than hand-cuffed the "criminals for peace"
and loaded them into a paddy-wagon. The Catonsville action
symbolized the high point of American Catholic resistance to
the Vietnam War in the 1960's. For Catholic peace activists,
Catonsville signalled a dramatic move to the left in their
resistance to war. After this action, two of the nine participants, Daniel Berrigan and his brother Philip emerged as
the architects of a new political and theological movement.

The American press labelled this movement the Catholic
Left, and used the term consistantly when describing events
related to the Berrigan brothers from Catonsville in 1968 to
the Harrisburg Seven Trial in 1972. The press also estimated
in 1972 that the Catholic Left had grown in size from the

241

Catonsville Nine to several hundred participants and several
thousand sympathizers in a church of 47,000,000 American
Catholics.[1]   The Berrigan Brothers and the Catholic Life
maintained a position of national prominence for the five
year period and represented the vanguard in the American
peace movement's efforts to stop the war in Vietnam.

The draft board raid at Catonsville marked a new
departure in the escalation of resistance on the part of
peace activists because the action was planned in secret and
destroyed government property.[2] The Catonsville Nine claimed
that the raid was a non-violent direct act of civil disobedience which had both secular and religious implications. By
attacking law and property, the bulwarks of a value system
which the participants believed lay at the roots of exploitation, racism, violence and war, they hoped to expose the evils
in the social value system of America. At the same time they
hoped to call the church to heed its message of justice and
peace. The participants dramatized prayer of civil disobedience at Catonsville attacked the false values of America,
especially the Vietnam war, while it proclaimed human life in
a Christian context.[3]

The idea for the destruction of draft files and the
organization of similar actions which would occur after
Catonsville were mainly the work of Philip Berrigan. He was
the organizer of Catonsville and as a peace activist, he was
there. But Philip remained in the background. It was his
brother, Daniel, who emerged as spokesman for the group and

who provided the rationale for such actions. The theological rationale for traditional non-violent resistance had already been articulated by Thomas Merton. But the monk had never left his monastery to participate in any act of non-violent resistance. Even Catholic Workers who had limited their actions to traditional forms of non-violent resistance were not participants at Catonsville, though some of them would follow the example of the Berrigans in subsequent draft board raids. As a writer, a poet, a theologian, and an activist, Daniel Berrigan was able to combine the tradition of the Catholic Worker, the activism of his brother Philip, and the contemplation and writing ability of his friend Merton.[4] Because of his writing and speaking ability, he was able to articulate for the American public a rationale for the action. By conveying sincerity and commitment through his participation, he also brought visibility and a following to the Catonsville action. Thus Daniel, who reconciled the paradoxes of the Catholic peacemaker within his own being, became a symbol of the possibilities and limits of the American Catholic peace movement as it confronted both church and state in resistance to the Vietnam War.

It is difficult to ascertain exactly what led the brothers to take such a daring risk at Catonsville. Some authors attribute it to the authoritarian character of their father or to the authoritarian structure of the Roman Catholic Church and its religious communities; and others attribute it to the "supposed sibling rivalry" between the Berrigan

brothers. Though these all may have contributed, the best
explanation lies in their faith in the Gospel message and
the combination of people and events that influenced their
thought and action. These experiences led them to new
thoughts and actions concerning the church and country they
loved.[5]

Philip was the youngest and Daniel the second youngest
of six sons born to Thomas and Frieda Berrigan. Thomas
Berrigan was a strong-authoritarian Irish Catholic who
enforced a rigid discipline in his home and had no rapport
with his sons. He was a great lover of poetry which he bel-
lowed through the house or silently attempted to write.
Ironically, Tom Berrigan was highly regarded in Syracuse for
his diligent work at the Light Company where he was employed
and for his involvement in social justice concerns in the
community. His home was always open to those who sought
relief, and extras were shared with the community, especially
during the depression years. The mother was the real spirit
in the family. A gentle, fragile, and humble woman of great
faith in God and people, she was able to instill confidence
and hope in her sons as they confronted each new situation.
Dan's position in the family was different from the other
boys; because he was pale and delicate, he helped with the
work inside the house while the stronger boys, like Philip,
did the outside work on their small farm. Daniel Berrigan
and his mother suffered greatly from the physical and psychological strains of the family.[6]

All the Berrigan brothers attended St. John the Baptist
Academy in Syracuse. Except for Daniel, the boys were average
students and participated mainly in sport activities. During
high school, Daniel wrote poetry, acted in plays, and learned
to dance. His enthusiasm for life even led him to become a
cheerleader, for which his brothers relentlessly chided him.
Toward the end of his high school years, Dan applied to the
Society of Jesus for acceptance. At first the Society would
not accept him and told him to go home and improve his Latin.
After a year of study, the rejection was rescinded and he
entered the Society of Jesus on August 14, 1939.

Daniel underwent the thirteen years of Jesuit training
with its emphasis on the intellectual and spiritual life.
The training during that time made no provisions for the
social apostolate except for three years reserved for teaching. Daniel later wrote of the effect the training had on
him:

> We were being asked to accept the truth that
> the past had something to offer living men.
> We could accept the truth, abstractly, but
> we could in fact offer men very little; for
> our theology, was not a living science. It
> was a dead one. . . . It was almost entirely
> an exercise in memory; it ignored living
> questions on principle; its venacular was
> almost as far from man's thought as its Latin;
> it had no urgent need to confront Protestant or
> Jewish traditions, except as opponents. And
> in moral questions, it gave a view of the world
> only as large or liberating as could be gained
> from the upper storeys of a Roman ivory tower.[7]

He went on to say, however, that it did do one thing, "it made
me teacheable." It also seems to have provided him with a

strong foundation of basic values and a sense of direction
which served as a sounding board to evaluate the onslaught
of everything new.

After ordination on June 21, 1952, Daniel went abroad
for his Tertianship. He studied at the Gregorian University
in Rome and at the Maison la Colombière, Paray le Monial in
France. It was during his stay in France that he associated
himself with the Worker Priest Movement. The impact of these
priests would shape the rest of Daniel's life.

The Worker Priest Movement was founded after World
War II under the guiding spirit of Emmanuel J. Cardinal
Suhard, Archbishop of Paris. The horrifying experiences of
Hitler's atrocities and the incredible inhumanity of World
War II in "Christian" Europe, coupled with the moral paralysis
of the churches in face of such a disaster had summoned a few
to a rethinking of the social dimensions of Christianity. The
Worker Priests rejected the Enlightenment notion that religion
was a personal private matter and emphasized an involvement
in temperal and social spheres. Their political philosophy
was largely Socialistic and anti-colonial. Association with
these men brought Dan into contact with the writings of progressive European theologians -- Dietrich Bonhoeffer, Henri
de Lubac, Yves Congar, and later with Teilhard de Chardin.
These contacts were to be among the most important influences
on Daniel Berrigan's later writings and actions. The French
underground experiences of some of the Worker Priests as
German prisoners affected Berrigan's theories of civil

disobedience; the progressive theologians' concepts of
Christianity demanding social involvement confirmed his
call to public action, and Teilhard de Chardin's optimistic
view of history would contribute to the eschatological
dimension that he would attribute to such actions as Catonsville.[8]

After returning from Europe in 1954, Daniel Berrigan
was assigned to teach high school boys at Brooklyn Preparatory.
His extracurricular interest in these years centered on combating poverty. He first began working with Puerto Ricans
in lower Manhattan and later became chaplain for the Young
Christian Workers, a Catholic group of high school students
involved in social justice concerns. In 1967, he was assigned
to teach theology at LeMoyne University in Syracuse. Besides
teaching theology and English, he continued his social
justice involvement by moderating a Professional Sodality,
a group of middle and upper class adults whose social action
he directed toward housing for the poor and interracial work
in the community. He also established an International House
on campus after President John F. Kennedy announced his Peace
Corps and Alliance for Progress. It was such projects which
brought Daniel Berrigan into a close working relationship with
his brother, Philip. This personal relationship would grow
during the years and be the most significant and sustaining
influence on both men. It would ultimately produce Catonsville and the Catholic Left.[9]

Upon graduation from high school, Philip worked for a
year scouring soot-caked locomotives at the New York Central
Yards to earn college money. He spent a semester at St.
Michael's College in Toronto before he was drafted in 1943.
The army served as the first major influence on Philip's life.
He underwent field artillery training in the Deep South --
Georgia, Florida, and North Carolina. Here he saw black
poverty and second class citizenship. Philip's own account
of his army career was written in a brief paragraph to the
religious community he later entered.

> Went overseas with a field artillery unit as
> a sargeant. While in Germany volunteered for
> officer's training in the infantry in the
> futile and foolish hope of seeing some action.
> By the time I was commissioned, the war had ended.[10]

Philip rarely speaks of his experience in the army and when
asked directly replies briefly or mentions some account of
racial discrimination he encountered. He was discharged in
1946 and enrolled at Holy Cross College in Worcester, Massachusetts, where he completed his B.A. degree on the G.I. Bill
of Rights. Upon graduation in 1950, he entered the Josephite
Fathers whose apostolate is service to the Negro. The third
youngest Berrigan son, Jerome, had already entered the same
community. Until Jerry left the community in 1957, Philip
had been closest to this brother. Philip entered the Society
of Saint Joseph because of their apostolate to the blacks and
his own identification with these people, because their period
of preparation for ordination was briefer than that of the

Jesuits, and perhaps most importantly, because his brother
Jerry was already a member of this society. When Jerry left
the Society of Saint Joseph just before ordination, he
married and built a home in Syracuse and adopted four children. In Syracuse Jerry continued to help the Negro by joining
the Catholic Interracial Council and worked with his brother,
Daniel, in the Professional Sodality. Philip continued his
studies and was ordained a priest in 1955. From 1956 until
1963, he taught in an all black high school, St. Augustine
in New Orleans. It was during these years that Phil and Dan
grew closer together as they shared ideas and activities concerning their students, and increased their involvement in
the Civil Rights Movement and the Liturgical Movement.

Philip Berrigan spent these years in New Orleans not
only in the classroom, but also in outdoor work, maintaining
the physical plant of the high school and repairing homes in
the black community. He spent hours of his free time organizing drives for clothes, food, and housing for the black
community. Obtaining first class citizenship for the black
people was his top priority. He often read and clipped
articles on current events in order to keep abreast of changes
in the Church and in American society. These years cannot be
underestimated in their impact on him as he moved from administering corporal works of mercy to the black community to
searching for ways to empower the black community to achieve
its own goals.[11] "Phil," as his friend James Forest has
written, "looks like an ad for a wheaties boxtop -- a Mr. All-

American." During these years he was known as a man's man,
courageous, strong, direct, fearless, and a man who constantly
confronted injustice. Thus, Philip Berrigan spent all his
time during these years teaching and working in the social
justice movement for black equality in the South. Daniel
Berrigan often sent his LeMoyne students to his brother's
high school to work in summer projects for the poor blacks
and aided him in securing college scholarships for the most
able black students.

There is no doubt that the general climate of evolving
social protext, especially the Civil Rights Movement, had an
influence on the Berrigan brothers, as on many thinking
Americans. The various church-related social action groups
had the greatest impact, especially the Southern Christian
Leadership Conference under the direction of Dr. Martin
Luther King. This group gave non-violent direct action and
civil disobedience a new dignity by the courage of a conscientious few in the midst of growing awareness of the urgent
need for massive social change.

Spurred on by such actions for social justice, the
Berrigan brothers confronted the question of civil disobedience for the first time in the summer of 1961. Along with
Richard Wagner, another Josephite priest, they decided to
participate in the Freedom Ride in Mississippi led by James
Farmer. For the first and last time they asked their religious
superiors for permission to follow their conscience in an act
of civil disobedience. Daniel Berrigan could not obtain

permission, but Philip Berrigan and Richard Wagner received affirmation from their religious Superior General, Father George O'Dea. The two priests got as far as Atlanta, Georgia, where a phone call prevented them from reaching Mississippi. CORE had released their names to the press two hours before their scheduled arrival. This exploitation of the priests' presence resulted in the Bishop of Jackson, the Most Reverend Richard Gerow, demanding the removal of the two priests from his diocese.[12] Obeying their religious superiors, the priests did not participate; but the experience left them no less convinced of the value and need for priests also to give such witness. Since civil disobedience was a matter of individual conscience, the priests never again asked their religious superiors for permission to follow their own consciences. Civil disobedience as a form of social protest would be applied by the Berrigan brothers without hesitation in the future.

It was also during the period of the late fifties and early sixties that the Berrigan brothers experienced the changes occurring in the Church. Prior to the Second Vatican Council, the new emphasis on the emerging layman and the Liturgical Movement occurred. It would be Daniel Berrigan who would rise to national prominence in the Liturgical Movement. Ironically, it was Philip Berrigan and not his brother who had first published a significant article on the topic in Worship magazine.[13] He lost interest in the Liturgical Movement, however, because he did not find it as important as the cause of social justice. He continued to devote his attention to the black community.

Liturgy, on the other hand, influenced Daniel Berrigan greatly and helped him to develop a stronger theological basis for his social involvement. At LeMoyne this enthusiasm for liturgy was reflected in the chapel he and his family built in the new International House on campus. The austere lines of the table altar and the stone floor were designed to emphasize the celebrant which in Berrigan's case sometimes led to excessive proportions of aesthetic and symbolic gestures. The significance of the Liturgical Movement resided in its new emphasis on the Paschal Mystery as an on-going reality at work in the lives of men and in their efforts to develop a new world. The sacraments, especially the Eucharist, were not merely a remembrance of God's past activity in Christ, but of God at work in Christ's new body, the community of discipleship, transforming the believing community and through them the world. Along with all of this was the liturgical movement's emphasis on salvation-history theology -- that in Jesus Christ the Kingdom was begun, and now history, through the actions of men, moved toward the fullness of the Kingdom of the day of love and justice and peace. It was this new emphasis that Daniel Berrigan used to explain the motivation behind acts of non-violent resistance. He extended the theology outward and not inward on a worshipping community. Thus, Berrigan used these theological emphases of the Liturgical Movement to move him toward more radical social

and political action. By acting with other persons in community against the evils of social injustice and eventually
against the evil of the war in Vietnam and his government
which perpetrated them and his church which was used to
sanction such evils, he believed that he was moving history
through such action toward the fullness of the Kingdom -- the
day of love and justice and peace.[14]

The ecumenical movement also beginning during this
period served to build an increased solidarity among men who
also held similar convictions about theology and action being
combined to fulfill the Kingdom. During the early sixties
at Mount Saviour Monastery, Daniel Berrigan along with Rev.
John Heidbrink, the Director of Church Relations for the
Fellowship of Reconciliation (FOR), led Roman Catholic and
Protestant retreats for clerics. It was this ecumenical
probing and inquiry which established their friendship. John
Heidbrink did help to liberate Berrigan in the area of ecumenical relations. Heidbrink would often accuse him of legalism
in the liturgy and of holding the Apostle Paul in such
reverence that he became the fourth member of the Trinity.
He also introduced him to FOR. Berrigan joined FOR in late
1962 and later, it provided him financial assistance for the
founding of a new Catholic peace organization. Heidbrink
wrote in a letter of the kind of changes Daniel Berrigan was
undergoing in the early sixties:

> Dan was, in the early sixties, a thorough-going
> artist with a sensitivity for the senuous which
> shocked me at times. He was moving into a Hebrew

> (biblical) grasp of reality in a unified
> matter-spirit unity. This was before the
> Teilhard manuscripts were released. But Dan
> sensed the organic relationship of matter
> and spirit and would begin soon his efforts to
> unite these substances so long divided. . . .
> Dan's ecclesiology underwent a massive change
> and it was then that his often bold and angry
> iconoclasm began and took such radical forms.[15]

These years at LeMoyne were also very productive
literarily for him and reflected the changes in his thought
concerning theology and social involvement. Berrigan became
most widely known during this period for his poetry; two books
were published, Time Without Number and Encounters. His first
prose work, The Bride: Essays in the Church reflected his
competence as a biblical scholar and liturgist. In these
writings he was concerned with exploring nature, the Church,
suffering, grace, sin, and the sacraments. His Thomism,
legalism, and his views about the dichotomy between the
spiritual and the natural were quite evident, especially in
his defense of the statement "there is no salvation outside
the Church" in The Bride. In later years, Dan referred to
The Bride as a "sin of his past."[16]

By 1961, however, in his prose work, The Bow in the
Clouds and especially in his book of poetry, The World For A
Wedding Ring, all dichotomy disappeared and the wedding of
the sacred and profane was finally achieved. Significantly,
this last book of poetry was dedicated to three Catholic
social activists: Tony Walsh, Dorothy Day, and Karl Meyer.
Suffering was no longer a spiritual agon for Dan, but a moment

of intense anxiety and ultimate rebirth. He found Christ in all nature and in the universe. He began to see the Church as a part of a larger movement to serve the world. He saw the realities behind the symbols which the Church had betrayed for the sake of acceptance and status. He also altered his view of authority and began to stress service. In his next book, They Call Us Dead Men, Dan attempted to place man in a concrete context of social involvement. From this book man emerges as a sacrament when he serves his brother and sister in need and the world. All issues are viewed as religious issues.

At this time he was also publishing in Worship, Critic, Perspectives, and Today. His topics ranged from sacred art, to the Christian and his times, to the role of the Church, to freedom, and to non-violence. The emphasis in all the writing was on man reaching the fullness of his humanity by consciously confronting things as they really are and trying to change them.

Many of the changes reflected in Dan's writing were the result of the knowledge he had gained while trying to serve the needs in the social apostolate. But even more important, he was observing, listening, and questioning every person and event that passed before him. He had a series of way stations that provided him these contacts. He maintained his relationship with Tony Walsh at the Benedict Labre House for the poor in Canada,[17] he would stop by the Catholic Worker, he would either make or give retreats at Mount Saviour Monastery in

Pine City, New York, and visit or address the Association
for International Development (AID) in Paterson, New Jersey.

The years at LeMoyne, however, also supplied negative
influences. Dan experienced increasing opposition from
influential people in the Syracuse community because of his
activities in Civil Rights. He was disappointed and angry
when the Jesuit censors refused to sanction publication of a
book he and his brother, Philip, had collaborated on. The
reason given was that Philip Berrigan's writing was too
secular, too hard hitting, and too radical on issues such as
civil rights.[18] Despite the anger, Daniel Berrigan accepted
the Jesuit censorship of Philip's writing. As a result,
Daniel wrote his own book, They Call Us Dead Men, and Philip
published his work, No More Strangers. Also, and perhaps
most difficult to bear, was the inhuman action and constant
opposition Dan received from his rector the last two years
at LeMoyne. In 1964 Dan explained this situation to his
provincial while he was on visitation at LeMoyne and asked
for a sabbatical. The request was immediately granted.

By 1964, both Berrigan brothers had begun to increase
their involvement in the issue of peace, especially opposition to the War in Vietnam. One reason for this increase of
concern was Pope John XXIII's encyclical, Pacem in Terris and
the Second Vatican Council's reiteration of Pope John XXIII's
social orientation. The Church at the time of the Council was
emphasizing that the church is a pilgrim people whose primary
task is the transformation of the social order in light of

the Gospel message. The Berrigans took this teaching of the
church seriously and sought ways or actions that symbolized
Christians' ability to break-out of their privatized spirituality and involve themselves with the great social and
political question facing collective mankind.

By 1963, Philip had become increasingly aware of the
issue of peace. He began to see the War in Vietnam as
diverting the energies of the American people and government
from the struggle for civil rights. He was also impatient
and dissatisfied with his effectiveness in the civil rights
movement while working out of a high school in New Orleans.
The increased emphasis on black separatism and militancy also
influenced his thoughts that he might do more not only for
civil rights but for his country as a whole if he devoted
his energies to trying to stop the War in Vietnam. Unsure
of his feelings and not desiring to leave the struggle for
civil rights, he first accepted an assignment as a fund
raiser for his religious community in New York City. During
this time he arranged for a consulting firm to study the
Josephite community and submit recommendations on how the
order could better fulfill its mission of service to the
black community. The consultants proposed that two million
dollars be raised to enable the Josephites to play a more prominent role in the fast developing civil rights revolution. But
the order's ruling council rejected the proposal, a setback that
finally convinced Berrigan that he could best accomplish his
goals on the edge of his community rather than try to change

the organization of the religious community itself.[19] While
fund raising he was also serving as a consultant to priests
in Harlem who had not yet freed themselves from an attitude
of protectors of the blacks. He was also often working with
John Grady, whose house became the center of many Berrigan
meetings.[20] In March, 1964, Philip Berrigan was assigned to
teach at Ephiphany Apostolic College in Newburgh. He left in
April, 1965, because the rightest community had harrassed
the seminary for maintaining him on its staff. They objected
to his positions and activities in civil rights and peace.
Philip Berrigan was assigned to a black parish in Baltimore,
St. Peter Claver. Greatly upset by the fact that his religious
superiors had acquiesed to the pressures of the people in
Newburgh, Philip called his brother Daniel to drive to
Baltimore with him so they could talk. It was at that time
that they made a solemn agreement that regardless of the
actions of the Church against them, they would not leave the
priesthood of their own volition.[21]

Prior to Philip's transfer to Baltimore, Daniel had
been revisiting France and other parts of Europe. While in
France during 1964, Daniel Berrigan was again affected by the
Worker Priest Movement and was overwhelmed by the changes in
it. The question of relevance began to loom large in his
thinking. The Worker Priests taught him that relevance needed
to be rooted in being brother to the world -- to serving those
in need. This was also the time when the memory of France's
involvement in Vietnam and Algeria still served as a depressant.

The Church's role had been mixed, but Berrigan soon learned that all respected European Catholics were pacifists and heavy supporters of the Fellowship of Reconciliation(FOR). After his stay in France he concluded that the Church in America was not really Christian for it often put him in a position of either choosing for the Church or for humanity. "From time to time, it is asked of man to choose between obedience on the one hand, and fidelity to the poor, or the Negro, or the workers, or the Algerians, or the Jews, or a hundred other actual men and situations," he wrote. "But I know, too, that Christ is in His Church; even though silenced, or put to shame, or drowned out by cynicism or politics or cowardice."[22]

More aware than ever of the issues of war and peace, Dan was asked by the FOR to join with twenty other Protestants and Catholics in a new experiment in peripatetic ecumenism through the Socialist Countries. These men were together for most of the summer of 1964. The tour included visits to Prague, Hungary, and the USSR. While in Prague, they attended the All Christian Peace Conference. Before leaving the Socialist countries, the FOR group decided on a series of resolves. The first and most significant was the "necessity of doing our own part in the peace movement in our churches at home." Another stressed the need for "imaginative and prophetic work at home."[23]

The time abroad had also included a visit to the Iona Island off the coast of Scotland and a trip to South Africa.

These experiences helped develop Daniel Berrigan's ideas on the Church and man and provided him with a new visition of America and its role in the world. He also felt that the times had changed enough to permit his ideas a possible area of implementation. He felt that the Vatican Council had stressed the need to remove the Church from the power system and according to Schema 13 encouraged the Christian to see the Church's issues as synonymous with man's and to start serving the world by applying the Beatitudes literally. Also the pressure of world conscience was upon the Church, allowing her to remove herself from methods of repression and coercion as evidenced in the Vatican II document on "Freedom of Conscience." This new vision of America and its role in the world would be applied to the war in Vietnam as it continued to be escalated.[24]

In September, 1965, Dan returned to the United States to serve as assistant editor of _Jesuit Missions_ magazine with its headquarters in New York. He again frequented Mount Saviour, AID, the Catholic Worker; but as a new man fortified by the European experience. The question now paramount in his mind was what should he do in face of the war. Already a member of FOR and with a group of Catholic Workers formed around him, recruited by his brother Philip, he conceived the idea of the Catholic Peace Fellowship (CPF) which in reality was an extension of FOR into an explicitly Catholic community. Dan and John Heidbrink worked out the structures of the CPF and raised enough money for the salary of the first director,

James Forest. Forest had been discharged from the Navy as a conscientious objector after two years of service, had served at St. Joseph's house of Hospitality on the Bowery in New York and was the managing editor of The Catholic Worker while also working for Liberation. Convinced by Philip Berrigan to assume the directorship of the CPF, he and Philip Berrigan along with Martin Corbin became the national co-chairmen.[25] Daniel Berrigan together with Dorothy Day, Archbishop Thomas Roberts, Thomas Merton, and a few others served as national sponsors.

Involvement in the peace issue did not mean the end of other participation. In March, 1965, both Berrigan brothers joined the Civil Rights group in Selma. They also continued their priestly functions of celebrating liturgy and counseling those with personal problems, but most of their energies were spent in working for peace, and developing the CPF. Both brothers spent as much time as possible writing and speaking on peace. While Daniel Berrigan was the best known nationally, Philip spent more time in the actual running of the CPF. Both men contributed most of what they earned on the road to the CPF,[26] and it in turn provided a community of conscience for them as for all the men involved. Who was influencing whom at this time is difficult to measure. Jim Forest and Tom Cornell both felt that they had contributed significantly toward Daniel Berrigan's becoming a full-blown activist. Certainly Philip Berrigan always was an activist.[27] In any event, Daniel was beyond the activism of these men as they all attest, for his action was always rooted in the theological, and his vision of the dimensions of each action went beyond history and gave the peace movement a prophetic eschatological quality.

In October, 1964 a number of clergymen felt compelled to protest the charges which had been lodged against dissenters, particularly against the young people opposed to the draft. About twenty clergymen of the New York area called a press conference. It was Rabbi Abraham Heschel who gave the most definitive assurances to the press when they were asked about continuing activities. So in a sense it might be said that he conceived the idea of forming an organization known as Clergy Concerned About Vietnam (CCAV). The group caucused on the question that afternoon and Rabbi Abraham Heschel, Father Daniel Berrigan, and Reverend Richard John Neuhause were chosen co-chairmen. The national CCAV group (later changed to CLCAV to include laymen) was not formed until January, 1966. Berrigan was actively engaged in planning and organization until he was sent on his Latin American journey. The CCAV held three or four meetings a month and held an "action" a month in New York City. These actions included public meetings, fasts, and beg-ins to protest the war in Vietnam.[28]

In March of 1965, after President Lyndon B. Johnson took a crucial escalatory step, ordering retaliatory strikes against North Vietnam, Philip and Daniel Berrigan were the only American Catholic priests to promise total "non-cooperation" with the nation's Vietnam policies by signing a "Declaration of Conscience." The statement advocated draft resistance. Among other signers were Dr. Martin Luther King and Bayard Rustin from the civil rights movement and Dr. Benjamin Spock from the peace movement. The repercussions of the act came in October, 1965, when David Miller, a former student of Dan's at LeMoyne and a member of the CPF burned his draft card after passage of the law that made such an act a felony. On November 6, 1965, Thomas Cornell, co-chairman of the CPF along with four other members of the American peace movement also burned their draft cards. The actions of these men, especially the Catholic Workers and CPF, Miller and Cornell, weighed heavily on the consciences of the Berrigan brothers. These men were risking so much and even going to jail for peace -- what were they as priests doing for peace?

In November, 1965, Daniel faced a crisis within the Society of Jesus just as Philip had previously met such a crisis at Newburgh -- the only difference was that the disciplinary action taken against Dan was to be more severe. It was not only to mean a transfer, but literally an exile to South America to silence him on the peace issue in the United States. Because of the contradictions in accounts in the New York Times, the National Catholic Reporter, and America, it was evident that there was a lot of two-facedness on the part of the Church authorities concerned. At the same time Dan received his news, two other Jesuit priests, Francis Keating and Daniel Kilfoyle of St. Peters College in New

Jersey were also silenced in their activities in the peace
movement. All three men agree that the best reporting was
done by John Leo from the National Catholic Reporter.[29] In
essence Dan was sent to Latin America as a result of pressure
and intervention by the New York chancery office.

On December 5, 1965, a New York Times ad appeared
entitled an "Open Letter to the Authorities of the Archdiocese
of New York and the Jesuit Community in New York." The ad
was financed by an ad hoc organization, the Institute for
Freedom in the Church, composed of lay Catholics who protest,
Dan said, "if someone gets kicked around." Without this public
protest and display of united effort for a man's freedom of
conscience within the Church, Dan would probably never have
been permitted to return to New York and to continue his peace
activities. The authorities of the Church could not silence
the conscience of Daniel Berrigan and never again would they
attempt to silence or discipline the Berrigan brothers in their
quest for peace. This would not be true, however, of the
government of the United States.

The exile in Latin America lasted three months. While
there Berrigan wrote Consequences, Truth and . . . in which he
presented the Church at the edge of new opportunities. To be
successful, he contended, the Church must be a revolutionary
force in society by rejecting power and prestige and chosing
to serve all of mankind by making institutions more human.
The exile served only to radicalize the thought process within
him and to intensify his commitment to peace. After Berrigan's

return he participated in many peace actions all over the
country, but especially in New York City. On March 30, 1966,
he participated in the Interfaith Peace March which included
a Prayer Service at St. Patrick's Cathedral in New York City.
On July 4, 1966, he spoke of the need to stop the bombing and
to begin negotiations with all parties of over 150 peace
groups that had assembled on 35th Street. However, by June,
1966, he was working mainly out of the CPF -- partly because
of his individual style and also because other organizations
such as CLCAV were too bureaucratic and would not move beyond
rhetoric.

Since April 24, 1965, Philip Berrigan had spent his
time working for housing for the blacks and for peace while
stationed at St. Peter Claver in Baltimore. In a desire to
escalate their resistance to the Vietnam War, Philip Berrigan
along with Robert Alpern, Thomas Lewis, Harry Trabold, and
James Harney formed the nucleus of a small peace group. This
group flourished and Bob Alpern became the director of SANE
in Baltimore. They first organized and practiced civil
disobedience on several occasions at Fort Myers, Virginia,
where most of the Joint Chiefs of Staff resided, but according to Berrigan there were no arrests because too many clergy
were present. In the summer of 1967, Philip Berrigan returned
to New York City to finish his second book, <u>A Punishment for
Peace</u> and in September he went back to Baltimore to seek a
more effective tactic to stop the war. The idea of bombing
draft boards was first contemplated by the small Baltimore

peace group but it was regarded as too violent. As members
of the white middle-class society they maintained that they
had no right to resort to violence; other options were still
open to them. Finally, Philip Hirchkopf, a Virginia lawyer
and head attorney for the Pentagon March in October came up
with the Post Christian Era symbolism of pouring blood on
the draft files.[30] Philip Berrigan along with three other
men from his Baltimore peace community readied themselves
for the action of pouring blood on 1-A draft files. Daniel,
of course, was told of the proposed action at the Custom's
House in Baltimore, but he did not feel free to join.[31]

While Philip Berrigan was busy through 1966 and 1967
in Baltimore attempting to form a small community of men who
desired to escalate the level of resistance to the war in
Vietnam, Daniel was continuing not only his peace activities
but also his writing. His poetry received increasing attention and criticism because it was said to have lost its
universal quality by alliance with a particular ideology.
Even No One Walks Waters was criticized in this manner by the
New York Times. His most unique book, Love, Love at the End,
a collection of poems, fables, and prayers received the
severest criticism because of its obscurity. He also was
finding difficulty locating a place for himself within the
Jesuit community. In September, 1967, Daniel Berrigan accepted
the offer to become the Associate Director for Service on the
Cornell United Religious Work staff. By this time Berrigan
felt that the contribution he could make to the specifically

Catholic structure was pretty well ended. In an article,
"Berrigan at Cornell" he explained his decision and went on
to state that the times called for Catholics to integrate
and reform themselves and make their values amenable to those
who were passionately interested in entering communion with
the Catholic tradition, and that mankind was in desperate
need of such resources. Yet, he also contended that the
Church and society were almost at the dead end of their
resources and that moral man would only take on an understanding of himself through the poet, the sacrificial student,
the Negro, and the inner-city community. This alone according to Berrigan would provide the humanness to which the
Gospel offers its widest options.[32]

His life at Cornell was associated with all and closed
to no one. His student contact was as wide and diverse as
the people at the university. He worked in the resistance
movement and still functioned within the CPF. Here again he
assumed the role of teacher with courses in modern drama and
the New Testament.

In October, 1967, Daniel Berrigan attended the March
on the Pentagon with the Cornell contingent. At midnight,
October 22, he was arrested at the Pentagon for a misdemeanor
for "refusing to move on when told" and was placed in jail
for the first time. In his "Letter from Three Jails" he
wrote that two reflections occurred to him: "1. Why was I so
long retarded from so crucially formative a happening? 2.
What's the big joke, You there?" On Friday, October 27, just

after his release, he heard a radio report of the arrest of his brother, Philip, and three others, for pouring blood on selective service files in Baltimore.

In February, 1968, Dave Dellinger of _Liberation_ called on Daniel Berrigan and Howard Zinn as representatives of the resistance in America to go to Hanoi to obtain the release of three war prisoners: Captain John D. Block, Major Norris M. Overly, and Ensign David P. Matheny. It was again time for Berrigan to witness the horrendous sights of poverty and death. But this time more trauma would result because he would be under the fire of his own country's bombs and witness the war atrocities caused by his fellow countrymen. He was to label Vietnam as the "land of burning children," a recurring theme to be used by the Catholic Left. As Berrigan reflected on why he had had this experience he wrote: "I do not as yet know what its import is but I shortly will. . . . To have seen the truth has its price attached."[33]

When Berrigan returned home he attended the trial of his brother, Philip, and wrote "My Brother, the Witness."[34] The trial resulted in a conviction of Philip Berrigan and the three others who had joined him. The trial was not widely publicized and Philip's testimony at the trial was direct, simple, and hard-hitting. There was no drama. Philip Berrigan just laid things out as he saw them. By Easter of 1968, he and Tom Lewis were planning a second action drawing on their experience from the October event. Philip Berrigan was doing most of the contact work, approaching people at Cornell, in

Mobile, in Boston, and in New York City. David Darst was
the contact in St. Louis and George Mische was instrumental
in getting the Melvilles into it. The idea of napalm came
from Tom Lewis and Philip Berrigan who saw first-hand that
the people did not perceive the symbol of blood-post-Christian
era, but were convinced that they could not miss the one of
napalm. It was Philip Berrigan's and Tom Lewis' courage and
constant reaffirmation of their presence in the action and of
the price they would have to pay that strengthened the wills
of the others. Daniel decided to be a part of the action
five days before the event occurred.[35] Even the night before,
however, he was still hesitant and informed his family that
if he did not call by ten in the morning, it meant that he
had decided to act. The final decision was an extremely
difficult one for Daniel Berrigan to make.

Many factors came into the final decision. For years
he had lived with the peace movement. He had tried every
legitimate means to bring about peace. His friends and followers had even been jailed with no cleric going with them.
He had written books and lectured widely on peace and as he
told his friend, Paul Mayer, "They slap me on the back and
tell me how great I am and nothing happens."[36] All of these
things were also true of his brother Philip, he realized, as
he attempted to make his decision. Daniel Berrigan had also
traveled around the world and had seen poverty and suffering
of the majority of men and could not help but compare it to
the affluence of America and America's erroneous foreign

policy. Though his brother Philip had been limited mainly
to sights of poverty in America especially black poverty,
Daniel knew that he had come to the same conclusions. Next,
Daniel Berrigan carried the Society of Jesus with him in his
every action. This was an extremely significant factor, for
relations with the Jesuits had become increasingly tenuous as
his actions for peace escalated. Yet, his brother had similar
experiences with the Josephites though they were a less
prestigous religious community. Finally, on the eve of the
Catonsville action, Philip and Daniel spent the night discussing the pros and cons of the action. With Philip's
emphasis on the practical and political and Daniel's emphasis
on the ideal and spiritual, it was a soul-searching event for
both brothers. The end result was that Daniel Berrigan joined
Philip and the seven others the next morning at Catonsville.
After the arrests, the nine were released, each on $2,500
bail. While awaiting the trial on October 7, 1968, the nine
began an extensive speaking tour to explain the reason for
Catonsville.

Ironically, the Jesuits did not evict Daniel Berrigan
from the community as a result of Catonsville. Rather, a
movement began among the rank and file to support him. The
Jesuits used the theme: "Our Brother Is In Need," and
stressed the right of freedom of conscience. The week the
trial began the Jesuit church and hall of St. Ignatius Parish
in Baltimore was used as the gathering place for the nine.
Religious services and rallies were held. Peace activists

from all over the United States came to participate in a public demonstration parade to protest the trial of the Catonsville Nine. The trial proceeded for three days during which time the defendants admitted that they had napalmed the files. Just before the verdict was returned, Federal Judge Roszel C. Thomsen engaged in a rather informal discourse with the Catonsville Nine. It seemed to be painful for the judge to arraign people whose intensity of moral passion and accumulated years of service to their fellowmen rendered them anything but "convicted felons." After all was said, Daniel Berrigan ended the trial the way he had ended the action at Catonsville by praying the Our Father.

The action and the trial of the Catonsville Nine left no doubt to many observers that their moral commitment to peace was so great it had called them forth to this ultra form of civil disobedience. Their moral commitment revealed to the public that they believed civil disobedience was now normative for those who seek to follow Christ. It was normative because the evils in America had become so great: the illegality and immorality of the war in Vietnam and its extension into the judicial system especially, and every aspect of American life necessitated such a response from a moral person. Through civil disobedience these people sought to overhaul the inefficient, cumbersome, and corrupt governmental machinery and its archaic policies of war, racism, and exploitation. Despite their moral plea, a verdict of guilty was returned against each defendant on each of three counts: destruction

of U. S. property, destruction of Selective Service records,
and interference with the Selective Service Act of 1967. The
convicted proceeded to appeal the decision.[37]

The action itself had been an open and peaceful violation of the law done in obedience to their conscience. It
was a so-called "stand-by" action where people openly remained
awaiting arrest. It was done because they believed their
moral witness would help society to change an unjust law, the
Selective Service Act of 1967 and an immoral policy, the War
in Vietnam. These protestors emulated Gandhi, Thoreau, and
Martin Luther King and other apostles of civil disobedience
who were prepared to go to jail for violating the law, even
though they thought the law was unjust.

Soon after Catonsville similar draft board actions
occurred in Milwaukee and Chicago, cities with traditionally
strong centers of the Catholic Worker from which participants
could easily be recruited. These actions were also stand-by
actions. Participants of draft board actions became known in
the press as members of the "Catholic Left" or the "Catholic
Resistance." These individuals prided themselves on individual acts of conscience and while they admired the Berrigans,
they considered neither them nor anyone else to be their
leaders per se.

At the time Catonsville occurred, publicity reached a
high point and focused on the Berrigan brothers. "Support
groups" surrounding the nine began to flourish and a defense
committee to raise funds for the trial was also formed.

Basically, the nine, the support groups, and the defense
committee began to promote itself as a Christian community.
It was a fragile group of volunteers who based their community on love and trust and advocated civil disobedience as
the form of protest against the war in Vietnam. Initiation
into the inner core of the community was an act of civil disobedience at a draft board. The action was meant to symbolize
their unwillingness to allow or permit the uncritical adaptation of Christianity to the society in which they lived.
Consequently, the emphasis was on Christianity's conflict
with the present war-making policy of their country.

In 1969 the Catholic Left underwent significant changes.
First, a group calling themselves the D.C. -- Nine raided the
Dow Chemical office in the nation's capital. This attack on
a corporation broadened the targets of the movement to include
corporations that produced war materials such as napalm for
use in the Vietnam War. Second, the members of the New York
Eight draft board group did not stand-by and await arrest
after their action. This group destroyed the draft files at
night and later "surfaced." The choice of a night tactic was
first used by the New York group to avoid any possible harm
to individuals in the Selective Service office at the time of
the raid. The New York Eight's tactics of "surfacing" consisted of calling a press conference and at it Reverend Neil
McLaughlin read a statement signed by the eight which claimed
moral responsibility for the draft board action.[38] Surprisingly
to the participants, no arrest followed. The reason was lack
of evidence.

This tact of "night actions" and "surfacing" was
adopted by subsequent groups, for example, the Boston Eight,
the Beaver Fifty-five, the East Coast Conspiracy to Save
Lives, the Flower City Conspiracy, and the Camden Twenty-eight.
The exact number of draft board actions to occur between
Philip Berrigan's first draft board raid at the Custom's
House in Baltimore on October 27, 1967, to the Camden Twenty-
eight action on August 22, 1971, is unknown. Theodore Glick,
a draft resister and participant in the East Coast Conspiracy
to Save Lives and the Flower City Conspiracy, and indicted
conspirator in the Harrisburg Trial, has estimated that over
250 draft board actions occurred during the time period.[39]

Besides the development of the night tactic for draft
board raids and raids on corporations one other raid of
significance occurred during the time period -- a raid on the
files of the FBI office in Media, Pennsylvania. This was a
night action, but no one ever surfaced to assume moral responsibility.[40]

As the number of actions increased and the members of
the resistance became more diverse, the term "Catholic Left"
began to lose its denominational significance. Many non-
Catholics joined the movement and did so from humanitarian
and political motivation. Change from the more traditional
stand-by action of civil disobedience to night actions and
surfacing signalled another departure in the Catholic Left.
Both represented a decline in emphasis on Christian witness
and symbolic action and a greater desire for political effectiveness.

The man who attempted to build this community of
resistance and to organize future draft board actions was not
Daniel Berrigan but his brother Philip. After Catonsville,
Daniel Berrigan returned to Cornell to resume his teaching
duties and to write and speak on behalf of the peace movement.
Philip Berrigan on the other hand, relieved of any specific
duty by his religious superior, resided at the Josephite
Provincialate in Baltimore. From this point of official
residence he spent most of his time traveling in hopes of
locating people who sympathized with the draft board action
and would be possible recruits for future actions. Philip
Berrigan believed the draft board community was too elitist
and wanted to widen it, but the lack of developing any tactic
beyond draft board and corporation raids limited the possibility. Catholicism and the Church were central to Philip
Berrigan's personal motivation for action, but he didn't make
this motivation a pre-requisite for participation. The only
requirement that he had was that participants shared his
political analysis and wanted to stop the war in Vietnam
through non-violent direct acts of civil disobedience. With
"night actions" and "surfacing" even the degree of risk and
assumption of personal responsibility was lessened as a prerequisite -- there was now a possibility that one would not
have to go to jail. The technique used by Berrigan for
building such a community of resistance was called a retreat,
one or more weekends to discover whether or not an individual
would engage in such an action. Philip Berrigan served as a

benevolent facilitator and counselor, being sure that people
of like-mind were brought together, that people's needs were
taken care of and that precautions and planning had been
carried out in full. The decision to act and the actual plans
of the action were worked out by the members themselves in
the group they had formed. Thus, technically, Philip Berrigan
was not the leader and not a participant in each action which
occurred.[41]

The switch to night actions and surfacing also reflected
a change in attitude concerning arrest and jail. Some members
were no longer willing to await arrest and go to jail for an
action they believed to be morally correct while the draft
and complicity of corporations continued unhampered in its
perpetuation of an immoral war. This change in the Catholic
Left also had its effect on the Berrigan brothers themselves.

By April 9, 1970, the appeals of both Berrigan brothers
had expired and they were to report to jail on that day.
Between October, 1967, and April, 1970, Philip Berrigan had
not spent a full year in jail and Daniel had spent only a few
days in jail. Both brothers agreed not to report, but rather
to appear publicly first and afterward be hauled away by
federal marshalls. Daniel Berrigan was to appear at the
Cornell Peace Rally on April 19, 1970, and Philip was to
appear at the Church of St. Gregory the Great in Manhattan's
Upper West Side two evenings later.

On April 19, 1970, Daniel Berrigan appeared before 10,000
people at the Cornell peace rally weekend called, "America is

Hard to Find" which was held in his honor. At the evening
"freedom Seder" Berrigan appeared and gave an impassioned
plea for resistance. A plan of escape through a huge
papier-mache figure of an apostle was suggested to him. In
five minutes, he decided to try the plan. In the darkness
of the auditorium he hopped into the figure and walked outside
into a truck. In minutes he was transferred to a car and
successfully began his four month underground escapade as a
fugitive from justice. The engineer of Daniel Berrigan's
underground existence was at this time the relatively unknown
Pakistani, Eqbal Ahmad, a fellow at Chicago's Adlai Stevenson
Institute for International Affairs.[42]

The FBI agents, embarrassed by his escape, began a
series of frantic searches for Daniel. Afraid that Philip
would attempt the same type of escape, they sought to capture
him before his appearance at the peace rally at 8:00 p.m. at
St. Gregory the Great Church. Philip along with David
Eberhardt, a fellow fugitive from the Baltimore Four draft
board conviction had slipped into the rectory before dawn on
April 21.

At mid-afternoon the FBI agents entered the rectory
and located Philip and David in a closet in the bedroom of
the pastor, Reverend Henry Browne. The closet was in reality
an "inner closet" which had been overlooked by all but one
agent.[43] The fugitives were taken to the Federal House of
Detention in New York City.

Despite the arrest over 500 people assembled at the
evening rally. Howard Zinn, a political science professor
at Boston University who had accompanied Daniel Berrigan on
the trip to Hanoi, Eqbal Ahmad, and Felipe Luciano, a Young
Lord, were the featured speakers. Over 100 FBI agents were
also present hoping to capture Daniel Berrigan. The pastor,
Henry Browne, presided over the rally and blended together
the menagerie of hippies, peace movement people, Black Panthers,
Young Lords, professors, middle-class sympathizers, nuns and
priests, FBI agents, and even a group of parishioners who
staged a counter-demonstration in protest of the church being
used as a sanctuary for Philip Berrigan.[44]

The next day Philip Berrigan and David Eberhardt were
taken to Lewisburg Federal Prison and placed in maximum
security for the four months that Daniel Berrigan was underground. The two men believed that prison officials were
unduly punishing them in order to put pressure on Daniel
Berrigan in the hope that he might give himself up.

Philip Berrigan had never considered the underground
as a viable political option for himself. And for the week
before they surfaced, Daniel and Philip engaged in heated
debates as to its viability. Daniel Berrigan strongly favored
it and Philip opposed it.[45] Philip Berrigan's arrest was no
shock, but the constant hassle of prison authorities and
being placed in maximum security at Lewisburg was. In fact
the imprisonment began to effect the psychological stability
of both Philip Berrigan and David Eberhardt. On July 20, 1970,

Dr. Rober Coles, a Harvard research psychiatrist examined both men and found it to be so.[46] Senator Charles Goodell of New York and others were recruited to confront the director of the Bureau of Prisons, Norman A. Carlson about the harrassment. In July, 1970, a demonstration at the prison was held to protest the maximum security confinement. There was no let up on the treatment by prison officials until Dan's capture. On August 25, 1970, Philip Berrigan was transferred to the federal prison in Danbury, Connecticut.

Because of Daniel Berrigan's talents as a writer, he viewed the underground as a means of amplifying -- not muting -- his propagandizing ability through the media. He believed the media would be more likely to publish the words of a fugitive priest than of a cleric not on the run. He also saw his fugitive status as a way to involve more and more middle-class people in a much deeper commitment to the peace movement by harboring him then they otherwise would make.[47] Thus, Berrigan mainly viewed the underground as an experiment -- he did not know what would happen.

While he was underground, both of these beliefs were realized. On April 26, 1970, the New York Times published an interview with him in a Manhattan walk-up apartment. The following month the Saturday Review featured Berrigan writing on the twenty-fifth anniversary of the death of Dietrick Bonhoeffer, a German Lutheran clergyman executed on Hitler's orders for his role in the resistance inside wartime Germany. In August, the premiere of his play, The Trial of the Catonsville

Nine occurred in Los Angeles. And on Sunday, August 2,
John C. Raines, an assistant professor of religion at Temple
University invited Daniel Berrigan to preach at his brother's
church, the First United Methodist in Germantown, Pennsylvania.
Berrigan's sermon lasted twenty minutes and received wide
press coverage and caused great embarrassment to the FBI.
During his four months underground, he stayed with thirty-
seven families and over two hundred people assisted in making
arrangements for his scenario.

But in August, Daniel Berrigan did not follow the
advice of his underground organizer, Eqbal Ahmad who had
warned him to stay away from life-time friends. Berrigan
went to the home of William Stringfellow and Anthony Towne
on Block Island, twelve miles off the coast of Rhode Island.
While staying there, he spent much of his time working on
his manuscript, The Dark Night of Resistance which he dedicated to his two friends: "To Bill and Tony, for I was
homeless and you gave me shelter." On August 11, FBI agents,
posing as bird-watchers, arrested him on Block Island.

The reason for the capture was that Sister Elizabeth
McAlister in her letters to Philip Berrigan at Lewisburg
prison had mentioned that Daniel Berrigan was going to stay
with William Stringfellow. At the time neither Elizabeth
McAlister nor Philip Berrigan knew that their smuggled letters
were being read by prison officials and FBI agents.[48]

The underground had been considered an experiment by
Daniel Berrigan and from the very beginning he did not know

how long it could be sustained. The successful four month
scenario had serious implications for the future of the
Catholic Left. First, it considerably escalated and intensified the widening gap between conscience and cooperation with
the government. The reason Berrigan gave for his underground
experiment was:

> Can Christians unthinkingly submit before such
> powers (war makers)? We judge not. The 'powers
> and dominations' remain subject to Christ; our
> consciences are in his keeping and no other. To
> act as though we were criminals before God or
> humanity, to cease resisting a war which has
> immeasurably widened since we first acted, to
> retire meekly to silence and isolation -- this
> seems to Phil and me a betrayal of our ministry.[49]

This action on the part of Daniel Berrigan offended not only
government authorities but also traditional adherents of civil
disobedience which demanded a willingness to go to jail for
violations of the law.

Second, it encouraged the over-reaction of government
officials who in the year of 1970 were filled with fear of
bombings and political kidnappings and security leaks in
Washington, D. C. The Watergate hearings in 1973 revealed
that the threat which the Berrigan brothers posed and the
fear that this engendered on the part of government officials
was greater than anyone imagined in 1970.

Third, Daniel Berrigan's writings during the underground repeatedly contended that the social institutions in
America were corrupt and that idolatry undergirded the value
system of America. The writings called no longer for reform,

but for revolution. The underground symbolized a radical
break of Berrigan with existing American institutions.

By August 25, 1970, both Philip Berrigan and Daniel
were behind bars in Danbury Federal Penitentiary. Ironically,
jail was not to mean silence and isolation for the Berrigans,
but rather a new and intensified position of national prominence. This change can be credited not to the Berrigan
brothers, but to the efforts of J. Edgar Hoover, Director of
the Federal Bureau of Investigation.

On November 27, before a Senate Appropriations Hearing
and to the press, Hoover hinted at an East Coast Conspiracy
to Save Lives which he alleged were planning to kidnap and
bomb and thus posed as a great threat to the internal security
of the United States. Seven weeks later on January 12, major
newspapers were called to send correspondents to a Justice
Department public information meeting. John W. Huske of the
department appeared carrying stacks of a four-page press
release and an eleven-page indictment. Both hand-outs made
no mention of Hoover's previous statement and his Senate
testimony outlining a plot and alleging it to be the work of
the East Coast Conspiracy to Save Lives.[50]

John Mitchell announced that six persons were indicted
on charges of plotting to blow up heating systems of federal
buildings in the nation's capital and also to kidnap Presidential Advisor Henry Kissinger. The six people who were
indicted were: Reverend Philip Berrigan, Sister Elizabeth
McAlister, Eqbal Ahmad, Reverend Neil McLaughlin, Reverend

Joseph Wenderoth, and Anthony Scoblick. The punishment indicated in the indictment if convicted of the kidnap conspiracy count was a maximum of life imprisonment and/or a general conspiracy conviction with a five year maximum in prison. Philip Berrigan and Elizabeth McAlister were also charged with three counts each of attempting to smuggle communications in and out of Lewisburg Penitentiary with a conviction of a single count punishable up to ten years imprisonment.

The indictment also combined a list of twenty-two overt acts beginning April 1, 1970, and named seven co-conspirators: Reverend Daniel Berrigan, Sister Jogues Egan, Sister Beverly Bell, Marjorie Shuman, an ex-nun, Paul Mayer, a former Benedictine monk, William Davidon, a Haverford physics professor, and Thomas Davidson, a twenty-five year old conscientious objector who lived in Washington, D. C. and worked with CLCAV and FOR.

Guy L. Goodwin was named the government's attorney. On the next day, January 13, Goodwin conducted a Grand Jury investigation in which Jane Hoover and Betsy Sandel, two Bucknell University students; Patricia Rom and Zoia Horn, two Bucknell University librarians, Mr. Robert Joynt and his sister Mrs. Patricia Chanel who lived near Washington, D. C., and Sister Jogues Egan, ex-provincial Superior of the Sisters of the Sacred Heart, were subpoenaed to testify. After being granted immunity, all testified before the grand jury except Sister Jogues Egan who was cited with contempt.

The efforts of her attorney, Jack Levine, a young Philadelphia lawyer, resulted in her case being heard by the Supreme Court.[51] In 1972, the Supreme Court rejected the stance taken by the Justice Department in the Jogues Egan contempt case. It established the precedent that grand jury witnesses threatened with contempt for refusing to testify could require the government to disclose whether they had been picked up on wiretaps or drop the contempt proceedings. It was a choice prosecutors did not make in this case.

The Jogues Egan Case became significant not only in legal history and subsequent Senate investigations of Watergate but also to a reconvening of the Harrisburg Grand Jury. Two weeks after the indictment had been issued, William S. Lynch, a forty-four year old lawyer and the most able prosecutor in the Criminal Division of the Justice Department was assigned to replace Goodwin as chief prosecuting attorney in the Harrisburg case. The reason for this change was the desparate desire on the part of J. Edgar Hoover, John Mitchell, and Rober C. Mardian, assistant Attorney General for the Internal Security division, to win the case.

Lynch agreed to take the case on the condition that he could issue a "superseding indictment." The new indictment was structured in such a way that the government would not have to prove either the kidnapping or the bombing allegation in order to obtain a conviction on the overall conspiracy charge. Draft board raids would be sufficient for conviction on the overall charge. The new indictment added two defendants,

Mary Cain Scoblick and John Theodore Glick, who was already
serving time for the Flower City Conspiracy draft board raid.
The indictment dropped as co-conspirators, Reverend Daniel
Berrigan, Paul Mayer, and Thomas Davidson. Thus, one Berrigan,
Daniel was subtracted from the case, but Glick joined Reverend
Joseph Wenderoth as the second member of the eleven-member
East Coast Conspiracy to Save Lives to be indicted. And
before the trial began Sister Susan Davis, another member of
the East Coast Conspiracy to Save Lives and John Swinglish,
head of the Catholic Peace Fellowship in Washington, D. C.
were added to the list of named co-conspirators. The new
indictment also included a maximum of five years imprisonment
upon conviction. The irony of the "superseding indictment"
was that it was issued without any new evidence being obtained.[52]
On April 20, ten days before it was issued, twenty-five persons were subpoened to testify before the grand jury in
Harrisburg. The people subpoened were all linked to the
Catholic Left through draft board raids or the Harrisburg
Defense Committee work. The exception was the in-laws of
Eqbal Ahmad, Mr. and Mrs. Abraham Diamond. Of the twenty-five
people subpoened only the Diamonds testified. Everyone else
refused to testify and seven of the twenty-five received contempt sentences. No one was placed in jail pending the
Jogues Egan case. As a result, no one cited with contempt,
except for Jogues Egan, ever went to jail. Because of the
silence of the subpoenaed, it also meant that no new information pertaining to the case was gained by the grand jury.

Despite these events, the superseding indictment was still
issued on April 30.

The indicted in the Harrisburg Eight case began meeting weekly at the Danbury Federal Prison to prepare their
defense. Three nationally known lawyers were selected by
the defendents.[53] Ramsey Clark, Leonard Boudin, and Paul
O'Dwyer. Before the trial began Theodore Glick was dropped
from the case because he wanted to defend himself. Finally
in January 25, 1972, the three month trial of the Harrisburg
Seven took place in the middle District of Pennsylvania.
Judge R. Dixon Herman, a Nixon appointee and former juvenile
court judge presided. Six of the seven indicted at the time
were Roman Catholic clergy -- priests and nuns -- members of
the new Catholic Left.

Central to the case of the Catholic team of prosecuters,
William Lynch, John Connally, and John Cattone were letters
between Philip Berrigan and Elizabeth McAlister written during
Berrigan's imprisonment. Boyd Douglas, a convict turned
informer had been the carrier of the letters. He had copied
the letters and turned the copies over to the FBI.[54] In
retrospect, since the public announcement of the marriage
of Elizabeth McAlister and Philip Berrigan on Memorial Day,
1973, the letters can now be viewed in their proper perspective. The letters can only be understood in terms of love,
fidelity, duty, and fantasy between a married couple dedicated
to a cause. These considerations far outweigh the apparent
political naïveté of the letters. If there had been no love

relationship there would not have been any letters. The
final judgment of Boyd Douglas' direct relationship with the
FBI as an informer, provacateur, and/or entrapper remained
unclear even at the end of the trial. The dramatic readings
of the letters and the lengthy testimony of Boyd Douglas provided the bulk of the testimony presented by the prosecution.

Ramsey Clark held the privilege of initiating the case
for the defense. He surprisingly stood up and declared:
"Your honor, the defendants will always seek peace, the defendants continue to proclaim their innocence -- and the defense
rests." This decision of silence on the part of the defense
had been made by a four to three vote on the part of the
defendants. Ahmad, Berrigan, and McAlister had voted against
it -- desiring to confront the government. Ironically, the
person who assumed the leadership in this final decision was
not the publicly acclaimed Philip nor the intellectual Eqbal,
but the small community of four lesser figures, the Scoblicks
and Reverends McLaughlin and Wenderoth. The four believed
that they made the decision by default of leadership. Ahmad
had looked to Berrigan as leader and because of Berrigan's
ambiguity between his commitment to resistance and his desire
to protect Elizabeth McAlister, he was unable to lead.[55]

The concluding arguments by the lawyers were made and
the judge charged the sequestered jury which had been carefully screened for any religious or political bias during
their selection. The verdict was a hung jury with a count
of ten to two in favor of acquittal. A mother of four sons

who were conscientious objectors to the war in Vietnam and a grocery store owner voted for conviction. Berrigan and McAlister were convicted of smuggling communications in and out of a federal prison. The outcome of the trial resulted in a legal and political victory for the defendants, and a setback for J. Edgar Hoover and President Nixon's Justice Department. Ironically, it was also the death-blow to what had come to be known as the Catholic Left.

The Harrisburg prosecution showed clearly by its presentation of evidence, really its lack of it, that the case would never have been brought to trial had not J. Edgar Hoover made his accusations against the Berrigan brothers. Four weeks after the trial had ended, Hoover died of natural causes -- a seventy-year-old heart giving out. The decision to prosecute illustrated how susceptible the career staff of the Justice Department could be to non-judicial influences of those running the department at any time. The tactic of a political trial was not new. It had been used in the recent past in the conspiracy trials of the Spock Trial, the Chicago Seven Trial, The Black Panther Trials, and after the Harrisburg Seven Trial it would be used again in the Angela Davis Trial and the Ellsberg Trial. Ironically, the government would lose every case in the courtroom. Yet, it would successfully accomplish the goal of eradicating dissident groups in American society. The government seemed to be losing every battle yet winning the war.

Through the pre-trial motions, the defense lawyers
were able to win victories through the courts to challenge
the illegal practices of the FBI and the Justice Department
such as the use of wiretapping, the use of an informer,
illegal search procedures, the use of the grand jury as a
fishing expedition, and the use of conspiracy laws for
political purposes. All such procedures indicated that the
Justice Department under President Nixon's Administration
had become highly politicized in its efforts to eradicate
dissent in the name of internal security and the law.[56]

Even the Bureau of Federal Prisons emerged as subject
to the Justice Department's pressure. For no given reason,
Philip Berrigan and David Eberhardt had been kept in maximum
security rather than the usual procedure for resistance to
the draft of minimum security at Lewisburg prison. And the
special study release program for prisoners, a rare privilege
granted by the U. S. Bureau of Prisons in Washington, D. C.
had been granted to an informer, Boyd Douglas who was paid
by the FBI for his information.[57]

All of these factors take on a new significance in
American history since the Senate Investigations of Watergate.
The politicization of American institutions revealed by
Watergate were already evident at the Harrisburg Seven trial
where the government served as prosecutor and not as defendant
in the case of Watergate.

During the trial there was no institutional Catholic
Church support for the defendants. There was personal support,

however, from members of the Church. Lawrence Cardinal
Sheehan, Archbishop of Baltimore, had visited the men in
jail and had designated the Archdiocesan lawyer, Francis X.
Gallagher to assume the duty of one of the defense lawyers.
There was also bail money provided and character defense
testimony given for the defendants by several priests in the
Archdiocese of Baltimore. Invididual Catholics and some
Catholic groups as well as many invididual Americans and
groups supported the Harrisburg Seven either through financial
donations or participation in functions planned by the publicly
accountable Harrisburg Seven Defense Committee. Over one
half million dollars was raised by the committee and all
except $20,000 was spent on trial expenses. The press again
came through with excellent coverage of the trial.[58]

Tragically, the government's use of a political trial
to destroy a dissident group in America, once again proved
effective. The demise of the Catholic Left and the Berrigan
brothers, however, had already occurred before the trial even
began. The American peace movement in general had begun to
recede before 1972. Though the Catholic Left and the Berrigan
brothers had been a separate group within that movement, and
often in an elitist manner felt that they were the peace movement in America, they relied heavily on the general anti-war
atmosphere. Once troop withdrawal began and the promise of
peace appeared imminent, the cause of the Catholic Left was
no longer of immediate concern to the public. The Harrisburg
Seven trial kept it before the public, but the end of the
trial abruptly signalled the end of a Catholic ultra-resistance.

The group itself also contained its own elements of self-destruction. One factor was that it was a voluntary association of very diverse, highly mobile and widespread people with no leader or organization to hold it together. Another element that weakened the group was that the members themselves became increasingly convinced that the tactic of draft board and corporation raids was no longer an effective means of stopping the war. And finally, the high price of long prison sentences was too great for many of its members to withstand. Thus, retreat from active resistance followed. This was especially evident with the seven who stood trial in Harrisburg and with the Berrigan brothers themselves.

Philip Berrigan returned to jail after the trial. Daniel Berrigan who was paroled during the trial, refused in any way to assume the role of leader for the peace movement in America and sought a new college teaching position. He did, however, continue to make public speaking engagements and even appeared on the Dick Cavett Show. On national television, he seemed to almost deliberately alienate his audience. The other defendants also seemed to seek retreat from the peace movement rather than continued involvement. The Scoblicks bought a small house in Baltimore and so did Reverends McLaughlin and Wenderoth. All four of these defendants sought normal lives in a changing neighborhood. Eqbal Ahmad returned to his work at the Adlai Stevenson Institute, and Elizabeth McAlister returned to her religious community and assumed a part-time teaching position in a small secular college in New Jersey. Elizabeth McAlister more so than the other defendants

continued to speak publicly about the future direction of
the peace movement. None of the defendants participated in
acts of civil disobedience against the war in Vietnam after
the trial and all seemed to seek a rather "normal living
situation" after the great publicity of the trial. They
seemed to want to convey to the American public that they
viewed the trial as an intrusion on their personal lives.[59]

Ironically, the prosecution of the Harrisburg Seven
had achieved a national prominence for these defendants in a
way that they could never have achieved by themselves.
Tragically in the process, the FBI director was revealed as
so powerful a man that the President of the United States
chose to ignore Hoover's blatant violation of the Bill of
Rights. Instead the Nixon Administration prosecuted the
seven in a vain attempt to show that the FBI director had his
facts right. Thus, not only Hoover, but the Justice Department and the Bureau of Federal Prisons resorted to acts in
the Harrisburg Seven trial which revealed itself not as a
nation built on a system of laws but so corrupt that it would
violate the law in order to prosecute so-called "law breakers."
Such actions seemed only to leave a pall of despair rather
than hope across the nation despite the acquital of the
defendants in the Harrisburg Seven Trial.

Thus, despite the efforts of the Berrigan brothers and
the Catholic Left to offer an effective peace witness that
would awaken the conscience of the public against the war in
Vietnam, the power of the United State's government in matters

related to war and peace overshadowed their attempts. The power of the government and their success at escalating the war best explains the Berrigan brothers' resistance and why they finally reached the level of ultra-resistance. The level of commitment required for such a peace witness also accounts for the Catholic Left's failure to build a broadly based community of resistance. Not many people were willing to risk arrest and face a jail sentence. The significance of the Berrigan brothers and the Catholic Left was that they did represent a willingness to offer such a peace witness in face of such power. Their witness offered an alternative to the government's policy of war-making. It gave hope to all Americans committed to peace and helped to keep the ideal of peace alive.

REFERENCES

[1] Jack Nelson and Ronald J. Ostrow, The FBI and the
Berrigans: The Making of a Conspiracy (New York, 1972), p. 14.

[2] It was not the Berrigans who launched the first
draft board raid, but a nineteen-year-old Minnesotan named
Barry Bondhaus. His eleven brothers and machinist father
helped him prepare for the 1966 action by collecting material
he would use. Bondhaus dumped two buckets of human feces
into a Selective Service filing cabinet. Although the protest, known as The Big Lake One, drew little press notice, it
was credited as "the movement that started the movement."
Nelson and Ostrow, FBI and Berrigans . . . , p. 14.

[3] Interview with Robert A. Ludwig, July 28, 1972. Ludwig
is a doctoral candidate at the Aquinas Institute of Theology
and is completing his dissertation on the theology of Daniel
Berrigan. He was most helpful in systematizing the influences
on and development of Daniel Berrigan's "political theology."

[4] In a letter to Representative William R. Anderson of
Tennessee, Daniel Berrigan cited Dorothy Day, founder of the
Catholic Worker Movement, and the late Thomas Merton, a Trappist monk, as having shaped his non-violence. Recalling that
he and Philip had attended a 1964 retreat conducted by Merton
on the "spiritual roots of protest," Daniel Berrigan said:
"I wrote him once that I could still remember the article of
his in the Catholic Worker that turned me from damp straw to
combustible man. . . . He got us started, after Dorothy Day.
The consequences are not theirs, but ours."

Berrigan told Anderson that Merton was shocked when he
and Philip joined in burning draft records. He said he thought
Merton "suffered the kind of electric shocks that come to a
man when his friends take him literally." Nelson and Ostrow,
FBI and Berrigans . . . , pp. 34-35.

[5] The most well-known biography of the Berrigan brothers
is that of Francine du Plessix Gray, Divine Disobedience:
Profiles in Catholic Radicalism (New York, 1970), pp. 130-210.
The chapter entitled "Berrigans" was reprinted from the New
Yorker, XLVI (March 14, 1970).

[6] Interviews with Mrs. Frieda Berrigan, Mr. and Mrs. James Berrigan, and Mr. and Mrs. Jerome Berrigan on November 1 and 2, 1968 in Syracuse, New York.

[7] Daniel Berrigan, S.J. "Reflections on the Priest as Peacemaker," Jubilee, XII (February, 1966), 25.

[8] Interview with Robert A. Ludwig, July 28, 1972.

[9] Daniel Berrigan, S.J., The World Showed Me Its Heart, a pamphlet published by the National Sodality Service Center, St. Louis, Missouri, 1966, 11. And interview with Jerome Berrigan on November 2, 1968, and visit to International House on LeMoyne campus, November 2, 1968.

[10] Interview with Reverend Matthew O'Rouke, S.S.J. and use of the file on Philip Berrigan, S.S.J. in the archives of the Josephite Provincialate in Baltimore, Maryland, on October 5, 1968. The quotation is cited in Nelson and Ostrow, FBI and Berrigans . . . , p. 40.

[11] From 1968 to 1972, the author was personally involved in the Catholic Left. Many statements and motivations attributed to Philip Berrigan came from conversations and correspondence with him through the years. The author's relationship with Daniel Berrigan was limited to two interviews, three letters of correspondence, and a proofreading by him of the author's M.A. thesis on Daniel Berrigan entitled "The Evolution of a Conscience."

[12] Interview with Reverend Richard Wagner, S.S.J., on October 6, 1968.

[13] Philip Berrigan, S.S.J., "The Challenge of Segregation," Worship, XXXV (November, 1960), 597-603.

[14] Interview with Robert A. Ludwig, July 28, 1972.

[15] Reverend John Heidbrink, a letter to author dated October 24, 1968, a copy of letter in the Jerome Berrigan residence in Syracuse, New York.

[16] Daniel Berrigan, S.J., A letter to his family from Eastern European trip in 1964 and now is at the Jerome Berrigan residence in Syracuse, New York.

[17]Interview with Tony Walsh on October 31, 1968.

[18]Interview with Daniel Berrigan, S.J., on November 27, 1968. The author read many letters of correspondence between Daniel and his religious superiors in the Society of Jesus. Upon Daniel's request these are not quoted directly and are paraphrased.

[19]Nelson and Ostrow, FBI and Berrigans . . . , p. 45.

[20]Interview with John P. Grady on October 6, 1968. Grady, a Catholic layman and father of five children has spent much of his time since the mid-1950's working with Daniel and Philip in their many projects.

[21]Interview with Sister Beverly Bell, S.N.D., on April 8, 1973. Philip Berrigan had told her this when they were discussing the viability of religious life.

[22]Daniel Berrigan, S.J., The World Showed Me . . . , pp. 25-26.

[23]Daniel Berrigan, S.J., a letter to his family from Eastern European trip in 1964, and is now at the Jerome Berrigan residence in Syracuse, New York.

[24]Many of Daniel's essays during this time reflect this attitude.

[25]Later Thomas Cornell also became a co-chairman.

[26]Philip Berrigan, S.S.J., letter to author, dated Monday, October 21, 1968 from Baltimore County Jail, a copy of it is at the Jerome Berrigan residence in Syrcause, New York.

[27]Interview with Thomas Cornell in summer of 1968.

[28]Reverend Richard J. Neuhause, letter to author dated October 21, 1968.

[29]Interviews with Francis Keating, S.J., and Daniel Kilfoyle, S.J., on October 6, 1968.

[30]Philip Berrigan, S.S.J., letter to author dated October 21, 1968.

[31]All three brothers, Phil, Jerry, and Dan when asked why Dan didn't participate responded the same way: "He (I) did not feel free to do it."

[32]Daniel Berrigan, S.J., "Berrigan at Cornell," Jubilee, XV (February, 1968), 29.

[33]Daniel Berrigan, S.J., Night Flight From Hanoi: War Diary With 11 Poems, (New York, 1968).

[34]Daniel Berrigan, S.J., "My Brother, the Witness," Commonweal, LXXXVIII (April 26, 1968), 181.

[35]Philip Berrigan, S.S.J., letter to author dated October 21, 1968.

[36]Interview with Paul Mayer, October 4, 1968.

[37]Daniel Berrigan, S.J., Trial of the Catonsville Nine (Boston, 1970).

[38]Interview with Reverend Neil McLaughlin, April 10, 1973.

[39]Interview with Theodore Glick, February 3, 1969. Estimates of the number of draft board raids that actually occurred varied with different members of the Catholic Left. Glick gave the highest estimate.

[40]William Hardy, the informer of the Camden Twenty-eight draft board raid, told the FBI that John P. Grady had confessed to him that he had engineered the raid at Media. Philadelphia Inquirer,(March 16, 1972), 1.

[41]These were the author's impressions after attending several such retreats.

[42]Nelson and Ostrow, FBI and Berrigans . . . , p. 60.

[43]Interview with Jay P. Dolan on January 8, 1972, who at the time of the search was in residence at St. Gregory the Great Rectory.

[44]Observations of the author who attended the rally.

[45] Interview with John P. Grady on April 21, 1970. Grady stayed with Philip much of the time that he was underground.

[46] Robert Coles and Daniel Berrigan, Geography of Faith (Boston, 1971). The Introduction provides Coles analysis.

[47] Nelson and Ostrow, FBI and Berrigans . . . , p. 56.

[48] No one knew exactly how the FBI found out about Daniel's existence at Block Island. After the letters were released by the prosecution at the Harrisburg Seven Trial, it was assumed that the letters provided the FBI with the knowledge.

[49] "Notes From the Underground; or I was a Fugitive from the FBI," Commonweal, XCII (May 29, 1970), 263-65.

[50] Nelson and Ostrow, FBI and Berrigans . . . , pp. 17-18.

[51] Interview with Jack Levine on April 22, 1971.

[52] Nelson and Ostrow, FBI and Berrigans . . . , p. 303.

[53] The process of selection of lawyers was tedious. For example, the Berrigan brothers met with Ramsey Clark who offered his services in the case. Personal and political motivations between them were discussed and not found to be in conflict. Interview with Reverend Neil McLaughlin at University of Notre Dame, October 15, 1971.

[54] Nelson and Ostrow, FBI and Berrigans . . . , pp. 111-28, presents lengthy excerpts of the letters. Nelson also treats Boyd Douglas on the witness stand in great detail, pp. 237-281. His book contains greater detail, more factual material, and more political analysis of the trial than does the more impressionistic character portrayals of the book by William O'Rouke, The Harrisburg 7 and the Catholic Left (New York, 1973).

[55] Interview with Reverends Neil McLaughlin and Joseph Wenderoth on February 17, 1973.

[56] Nelson and Ostrow, FBI and Berrigans . . . , pp. 303-06.

[57] <u>Ibid</u>., pp. 302-03.

[58] <u>Ibid</u>., p. 215.

[59] Interviews limited to Reverends Neil McLaughlin and Joseph Wenderoth and Anthony and Mary Scoblick. There was no interviewing of Eqbal Ahmad and conversations with Sister Elizabeth McAlister stressed continuing to work for peace and the need to keep building small communities of resistance.

CONCLUSION

Although it was the single largest religious denomination in the United States, the Catholic Church did not foster
a peace movement of any significant size or visibility until
the 1960's. The Vietnam War was the principal catalyst for
the change in the Catholic community, but the roots of this
transformation can be traced back to the 1920's when the first
Catholic organization for peace was established. This pioneer
organization, the Catholic Association for International Peace
(CAIP), came into existence in 1928. The Association was
founded by leading American Catholic Church liberals under
the leadership of Reverend John A. Ryan. Desiring America's
entrance into the League of Nations after World War I, Ryan
founded the CAIP to help combat isolationism and promote international peace among Catholics. With the defeat of the League
and the rise of nazism and fascism, their focus of attention
became the issue of war.

From its very beginning the Association, consisting of
never more than 500 members, spent its energies on committee
work, writing position papers, speaking engagements, conferences,
and lobbying as the best means of applying Catholic teaching
to international relations. The CAIP wholeheartedly endorsed
the normative Catholic position of the just war ethic as the

basic criteria for its work. Though an independent organization, the CAIP relied heavily on the National Catholic Welfare Conference, the central organization of the American
hierarchy, for assistance in its labors for peace.

The irony of the CAIP was that during its forty years
of existence from 1928 to 1968 its attempts to promote international peace always resulted in the sanctioning of war.
The Association endorsed the United States' involvement in
World War II, the Korean war, and the War in Vietnam. During
World War II, it did not raise any objections to obliteration
bombing nor to the dropping of the atomic bomb on Hiroshima
and Nagasaki. The CAIP justified all these positions as a
peace group by the application of the just war criteria.

The only other group of Catholics that offered a peace
witness in America prior to World War II was the Catholic
Worker. It had been formed in 1933 by Peter Maurin and Dorothy
Day, not as a peace group, but as a movement that would
witness to a radical Catholic vision of society. Its aim
was a human and social revolution that would come from the
timeless qualities of the human spirit and not from the array
of events of a world in process. The main belief of the
Worker was that the Church was the heart of the hoped-for
new life. Their work centered on applying the corporal works
of mercy and finding ways to aid the oppressed.

When war did erupt, first in the Spanish Civil War and
then World War II, the Catholic Worker ideal prompted Dorothy
Day to proclaim pacifism. It was never clear in the early

years exactly what Catholic pacifism meant, but it was sufficient as an ethic for the Catholic Worker to oppose war even after it was declared by the United States government. The Catholic Worker was the only Catholic group to offer a peace witness during World War II. This peace witness was maintained in all subsequent wars. Thus, the only Catholic group in American history that offered a peace witness while the nation was at war prior to Vietnam was the Catholic Worker.

It must be pointed out that most of the members of the Worker were more than willing to accept military service during World War II. Yet, at the same time some members did become conscientious objectors (CO's). The significant aspect of the Catholic Worker was that it was again the first and only group of Catholics during World War II to support Catholic conscientious objection. Though the CAIP did not deny the right of a Catholic to be a CO, it did nothing to affirm it.

Conscientious objection was the main way for an individual to offer a peace witness during a time of war. Individual Catholics scattered throughout America were CO's in World War II and in the Vietnam War. They came from various backgrounds, gave different reasons for their position, and became various types of CO's. In World War II there were 223 Catholic CO's who registered their dissent within the law and were granted CO status and performed their alternative service in the Civilian Public Service camps; there were 61 known Catholic CO's who were sent to prison either because

they were not granted CO status or would not cooperate in
any way with the military; the number of Catholic CO's who
entered the service and were classified non-combatants is
unknown. Though only 1.3% of the CO population in Civilian
Public Service were Catholic it was an increase in light of
the four known Catholic CO's in World War I. But by August
of 1970, 7.8% of all men granted CO status under the draft
regulations for alternative service during the War in Vietnam
were Catholic. There are no statistics available on the
number of Catholic CO's during the War in Vietnam who were in
prison, or the number who burned their draft cards or turned
them in, or the number who fled to Canada. There is also no
record of the religious motivation or reasons for their CO
position. The extent to which the unpopularity of the War
in Vietnam influenced their decision to become CO's is a
factor that cannot be determined.

The change that had occurred in the Catholic Church
during the Vietnam War can more readily be documented. In
1968 the American Catholic hierarchy came out in support of
the right of a Catholic to become a conscientious objector.
The Second Vatican Council had already done this and all
during the 1960's Catholic groups such as the Catholic Worker
and its offsprings, PAX and the CPF, had encouraged all forms
of conscientious objection. The CAIP had also come out for
the first time in support not only of conscientious objection
but also of selective conscientious objection (SCO). The
issue of SCO gave the just war theory its last surge of

relevance. The right of the individual to object to certain
wars and not all wars was the difference. The Catholic hierarchy also supported SCO, but the position was defeated in
the courts.

Though conscientious objection was the main way that
an individual opposed war, a new tactic, non-violent resistance, was developed after World War II. This tactic could
be applied by individuals and groups alike. Ammon Hennacy
brought the practical application of non-violent resistance
to the Catholic Worker and during the 1950's it marked a new
departure in the type of peace witness that Catholics would
offer.

Pacifism narrowly defined meant opposition to war and
its main form of expression during a time of war was conscientious objection. Non-violent resistance when applied to
the issue of war and peace differed from pacifism in so far
as its aim was to posit a direct action for peace. It also
had within it an element of coercion. There were many different actions that qualified under its heading, but its main
thrust came from acts of civil disobedience. A law would be
broken because it was in conflict with a higher law. Individuals who performed such acts would assume personal
responsibility for their actions and accept the consequences
of a trial and often jail. The Catholic Worker's yearly
non-violent resistance to New York City's air raid drills
during the late 1950's received such publicity that the group
became known for its non-violent resistance.

The action had been ultimately performed to protest nuclear warfare. The Catholic Worker opposed nuclear warfare as it had opposed all modern warfare and in practice had adopted non-violent resistance as a way to oppose the new threat. The threat of nuclear warfare during the Cold War era did not seem to produce any immediate change in the thought and practices of other American Catholics. Only one Catholic theologian, Thomas Merton, attempted to develop a rationale for nuclear pacifism. Impressed by the writings of British Catholics on nuclear pacifism, he attempted to edit a book on nuclear pacifism presenting the writings of Catholics. Merton admitted in the Introduction to his book, Breakthrough to Peace: Twelve Views on the Threat of Thermonuclear Extermination that he was unable to find any Catholic, except Gordon Zahn, to counter the written and spoken statements of Catholic nuclear realists. Their position had clearly been set forth in the book, Morality and Modern Warfare, edited by William Nagle, a leading member of the CAIP. The threat of nuclear warfare, however, had not produced the same response of nuclear realism among Catholics throughout the rest of the world.

This was first evident when the head of the Catholic Church, Pope John XXIII, wrote his encyclical, Pacem in Terris. He indicated that the normative just war position was no longer adequate to meet the new threats of human annihilation and called for a new theology of peace. The difficulties of the Church in implementing his plea were clearly evident at

the Second Vatican Council. Only one member of the American
hierarchy, Joseph Cardinal Ritter, showed any willingness to
condemn nuclear warfare at the risk of confronting the United
States' policy. The role of the American Catholic peace
movement at the Council was equally limited.

No member of the Catholic hierarchy had any difficulty
condemning a total nuclear war that would annihilate the
human race, but they would not condemn the limited use of
nuclear warfare. There were some bishops from other parts of
the world who wanted the condemnation of the use of thermonuclear weapons under any circumstances but they were not in
the majority. The Council Fathers were, however, willing to
endorse a clear statement of support for the individual's
right to become a conscientious objector to war.

These debates at the Council resulted in the first
serious challenge in centuries to the normative just war
tradition. The failure to condemn the use of thermonuclear
weapons revealed to some Catholics the bankruptcy of the just
war theory. The statement on conscientious objection was
not based on the just war, but on the dignity and freedom of
the individual. In both cases, the Council Fathers admitted
the inadequacy of the just war theory and called for a new
theology of peace. They could only point to the Gospels,
the dignity of man, and non-violence as the basis for its
development. The Council did not completely shut the door
on the just war theory, but it did open the door for Catholics
to search for new ways to become peacemakers.

The impact of the statements of Vatican II were
clearly reflected among the American Catholic hierarchy during the Vietnam War. In 1968 the American hierarchy for the
first time in its history came forth with a statement of
support for conscientious objection. At the same time it
would not condemn the actions of the United States government
in its war-making policy in Vietnam.

The American Catholic peace movement also reflected
the Council's call for peace based on the Gospels, the
dignity of man, and non-violence. In fact, non-violence
characterized the two most significant and innovative aspects
of the entire American peace movement during the Vietnam War.
Both innovations were initiated by Catholics. The first
occurred when a young Catholic Worker, David Miller, burned
his draft card in 1965. The action symbolized a new level
of non-violent resistance by the individual in response to
the draft. It was a dramatic gesture that gave birth to the
Resistance Movement. Mass demonstrations and peace rallies
often incorporated such action.

The destruction of draft files went one step further
and moved to the level of ultra-resistance. The Catonsville
Nine draft board action gave birth to the Catholic Left and
the Berrigan brothers emerged as its leaders. Though differences in religion and motivation existed within the
Catholic Left, all participants agreed that the action not
only challenged the war and the military, but both church and
state in America. The implications of this kind of group

action were revolutionary. The Catholic Left emphasized
values and not concrete practical operations of the way
church and state functioned in American society. The result
was a strong theological prophetic witness on their part
rather than any effective political consequences. The actions
did not achieve the immediate goal of the peace movement --
stopping the war. It did, however, reveal the deep commitment
of the participants in the Catholic Left. At its best, it
showed how far both church and state in America had removed
themselves from the ideals of justice and peace. The Catholic
Left could find no effective way to build a revolutionary
non-violent movement in America that would be strong enough
to return both church and state to the ideal.

The activities of American Catholic peacemakers over
the past forty years brings forth few definite conclusions.
All that can be said is that Catholic concern for peace was
a post-World War I phenomenon in American history. Catholics
who accepted the normative just war tradition as their ethic,
with only a few individual exceptions of conscientious objectors, were not able to maintain a peace witness when their
government was involved in war. This was true whether the
war was very popular as in World War II or when it was
unpopular as in Vietnam.

There was only one Catholic group, the Catholic Worker,
that maintained its peace witness at all times. This pattern
of persistence leads to the conclusion that the only Catholic
peace movement in American history was that which came from

the Catholic Worker and the groups it gave birth to: PAX
and CPF. Also, it was not the just war ethic, but the
ethics of pacifism and non-violent resistance that fostered
a peace witness even during a time of war. With the combination of these facts plus the threat of nuclear warfare, it is
only fitting that the CAIP ceased to exist in 1968. Such
conclusions lead to basic questions about the relationship
of the Catholic religion to the American way of life and
about the future of the American Catholic peace movement.

It is evident from this study that a basic tension
exists within the Catholic Church between its prophetic and
adaptive roles in society. In its prophetic role, the Church
presents the ideal of Christianity enunciated concisely in
the Sermon on the Mount: "Blessed are the peacemakers for
they shall be called sons of God." Inspired by this ideal
Catholicism can be a force within society that challenges
and seeks to bring the historical reality of society into
conformity with the Gospel message. At the same time, since
the Church is also a part of the historical reality it has
to adapt itself to the cultural situation in order to survive.
The adaptation is done with the hope that the ideal may still
be proclaimed. But there remains the ongoing dilemma of
trying to make the ideal operative and effective in a world
scarred by man's passion for war.

This tension was clear from the very origin of Catholic
concern for peace in America. The CAIP represented the adaptive approach and the Catholic Worker represented the prophetic

approach. What the past forty years has indicated is that
the strength of the United States government in terms of
political reality is so powerful that when a group of Catholics,
such as the CAIP attempted to bring the normative just war
tradition to bear on the moral issue of war and peace, it
resulted only in a sanctioning of the government's political
decision in favor of war. With the development of thermonuclear weapons, the bankruptcy of this ethic and the power
of the state became even clearer. For the Catholic Church in
America there was no adaptation only absorption. Thus, the
government became the absolute power and the moral arbitrator
in the area of war and peace when the Church attempted to
apply the just war ethic.

The Catholic Worker, on the other hand, as a prophetic
group was committed to witnessing to the ideal. It embraced
pacifism and regardless of the political consequences witnessed
to the supremacy of the ideal in their lives. By this choice
they were able to challenge the United States government and
affirm the ideal of the Gospels as the final moral arbitrator
even in the political realm of war. The choice that it left
open to the Church, however, was for it to develop a proscription against war in its ethic. But the leaders of the Church
refused to do this.

All that the Church was able to do in face of the
political reality was to admit to the weakness of the just
war and hope that its members would work toward the development of a new peace ethic. Thus, the Church placed the burden

of such a development on individuals and fortified them
with affirmations of their dignity and freedom. It would
not judge the motivation of nations, thus it continued to
presuppose that nations were moral and had certain rights
such as the right to self-defense and self-preservation.
The Catholic Church after Vatican II continued to affirm
both its prophetic and adaptive roles. By doing so, it
increased the desire on the part of its prophetic peacemakers to become more politically effective and forced the
realization of just war peacemakers to admit the inadequacy
of their ethical position. The result of these events were
the collapse of the CAIP and the discouragement and despair
that filled the Catholic Left at their political ineffectiveness. When the Nixon administration finally stopped American
involvement in Indo-China and withdrew American troops, the
political reality of war was no longer present and the
Catholic peace movement virtually disappeared. A new low
ebb of peace activity occurred throughout all America. The
Catholic Worker, PAX, and the CPF continued to exist.

The only clear indications for the future were that
never again would a Catholic peace organization solely base
its position on the just war ethic. Also, Catholic pacifist
and resistance groups would go in two directions -- one
would stress prophetic witness and the other would stress
political effectiveness. Regardless of their direction, the
Catholic Left had achieved certain victories in both areas
during the Vietnam era. Prophetically, they had demonstrated

the deepest level of commitment and willingness to assume
daring risks and long prison sentences. Politically, they
had increased in size and had achieved victories in the
courts both by wire-tapping decisions and by the hung jury
at Harrisburg. The War in Vietnam had provided a political
arena in which to act. The problem now facing them was what
could they do during a time of peace to keep their peace
witness alive?

APPENDIX I

CAIP PAMPHLETS
1928 to 1949
Located in the Archives, Marquette University

Agriculture and International Life, Rev. Dr. Edgar
Schmiedeler, O.S.B., and Subcommittee on Agriculture,
Washington, D. C., 1937.

America's Peace Aims, A Committee Report, Washington,
D. C., 1941.

American Agriculture and International Affairs, Rev.
Francis J. Haas, Ph.D., Washington, D. C., 1930.

Arbitration and the World Count, Charles G. Fenwick,
Ph.D., and International Law and Organization Committee,
Washington, D. C., 1937.

The Catholic Church and Peace Efforts, William F.
Roemer, Ph.D., John Tracy Ellis, Ph.D., and the History
Committee, Washington, D. C., 1934.

Catholic Life in the West Indies, Richard Pattee and
the Inter-American Committee, Washington, D. C., 1946.

Catholic Organization for Peace in Europe, Mary
Catherine Schaefer, M.A., and the Europe Committee, Washington,
D. C., 1935.

The Catholic Revival in Mexico, Richard Pattee and the
Inter-American Committee, Washington, D. C., 1944.

Causes of War, Parker Thomas Moon and the Committee
on Sources of International Enmity and Security, Old and New;
Rev. Joseph F. Thorning, S.J., and the Europe Committee,
Washington, D. C., 1937.

The Church and the Jews (A Memorial Issued by Catholic
European Scholars), English Version by Rev. Dr. George Feige,
Washington, D. C., 1937.

The Ethics of War, Rev. Cyprian Emmanuel, O.F.M., and
Committee on Ethics, Washington, D. C., 1932.

Europe and the U. S., Elements in Their Relations, Rev.
R. A. McGowan and European Committee, Washington, D. C., 1931.

313

International Economic Life, by the Committees on Ethics and Economic Relations, Washington, D. C., 1934.

International Ethics, Right Rev. John A. Ryan, D.D., and Ethics Committee, Washington, D. C., 1928.

The International Trade Organization, Sr. Thomasine, O.P., and Subcommittee on Economic Life, Washington, D. C., 1948.

An Introduction to Mexico, Anna Dill Gamble, Rev. R. A. McGowan and the Latin American Committee, Washington, D. C., 1936.

Latin America and the U. S., A Preliminary Report of the Committee on Latin-American Relations, Washington, D. C., 1929.

Manchuria, The Problem in the Far East, Elizabeth M. Lynsky, Ph.D., and Asia Committee, Washington, D. C., 1934.

The Marshall Plan, Dr. Helen C. Potter and the Subcommittee on Economic Life.

The Morality of Conscientious Objection to War, Rev. Cyprian Emmanuel, O.F.M., Ph.D., and the Committee on Ethics, Washington, D. C., 1941.

National Attitudes in Children, Rev. Maurice S. Sheehy, Ph.D., and National Attitudes Committee, Washington, D. C., 1932.

The Obligations of Catholics to Promote Peace, A Report of the Ethics Committee, Washington, D. C., 1940. *The Rights of Peoples*, A Report of the Ethics Committee and the Joint Policy Committee, Washington, D. C., 1940.

A Papal Peace Mosaic (Excerpts from Messages of Popes Leo XIII, Pius X, Benedict XV, Pius XI and Pius XII), compiled by Henry C. Koenig, S.I.D., Washington, D. C., 1944.

Patriotism, Nationalism and the Brotherhood of Man, A Report of the Committee on National Attitudes, Carlton J. H. Hayes, Chairman, Washington, D. C., 1937.

A Pattern for Peace and the Papal Peace Program, John Courtney Murray, S.J., and the Ethics Committee, Washington, D. C., 1944.

Peace Action of Pope Ben XV, A Summary by the History Committee of Friedrich Ritter Von Lama's "Die Friedensvermittlung Papst Benedikt XV, und ihre Vereitlung dusch den deutschen Reichskanzler Michaelis," Washington, D. C., 1934.

A Peace Agenda for the United Nations, A Report by Post-War World Committee, Washington, D. C., 1943.

Peace in the Atomic Age, Reports by: Rev. Wilfred Parsons, S.J., and the Ethics Committee, Rev. Edward A. Conway, S.J., Thomas H. Mahoney and the Post-War World Committee, Washington, D. C., 1947.

Peace Education in the Curriculum of the Schools, Right Rev. Msgr. John M. Wolfe, S.I.D., Ph.D., and Peace Education Committee, Washington, D. C., 1934.

The Pope Speaks on Peace (Excerpts from Papal Pronouncements 1944-48), Thomas P. Neill, Ph.D. (ed.), Washington, D. C., 1949.

Puerto Rico and the U. S., Elizabeth M. Lynsky, Ph.D., and Committee on U. S. Dependencies, Washington, D. C., 1931.

Relations Between France and Italy, Patrick J. Ward and the Europe Committee, Washington, D. C., 1934.

Symposium on Africa, A Statement by the Subcommittee on Africa and Papers by: Rev. Martin J. Bane, S.M.A.; Rev. Francis J. Gilligan, S.I.D.; Sr. Helen Angela Hurley, C.S.J., Washington, D. C., 1947.

Tariffs and World Peace, Rev. Thomas F. Divine, S.J., and Economics Committee, Washington, D. C., 1933.

Timeless Rights in Modern Times (Commentaries on the NCWC's Declaration of Human Rights), Rev. Wilfred Parsons, S.J., Rev. John M. Paul, C.S.P., and the Ethics Committee, Washington, D. C., 1948.

Transition from War to Peace, A Report by the Post-War World Committee, Washington, D. C., 1943.

The United Nations Charter, Thomas H. Mahoney and Post-War World Committee, Washington, D. C., 1945 and 1946.

The United States and the Dominican Republic, Elizabeth W. Loughram and the Latin-American Committee, Washington, D. C., 1936.

Francis De Vitoria, Founder of International Law, C. H. McKenna, O.P., Washington, D. C., 1930.

War and Peace in St. Augustine's "De Civitate Dei," Rev. F. E. Touscher, O.S.A., S.I.M., and Ethics Committee, Washington, D. C., 1934.

The World Society, A Joint Report, Washington, D. C., 1941.

APPENDIX II

ACCO PEACE BIBLIOGRAPHY FOR CATHOLIC CO'S

Books and Pamphlets

Attwater, Donald. <u>Bombs, Babies and Beatitudes</u>, PAX Pamphlet.

Berdyaev, Nicholas. <u>War and the Christian Conscience</u>, PAX
    Pamphlet.

—————————. <u>Slavery and Freedom</u> (Centenary Press).

Cahill, Rev. L., S.J. <u>Framework of a Christian State</u>.

Dawley, Rev. P. A., Ph.D. "The Conditions of a Just War,"
    <u>This War and Christian Ethics</u> (Blackwell, Oxford, 1940).

Eppstein, J. <u>The Catholic Tradition of the Law of Nations</u>.

—————————. <u>Must War Come?</u> (Burns Oates & Washbourne).

<u>Evolution of Peace</u>, Pamphlet (Stormont Murray, London, England).

Fitzroy, Mark. <u>War, Conscience and the Rule of Christ</u>, PAX
    Pamphlet.

Furfey, Rev. Paul Hanly. <u>Fire on the Earth</u> (The Preservation
    Press, Silver Spring, Md.).

—————————. <u>This Way to Heaven</u> (The Preservation
    Press).

—————————. <u>Catholic Extremism</u>, Pamphlet (The
    Preservation Press).

Gillis, Rev. J. M., C.S.P. <u>This Our Day</u> (Paulist Press, New
    York, 1933).

Hugo, Rev. John J. <u>Weapons of the Spirit</u> (The Catholic Worker
    Press, 1943).

Kossak, Zofia. <u>Blessed are the Meek</u> (A Historical Nove., Roy).

Le Messurier, Rev. R. H. <u>Christianity in the Post-War World</u>
    (Holy Cross Vicarage, 47 Argyle Sq., London, England).

316

Lord, Rev. Daniel A., S.J. So You Won't Fight Eh?, Pamphlet
(The Queen's Work, St. Louis, Mo., 1939; 2nd ed., 1941).

MacManus, Theodore. What Shall It Profit?

O'Connor, Rev. Wm. R. The Layman's Call (P. J. Kenedy, New
York).

O'Toole, Rt. Rev. Msgr. George Barry, Ph.D., S.T.D. War and
Conscription at the Bar of Christian Morals, Pamphlet
(The Catholic Worker Press, 1941).

PAX Bulletin. (Green End, Radnage, High Wycombe, Bucks,
England).

Principles of Peace: Peace Pronouncements of the last Popes
(Bruce Publishing Co., Milwaukee).

Stratmann, Rev. Franziskus, O.P. Peace and the Clergy
(Translated from the German by Conrad M. R. Bonacina).

_____. The Church and War (Sheed & Ward).

Sturzo, Don Luigi. Morality and Politics, PAX Pamphlet.

Vann, Rev. Gerald, O.P. Morality and War (Burns Oates).

_____. The Psychology of War-Mongering (Sands,
London).

_____. Common Sense, Christianity and War, PAX
Pamphlet.

Watkin, E. I. The Catholic Centre.

_____. The Crime of Conscription, PAX Pamphlet.

Articles

Attwater, Donald. "This War Business," The Catholic World
(April, 1937).

_____. "War and Christian Ethics," A Symposium, 1940.

Benignus, Bro., F.S.C. "America and the War: The Moral
Question," The Catholic World (October, 1941).

Cawley, S. "The Church and War," The Catholic World
(December, 1938).

318

Cerejeira, Cardinal, Patriarch of Lisbon, Portugal. "Address to his Clergy and People," Commonweal (January 6, 1939).

Ducey, W. Michael, O.S.B. "Peace and the Roman Missal," Commonweal (February 9, 1940).

Duffy, Rev. Clarence. "Peace--Peace--Peace," The Catholic Worker (June, 1943).

Editorial, "Salesmen of Mars," The Catholic World (October, 1934).

_____. "The Real Problem in Spain" (June, 1937).

_____. "Who Wants War?" (February, 1937).

Faulhaber, Cardinal. "Toward a New Ethic of War," Der Friedens Kaempfer (March, 1932).

Gigon, H. "Thomas Aquinas and the Problem of War," The Catholic World (May, 1939).

Gill, Eric. "Who Wants Peace?" The Catholic CO (September, 1943).

Gillis, Rev. J. M., C.S.P. "Defense of What?" The Catholic World (October, 1941).

_____. "Shall We Abrogate International Law?"

Hugo, Rev. John J. "Catholics Can be Conscientious Objectors," The Catholic Worker (May and June, 1943).

_____. "The Gospel of Peace" (beginning September, 1943).

_____. "Weapons of the Spirit" (beginning November, 1942).

Innitzer, Cardinal. "The Holy Year and Peace," Schoenere Zukunft (March 4, 1933).

McCawley, James. "War versus Conscience," The Catholic World (January, 1940).

McNabb, Rev. Vincent, O.P. "Just Self-Defense: No War," Blackfriars (January, 1941).

_____. "Meditation on Peace," Blackfriars (December, 1936).

_____. "Some Principles of Peace," Blackfriars (February, 1939).

Moore, H. G. "Catholic C.O.'s in the Last War," PAX Bulletin (September, 1943).

O'Connor, Rev. Wm. R., S.T.L. "Argument against War, and Conscientious Objectors," The Catholic Worker (July-August, 1942).

_____. "Defending Christendom?" The Irish Monthly (February, 1941).

Orchard, Rev. W. E. "Catholic Pacifism," The Catholic Worker (January, 1942).

_____. "Cut Roots of War" (May, 1942).

_____. "Pacifist Problems" (February, 1942).

_____. Article in Commonweal (October 28, 1941).

O'Toole, Rt. Rev. Msgr. George Barry, Ph.D., S.T.D. Article in The Washington Post (May 10, 1941).

Pauper, Brother. The Old Testament Preparation of the Gospel of the Gospel of Peace, Pamphlet, The Catholic Pacifists' Association.

Peregrinus, Bro. "Patristics and Peace," The Catholic Worker (June, 1943).

_____. "The Pacific Crusaders," The Franciscan Review (beginning June, 1943).

_____. "Evangelical Pacifism in the Age of St. Francis," The Catholic C.O. (January, 1944).

Quinn, Edward. "The Catholic and the Secular Approach," Blackfriars (December, 1936).

Stratmann, Rev. Franziskus, O.P. "PAX CHRISTI IN REGNO CHRISTI," Blackfriars (December, 1936).

Sturzo, Don Luigi. "The Modern Wars and the Catholic Thought," Review of Politics (Notre Dame, Indiana, 1941).

_____. "The Risks of Peace, Blackfriars (December, 1936).

Styles, W. A. L., M.D. "What Price War?" The Franciscan Review (September, 1944).

Vann, Rev. Gerald, O.P. "IN TEMPORE BELLI" (October, 1939).

_____. "Patriotism and the Life of the State" (January, 1940).

320

————————. "The Ethics of Modern War" (December, 1936).

————————. Article in The Dublin Review (April, 1939).

Watkin, E. I. "Catholics Can't Fight," The Catholic Student (New York, 1936).

————————. "War and Peace," Colosseum (September, 1936).

White, Rev. Victor, O.P. "War and the Early Church" (September, 1939).

————————. "Wars and Rumours of War" (June, 1939).

Zahn, Gordon. "War Brings Atrocities," The Catholic Worker (May, 1944).

BIBLIOGRAPHY

A Note on the Sources

In an attempt to locate the origins of the American
Catholic peace movement that emerged during the Vietnam Era,
I was able to locate two possible antecedents: the Catholic
Association for International Peace (CAIP) and the Catholic
Worker Movement. Though the latter proved to be the leaven
within American Catholicism that fostered the phenomena in
the 1960's both groups had to be presented in order to provide
a full understanding of the Catholic peace witness.

The Catholic Worker Movement

One of the principal sources used in the preparation
of this study were Dorothy Day's published writings about
her life in the Catholic Worker Movement: _From Union Square
to Rome_, (Maryland, 1939), _Houses of Hospitality_, (New York,
1939), _The Long Loneliness_, (New York, 1952), and _Loaves and
Fishes_, (New York, 1963). Ammon Hennacy's _The Autobiography
of a Catholic Anarchist_, (New York, 1954) was also very
helpful. The latest edition of the book appears under the
title, _The Book of Ammon_, (Salt Lake City, 1970). Most
essential to any study pertaining to the Catholic Worker is
its newspaper, _The Catholic Worker_. I first used the copies

of the newspaper located at St. Charles Borromeo Seminary
Archives in Philadelphia. Significantly, issues published
during World War II were missing. The complete newspaper is
available on microfilm at the University of Notre Dame. It
should also be noted that The Catholic Worker Vols. 1-27
(1933-1961) has been reprinted in four volumes with an
Introduction by Dwight MacDonald by the Greenwood Press of
Westport, Connecticut. The manuscript collection of the
Catholic Worker papers, correspondence, etc., is at Marquette
University. They were donated by Dorothy Day and remain
closed. I was not able to consult them. Only one historian,
William D. Miller has been granted entry. His recent book,
A Harsh and Dreadful Love: Dorothy Day and the Catholic
Worker Movement, (New York, 1973) has been a valuable aid.
It must be pointed out that Day and Miller both contend there
is no pertinent information on peace in the collection. There
is also an unpublished Ph.D. dissertation, 1973, from Case
Western Reserve by John L. LeBrun entitled "The Role of the
Catholic Worker Movement in American Pacifism, 1933-1972"
that is helpful.

The Catholic Association for International Peace

The principal source for a study of the CAIP is the
CAIP collection located in the archives of Marquette University.
Although these papers are open to the public, the material has
rarely been consulted. There are, however, significant gaps
such as the post-World War II period. There are additional

papers of the CAIP within the United States Catholic Conference
archives located at The Catholic University of America, but
these have not yet been made available to scholars. The
Catholic University of America also possesses the John A.
Ryan papers, a limited portion of which were pertinent to
this study. In Appendix I of this dissertation there is a
list of CAIP pamphlets published from 1928-1949 which I
compiled.

Conscientious Objection

In Appendix II there is a reading list published in
the newspaper of the Association of Catholic Conscientious
Objectors (ACCO) during World War II. A comparison of titles
provides keen insights into the differences between both
groups and is a good aid in future Catholic peace studies.

The ACCO newspaper is located at the Catholic Worker
house of hospitality on 1st Street in New York City. Much of
the data on Catholic CO's in this study was obtained from it.
This material is also available on microfilm from the University
of San Francisco. The other information was located at the
Peace Collection, Swarthmore College. The accumulative files
at Swarthmore cover the ACCO, the CAIP, the Catholic Worker,
and the complete files of the NSBRO. They also have the U.
S. Selective Service Systems report published in 1950 on
Conscientious Objection, Vols. I and II. A copy of Gordon
Zahn's unpublished Ph.D. dissertation from Catholic University
in 1953, A Descriptive Study of the Sociological Backgrounds

of CO's during World War II is also there. The writings of
John Courtney Murray on Selective Conscientious Objection
(SCO) are located in the archives of Woodstock College
presently situated in New York City. Arthur Sheehan, director of the ACCO, and Gordon Zahn, a Catholic CO during World
War II, provided significant information through interviews
and correspondence.

Thomas Merton

On the Thomas Merton section of this study the main
sources were Merton's writings on peace and these are listed
in the footnotes to Chapter IV. There is also correspondence
between James Forest and Thomas Merton during the last ten
years of Merton's life which are located at Regina Laudis
Monastery in Bethlehem, Connecticut. With James Forest's
permission I had access to these valuable letters from Thomas
Merton. Also contained in the collection are many of Merton's
unpublished writings on peace that he mimeographed and circulated among friends.

The Second Vatican Council

Another valuable source were the writings and correspondence of James Douglas during his intervention at Vatican
II. Mr. Douglas gave this collection to me and it proved to
be very helpful. His book, The Non-Violent Cross, (New York,
1966) provides his theological reflections on his experience
at the Second Vatican Council.

PAX

There is also much valuable material, especially correspondence in the possession of Eileen Egan, director of PAX. I was not, despite the intervention of Gordon Zahn, granted access to these sources.

The Berrigan Brothers and the Catholic Left

The main sources for Chapter VII of this study were obtained from my friendship with and personal involvement in the Catholic Left. Emphasis must be placed on the published writings of the Berrigan brothers and their conversations and writings to me. Jerome and Carol Berrigan provided me with hospitality and access to their personal archives on Daniel and Philip Berrigan. One of the most touching experiences that I had was a four hour conversation with their mother, Mrs. Frieda Berrigan, when she swore me to secrecy and proceded to talk about her two sons, Daniel and Philip.

Oral Interviews

Since I was privileged to interview many of the people mentioned in this study, I will just name the few whom I found to be most helpful: Daniel and Philip Berrigan, leaders of the Catholic Left during the Vietnam Era; Henry Browne, pastor of St. Gregory the Great Church in New York City; Thomas Cornell, a Catholic Worker, a draft card burner, and cirector of the CPF until the present time; Dorothy Day, co-founder of the Catholic Worker Movement; Eileen Egan, a

Catholic Worker and founder of PAX; Paul Hanley Furfey, a
spiritual advisor to the Catholic Worker Movement and professor
emeritus from the sociology department of The Catholic
University of America; James Forest, a Catholic Worker,
director of the CPF, and draft file raider in Milwaukee;
John Peter Grady, devoted friend of the Berrigan brothers and
prominent organizer of the Catholic Left; Patrick McDermott,
former director of the Department of Justice and Peace for the
United States Catholic Conference; Archbishop Thomas Roberts,
leading pacifist member of the British Catholic hierarchy;
and George Shuster, prominent member of the CAIP and present
advisor to the president of the University of Notre Dame.

Secondary sources of any pertinent relevance to this
study have been cited in the footnotes of this dissertation.

THE AMERICAN CATHOLIC TRADITION

An Arno Press Collection

Callahan, Nelson J., editor. **The Diary of Richard L. Burtsell, Priest of New York.** 1978

Curran, Robert Emmett. **Michael Augustine Corrigan and the Shaping of Conservative Catholicism in America, 1878-1902.** 1978

Ewens, Mary. **The Role of the Nun in Nineteenth-Century America** (Doctoral Thesis, The University of Minnesota, 1971). 1978

McNeal, Patricia F. **The American Catholic Peace Movement 1928-1972** (Doctoral Dissertation, Temple University, 1974). 1978

Meiring, Bernard Julius. **Educational Aspects of the Legislation of the Councils of Baltimore, 1829-1884** (Doctoral Dissertation, University of California, Berkeley, 1963). 1978

Murnion, Philip J., **The Catholic Priest and the Changing Structure of Pastoral Ministry, New York, 1920-1970** (Doctoral Dissertation, Columbia University, 1972). 1978

White, James A., **The Era of Good Intentions: A Survey of American Catholics' Writing Between the Years 1880-1915** (Doctoral Thesis, University of Notre Dame, 1957). 1978

Dyrud, Keith P., Michael Novak and Rudolph J. Vecoli, editors. **The Other Catholics.** 1978

Gleason, Philip, editor. **Documentary Reports on Early American Catholicism.** 1978

Bugg, Lelia Hardin, editor. **The People of Our Parish.** 1900

Cadden, John Paul. **The Historiography of the American Catholic Church: 1785-1943.** 1944

Caruso, Joseph. **The Priest.** 1956

Congress of Colored Catholics of the United States. **Three Catholic Afro-American Congresses.** [1893]

Day, Dorothy. **From Union Square to Rome.** 1940

Deshon, George. **Guide for Catholic Young Women.** 1897

Dorsey, Anna H[anson]. **The Flemmings.** [1869]

Egan, Maurice Francis. **The Disappearance of John Longworthy.** 1890

Ellard, Gerald. **Christian Life and Worship.** 1948

England, John. **The Works of the Right Rev. John England, First Bishop of Charleston.** 1849. 5 vols.

Fichter, Joseph H. **Dynamics of a City Church.** 1951

Furfey, Paul Hanly. **Fire on the Earth.** 1936

Garraghan, Gilbert J. **The Jesuits of the Middle United States.** 1938. 3 vols.

Gibbons, James. **The Faith of Our Fathers.** 1877

Hecker, I[saac] T[homas]. **Questions of the Soul.** 1855

Houtart, François. **Aspects Sociologiques Du Catholicisme Américain.** 1957

[Hughes, William H.] **Souvenir Volume. Three Great Events in the History of the Catholic Church in the United States.** 1889

[Huntington, Jedediah Vincent]. **Alban: A Tale of the New World.** 1851

Kelley, Francis C., editor. The First American Catholic Missionary Congress. 1909

Labbé, Dolores Egger. **Jim Crow Comes to Church.** 1971

LaFarge, John. **Interracial Justice.** 1937

Malone, Sylvester L. **Dr. Edward McGlynn.** 1918

The Mission-Book of the Congregation of the Most Holy Redeemer. 1862

O'Hara, Edwin V. **The Church and the Country Community.** 1927

Pise, Charles Constantine. **Father Rowland.** 1829

Ryan, Alvan S., editor. **The Brownson Reader.** 1955

Ryan, John A., **Distributive Justice.** 1916

Sadlier, [Mary Anne]. **Confessions of an Apostate.** 1903

Sermons Preached at the Church of St. Paul the Apostle, New York, During the Year 1863. 1864

Shea, John Gilmary. **A History of the Catholic Church Within the Limits of the United States.** 1886/1888/1890/1892. 4 Vols.

Shuster, George N. **The Catholic Spirit in America.** 1928

Spalding, J[ohn] L[ancaster]. **The Religious Mission of the Irish People and Catholic Colonization.** 1880

Sullivan, Richard. **Summer After Summer.** 1942

[Sullivan, William L.] **The Priest.** 1911

Thorp, Willard. **Catholic Novelists in Defense of Their Faith, 1829-1865.** 1968

Tincker, Mary Agnes. **San Salvador.** 1892

Weninger, Franz Xaver. **Die Heilige Mission** *and* **Praktische Winke Für Missionare.** 1885. 2 Vols. in 1

Wissel, Joseph. **The Redemptorist on the American Missions.** 1920. 3 Vols. in 2

The World's Columbian Catholic Congresses and Educational Exhibit. 1893

Zahm, J[ohn] A[ugustine]. **Evolution and Dogma.** 1896